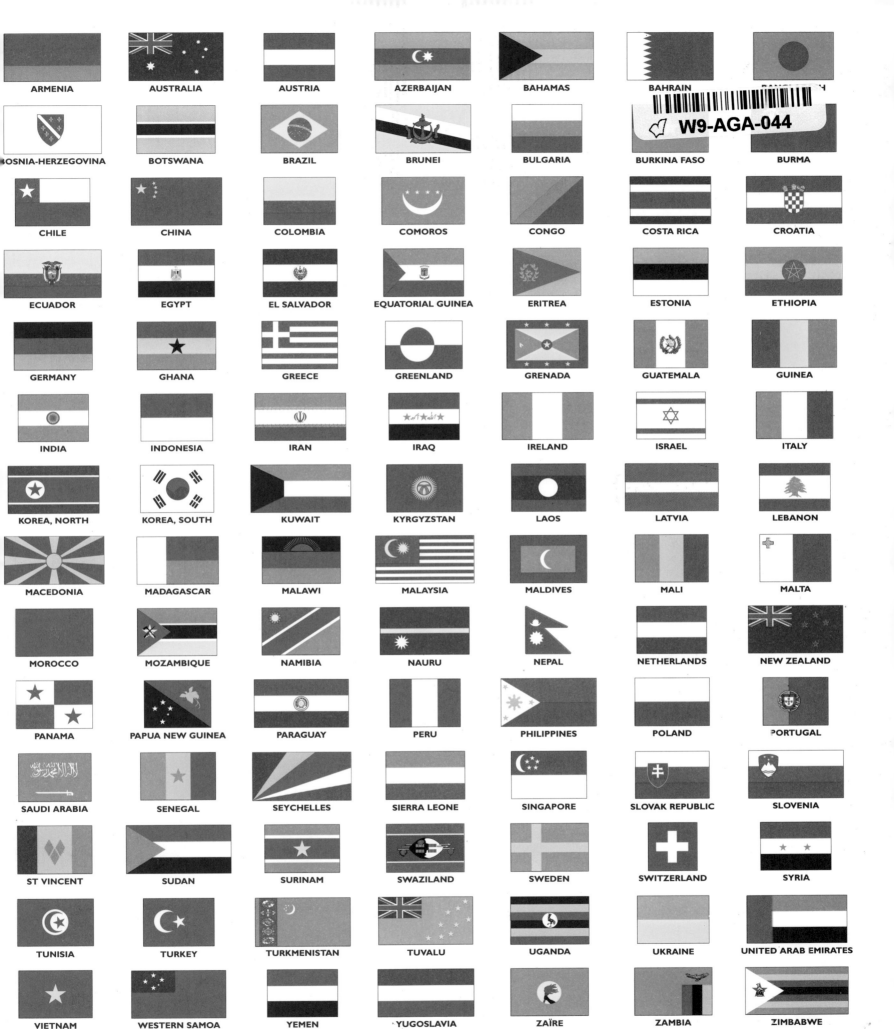

ARMENIA

AUSTRALIA

AUSTRIA

AZERBAIJAN

BAHAMAS

BAHRAIN

BANGLADESH

BOSNIA-HERZEGOVINA

BOTSWANA

BRAZIL

BRUNEI

BULGARIA

BURKINA FASO

BURMA

CHILE

CHINA

COLOMBIA

COMOROS

CONGO

COSTA RICA

CROATIA

ECUADOR

EGYPT

EL SALVADOR

EQUATORIAL GUINEA

ERITREA

ESTONIA

ETHIOPIA

GERMANY

GHANA

GREECE

GREENLAND

GRENADA

GUATEMALA

GUINEA

INDIA

INDONESIA

IRAN

IRAQ

IRELAND

ISRAEL

ITALY

KOREA, NORTH

KOREA, SOUTH

KUWAIT

KYRGYZSTAN

LAOS

LATVIA

LEBANON

MACEDONIA

MADAGASCAR

MALAWI

MALAYSIA

MALDIVES

MALI

MALTA

MOROCCO

MOZAMBIQUE

NAMIBIA

NAURU

NEPAL

NETHERLANDS

NEW ZEALAND

PANAMA

PAPUA NEW GUINEA

PARAGUAY

PERU

PHILIPPINES

POLAND

PORTUGAL

SAUDI ARABIA

SENEGAL

SEYCHELLES

SIERRA LEONE

SINGAPORE

SLOVAK REPUBLIC

SLOVENIA

ST VINCENT

SUDAN

SURINAM

SWAZILAND

SWEDEN

SWITZERLAND

SYRIA

TUNISIA

TURKEY

TURKMENISTAN

TUVALU

UGANDA

UKRAINE

UNITED ARAB EMIRATES

VIETNAM

WESTERN SAMOA

YEMEN

YUGOSLAVIA

ZAÏRE

ZAMBIA

ZIMBABWE

FACTS ON FILE

Children's
atlas

WITHDRAWN

David and Jill Wright

☑® Facts On File, Inc.

CONTENTS

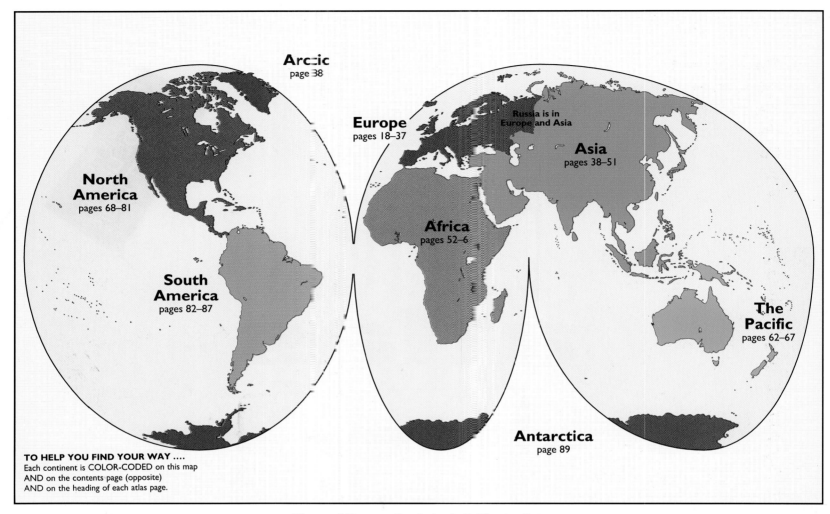

Arctic
page 38

Europe
pages 18–37

Russia is in
Europe and Asia

Asia
pages 38–51

North
America
pages 68–81

Africa
pages 52–6

South
America
pages 82–87

The
Pacific
pages 62–67

Antarctica
page 89

TO HELP YOU FIND YOUR WAY ....
Each continent is COLOR-CODED on this map
AND on the contents page (opposite)
AND on the heading of each atlas page.

TO RACHEL AND STEVEN

EXECUTIVE EDITOR Caroline Rayner

ART EDITORS Alison Myer, Karen Ferguson

EDITOR Kara Turner

PICTURE RESEARCH Liz Fowler

Text © 1987, 1997 David and Jill Wright
Maps © 1987, 1997 George Philip Limited
Cartography by Philip's

First published in the United States of America
by Facts On File, Inc.

First published in Great Britain by George Philip Limited

Facts On File, Inc.
11 Penn Plaza
New York, NY 10001

Library of Congress Cataloging-in-Publication Data
Wright, David, 1939–
   Facts On File children's atlas / David and Jill Wright.
     p. cm.
   "Cartography by Philip's" — Copyright .
   Includes index.
   Summary: Text, photography, maps, and charts cover
people and places by continent, providing population
statistics, national flags, currency, stamps, etc.
   ISBN 0-3160-3713-2
   1. Children's atlases. [1. Atlases.] I. Wright Jill, 1942–
II. George Philip Ltd. III. Title, IV. Title: Children's atlas.
G1021. W636 1997 <G&M>
912—DC21
                                          97–14954

Facts On File books are available at special discounts
when purchased in bulk quantities for businesses,
associations, institutions or sales promotions.
Please call our Special Sales Department in New York
at (212) 967–8800 or (800) 322-8755.

You can find Facts On File on the World Wide Web at
http://www.factsonfile.com

ISBN 0-8160-3713-2

Printed in Hong Kong

10 9 8 7 6 5 4 3 2

FRONT COVER PHOTO ACKNOWLEDGEMENTS:
Colorsport /Bryan Yablonsky center left
Robert Harding Picture Library bottom right,
/Thomas Laird top right
Image Bank /Harald Sund top left
Tony Stone Images center right

OUR PLANET EARTH

Our Earth is made of layers of rock. The diagram below shows the Earth with a slice cut out. The hottest part is the core, at the center. Around the core is the mantle.

The outer layer, the crust, is quite thin under the oceans, but it is thicker under the continents. Scientists now know that the Earth's crust is cracked, like the shell of a hard-boiled egg that has been dropped. The cracks are called faults. The huge sections of crust divided by the faults are called plates and they are moving very, very slowly. The continents have gradually moved across the Earth's surface as the crustal plates have moved. Sudden movements near the faults cause volcanic eruptions or earthquakes.

CRUST **MANTLE**

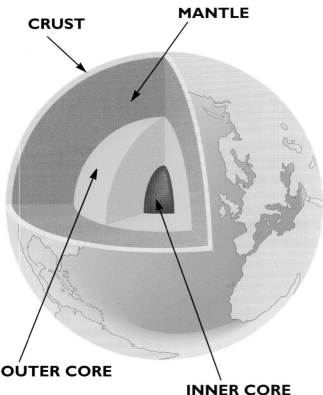

OUTER CORE

INNER CORE

The Earth from space: this satellite image shows Africa, Arabia and Antarctica. The Sahara Desert is free of cloud and all sunny. Some of the white clouds near the Equator show thunderstorms. In the far south, the Antarctic ice is even whiter than the cloud.

Can you name the oceans to the west (left) and to the east (right) of Africa? The map on page 7 will help you.

FACTS ABOUT THE EARTH

DISTANCE AROUND THE EQUATOR 24,902 miles
DISTANCE AROUND THE POLES 24,860 miles
DISTANCE TO THE CENTER OF THE EARTH 3958 miles
SURFACE AREA OF THE EARTH 196,936,000 square miles
PROPORTIONS OF SEA AND LAND 71% sea; 29% land
DISTANCE FROM THE EARTH TO THE SUN 93,210,000 miles
  (It takes 8½ minutes for the Sun's light to reach the Earth.)
DISTANCE FROM THE EARTH TO THE MOON 238,906 miles
THE EARTH TRAVELS AROUND THE SUN at 66,490 miles per hour, or nearly 19 miles per second
THE EARTH'S ATMOSPHERE is about 109 miles high
CHIEF GASES IN THE ATMOSPHERE Nitrogen 78%; oxygen 21%
AVERAGE DEPTH OF SEA 12,800 feet
AVERAGE HEIGHT OF LAND 2,900 feet

It takes 365¼ days for the Earth to travel all the way round the Sun, which we call a year. Every four years we add an extra day to February to use up the ¼ days. This is called a Leap Year. The Earth travels at a speed of more than 66,000 miles an hour. (You have traveled 370 miles through space while reading this!)

As the Earth travels through space, it is also spinning round and round. It spins round once in 24 hours, which we call a day. Places on the Equator are spinning at 1030 miles an hour. Because of the way the Earth moves, we experience day and night, and different seasons during a year (see page 13). No part of our planet is too hot or too cold for life to survive.

Our nearest neighbor in space is the Moon, 238,906 miles away. The first men to reach the Moon took four days to travel there in 1969. On the way, they took photos of the Earth, such as the one on the left. The Earth looks very blue from space because of all the sea. It is the only planet in the Solar System with sea. Look at the swirls of cloud, especially to the south of Africa. These show that the Earth has an atmosphere. Our atmosphere contains oxygen and water vapor, and it keeps all living things alive. The diagrams below show all the planets of our Solar System.

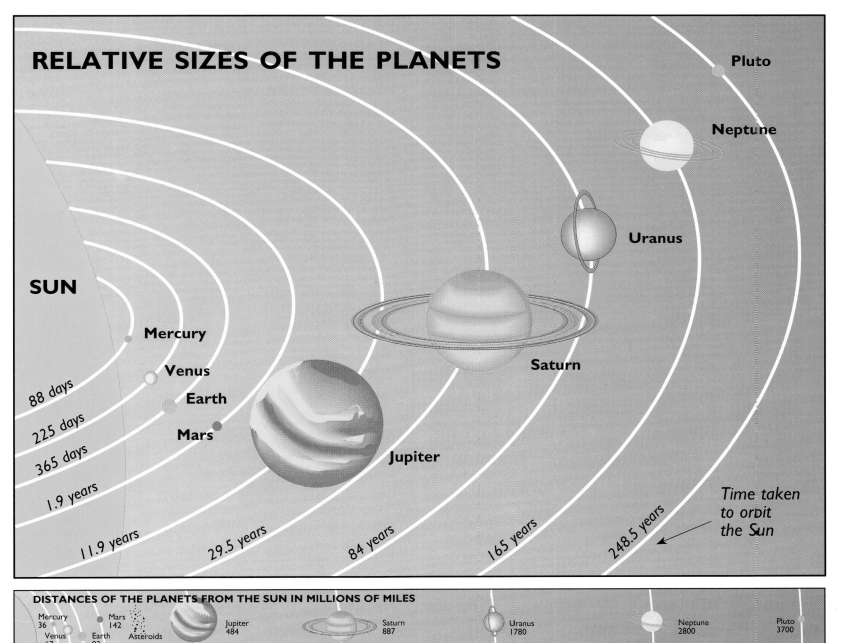

RELATIVE SIZES OF THE PLANETS

Pluto

Neptune

Uranus

SUN

Mercury

Saturn

Venus

Earth

88 days

Mars

225 days

Jupiter

365 days

1.9 years

11.9 years

29.5 years

84 years

165 years

248.5 years

Time taken to orbit the Sun

DISTANCES OF THE PLANETS FROM THE SUN IN MILLIONS OF MILES

| Mercury 36 | Mars 142 | | Jupiter 484 | Saturn 887 | Uranus 1780 | Neptune 2800 | Pluto 3700 |
| Venus 67 | Earth 93 | Asteroids | | | | | |

MOUNTAINS, PLAINS AND SEAS

The map shows that there is much more sea than land in the world. The Pacific is by far the biggest ocean; the map splits it in two.

The mountains are shown with shadows on this map. Look for the world's highest mountain range – the Himalayas, in Asia. There are high mountains on the western side of both American continents. Most of the world's great mountain ranges have been made by folding in the Earth's crust.

Desert areas are shown in orange. The green expanse across northern Europe and northern Asia is the world's biggest plain.

Mountains and plains – but in which country? (Answer on page 96.)

Farming the Great Plains of North America. *The Plains cover large areas of the USA and Canada. This land in Alberta, Canada, has just been harvested. The almost flat land of the Great Plains ends where the Rocky Mountains begin.*

Scale along the equator 1:116 000 000

| 0 | 1000km | 2000km | 3000km | 4000km | 5000km |

1cm on the map = 1160 km on the ground

| 0 | 1000 miles | 2000 miles | 3000 miles |

1 inch on the map = 1860 miles on the ground

WORLD RECORDS: LARGEST • LONGEST • HIGHEST • DEEPEST

LARGEST OCEAN Pacific, 69,356,000 sq miles

DEEPEST PART OF OCEANS Mariana Trench, 36,050 feet (Pacific)

LARGEST LAKE Caspian Sea, 139,266 sq miles (Europe and Asia)

DEEPEST LAKE Lake Baykal, 6365 feet (Russia)

LONGEST RIVERS Nile, 4145 miles (Africa); Amazon, 4006 miles (South America); Yangtze, 3960 km (Asia)

LARGEST ISLANDS Australia, 2,967,900 sq miles; Greenland, 840,000 sq miles

LARGEST DESERT Sahara, 3,243,240 sq miles (Africa)

HIGHEST MOUNTAIN Everest, 29,028 ft (Asia)

LONGEST MOUNTAIN RANGE Andes, 4474 miles (South America)

LONGEST GORGE Grand Canyon, 217 miles (North America)

HIGHEST WATERFALL Angel Falls 3212 feet (Venezuela, South America)

THE COUNTRIES OF THE WORLD

The United Nations flag – but what do the symbols mean? *(Answers on page 96.)*

Five of the continents of the world are divided into countries. Most countries are now independent and manage their own affairs. A few of the smaller countries and islands are still ruled by another country.

Look at the boundaries between countries. Some follow natural features, such as rivers or mountain ranges. Straight boundaries were drawn for simplicity. But in many places they separate people of the same language or tribe, and this can create problems.

Remember – no world map on flat paper can show both the size *and* the shape of a country correctly – only a globe is really accurate.

The United Nations building, in New York City. The world's problems are discussed here – and sometimes solved. Almost every country has a representative at the United Nations.

RUSSIA

Alaska (U.S.A.)

CANADA

UNITED STATES OF AMERICA (U.S.A.)

Greenland

Bermuda

Tropic of Cancer

Hawaiian Islands

BAHAMAS

MEXICO

CUBA

JAMAICA

DOMINICAN REPUBLIC

BELIZE

HAITI

PUERTO RICO

GUATEMALA

HONDURAS

EL SALVADOR

NICARAGUA

TRINIDAD & TOBAGO

COSTA RICA

VENEZUELA

GUYANA

PANAMA

SURINAM

COLOMBIA

French Guiana

Equator

ECUADOR

BRAZIL

PERU

BOLIVIA

Tropic of Capricorn

FRENCH POLYNESIA

PARAGUAY

KEY

ARM. = ARMENIA	LUX. = LUXEMBOURG
AZER. = AZERBAIJAN	MAC. = MACEDONIA
B. = BHUTAN	MOL. = MOLDOVA
B.-H. = BOSNIA-HERZEGOVINA	N. = NETHERLANDS
BUR. = BURUNDI	R. = RWANDA
BEL. = BELGIUM	SL. = SLOVENIA
CRO. = CROATIA	S. = SWITZERLAND
L. = LEBANON	U.A.E. = UNITED ARAB EMIRATES
LITH. = LITHUANIA	YUGO. = YUGOSLAVIA

CHILE

URUGUAY

ARGENTINA

Scale along the equator 1:116 000 000

0   1000km   2000km   3000km   4000km   5000km

1cm or the map = 1160 km on the ground

0   1000miles   2000 miles   3000 miles

1inch on the map = 1860 miles on the ground

Falkland Islands

South Georgia

WHICH ARE THE WORLD'S BIGGEST COUNTRIES?

Only five of the "top ten" countries with large populations are also among the "top ten" biggest countries.

TOP TEN COUNTRIES BY SIZE (SQUARE MILES)					
1	Russia	6,592,800	6	Australia	2,967,893
2	Canada	3,851,788	7	India	1,269,338
3	China	3,705,386	8	Argentina	1,068,296
4	USA	3,618,765	9	Kazakstan	1,049,150
5	Brazil	3,286,472	10	Sudan	967,493

TOP TEN COUNTRIES BY POPULATION (UN FIGURES)					
1	China	1227 million	6	Russia	148 million
2	India	943 million	7	Pakistan	144 million
3	USA	264 million	8	Japan	125 million
4	Indonesia	199 million	9	Bangladesh	118 million
5	Brazil	161 million	10	Mexico	93 million

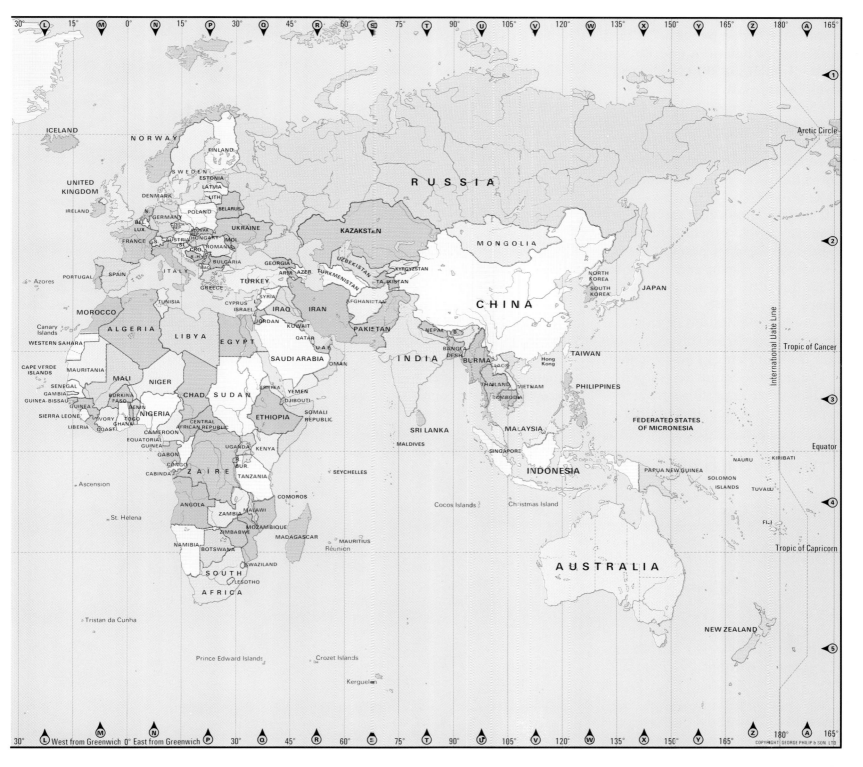

PEOPLE OF THE WORLD

There is *one* race of people: the human race. In Latin, we are all known as *Homo sapiens* – "wise person." The differences between people, such as dark or light skin, hair and eyes, are small.

The smaller map (below) shows the rich and the poor countries of the world. In any one country there are rich and poor people, but the difference between countries is even greater.

The map shows that the richest countries are in North America, northwest Europe, parts of the Middle East, Japan and Australia. Here, most people usually have enough to eat. They can buy a variety of different foods; they can go to a doctor when they need to, and the children can go to school.

The poorest countries (shown in dark green) are in the tropics – especially in Africa and southern Asia. Life in these countries is very different from life in the rich world. Many people struggle to grow enough food, and they are often hungry. People who do not have enough to eat find it difficult to work hard and they get ill more easily. They do not have enough money to pay for medicines or to send their children to school to learn to read and write. Some of the poorest people live in shanty towns in or near large cities.

But many people in the tropics do manage to break out of this "cycle of poverty." They now have a better diet, and more and more people can obtain clean water. Primary schools now teach most children to read and write and do simple math – though there are few books and classes may be very large. In many places, village health workers are taught to recognize and treat the common diseases.

Crowded and poor: a shanty town in Brazil. *These shanties on a steep hillside in Rio de Janeiro were built by people who have nowhere else to live. Some of them have low-paid jobs, but others have to beg to get enough to eat.*

THIRD WORLD AID

Watering onions in The Gambia, West Africa. This boy's watering-can was given by a charity to help the family grow more food. The onions can be sold to people living in the city. Many schemes like this are helped by money given by the rich countries of the world.

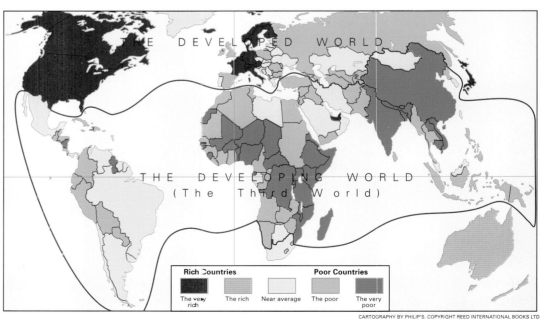

THE DEVELOPED WORLD

THE DEVELOPING WORLD
(The Third World)

Rich Countries			Poor Countries	
The very rich	The rich	Near average	The poor	The very poor

The map on this page shows where the world's people live. Most of the world has very few people: large areas are shown in yellow.

These areas are mostly desert, or high mountains, or densely forested, or very cold. Over half the world's people live in the lowlands of south and east Asia. Other crowded areas are parts of northwest Europe and the Nile Valley. The most crowded places of all are the big cities.

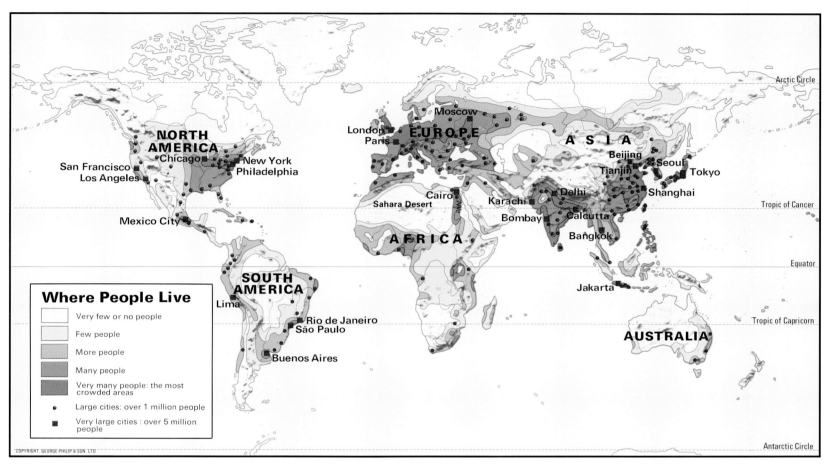

Where People Live

- Very few or no people
- Few people
- More people
- Many people
- Very many people: the most crowded areas
- • Large cities: over 1 million people
- ■ Very large cities: over 5 million people

COPYRIGHT GEORGE PHILIP & SON LTD

Empty and poor: *nomads meet in the desert in Western Sahara. It is hot and dusty and there is no shade.*

Crowded and rich: New York City. *The offices of Manhattan Island, in the center of New York, are crowded with workers during the day, but are empty at night. Only the richest people can afford to live in apartments here.*

COLD AND HOT LANDS

Five important lines are drawn across these maps of the world: the Arctic and Antarctic Circles; the Tropics of Cancer and Capricorn; and the Equator. They divide the world roughly into *polar*, *temperate* and *tropical* zones.

The *polar* lands remain cold all through the year, even though the summer days are long and some snow melts.

The *temperate* lands have four seasons: summer and winter, with spring and autumn in between. But these seasons come at different times of the year north and south of the Equator, so children in New Zealand open their Christmas presents in midsummer.

The *tropical* lands are always hot, except where mountains or plateaus reach high above sea level. For some of the year the sun is directly overhead at noon (local time).

The map on THIS page shows the world in June. Hardly anywhere is very cold (except for Antarctica in midwinter, of course). Most of the very hot areas in June are NORTH of the Equator.

The December map (opposite page) is very different. Both Canada

Arctic winter. *Winter begins early in Greenland. This fishing boat is frozen in the harbor at Angmagssalik, near the Arctic Circle. There are 24 hours of dark and cold at Christmas. Yet by June, the ice will have melted, and there will be 24 hours of daylight.*

and Russia are VERY cold. Most of the hottest areas in December are SOUTH of the Equator, near the Tropic of Capricorn.

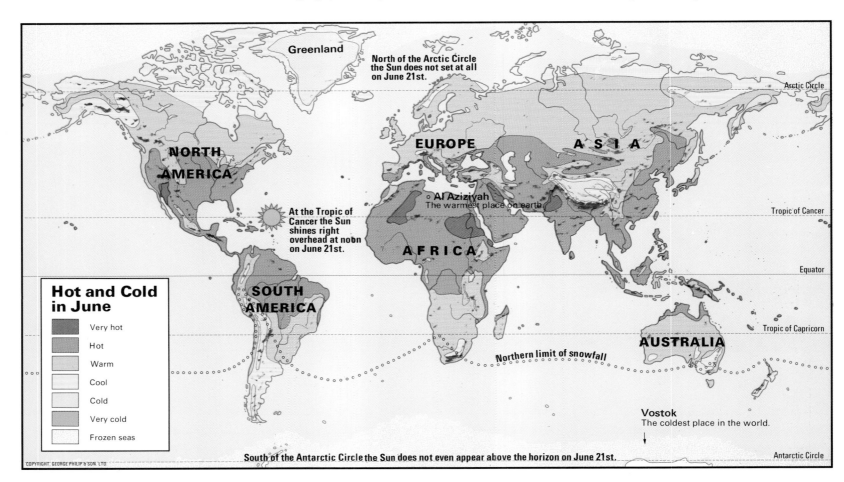

Greenland

North of the Arctic Circle the Sun does not set at all on June 21st.

Arctic Circle

NORTH AMERICA

EUROPE

ASIA

○ Al Aziziyah
The warmest place on earth.

At the Tropic of Cancer the Sun shines right overhead at noon on June 21st.

Tropic of Cancer

AFRICA

SOUTH AMERICA

Equator

Hot and Cold in June

- Very hot
- Hot
- Warm
- Cool
- Cold
- Very cold
- Frozen seas

Northern limit of snowfall

AUSTRALIA

Tropic of Capricorn

Vostok
The coldest place in the world.

South of the Antarctic Circle the Sun does not even appear above the horizon on June 21st.

Antarctic Circle

COLD & HOT LANDS FACTS

HOTTEST RECORDED TEMPERATURE
136.4°F at Al Aziziyah in Libya

COLDEST RECORDED TEMPERATURE
−128.6°F at Vostok in Antarctica

**GREATEST CHANGE OF TEMPERATURE
AT ONE PLACE IN A YEAR**
From −94°F to +98°F at
Verkhoyansk in Siberia, Russia

HIGHEST RAINFALL IN ONE MONTH
366 inches in one month at Cherrapunji,
India *

HIGHEST RAINFALL IN ONE YEAR
1043 inches in one year at Cherrapunji *

MOST RAINY DAYS
350 days in a year at Mount Wai-'ale-'ale
in Hawaii *

WETTEST PLACE ON AVERAGE
Over 463 inches of rain a year at
Tutunendo, Colombia *

DRIEST PLACE In the Atacama Desert,
northern Chile: no rain for 400 years! *

MOST THUNDER 322 days in a year with
thunder at Bogor in Java, Indonesia

* See map on page 14.

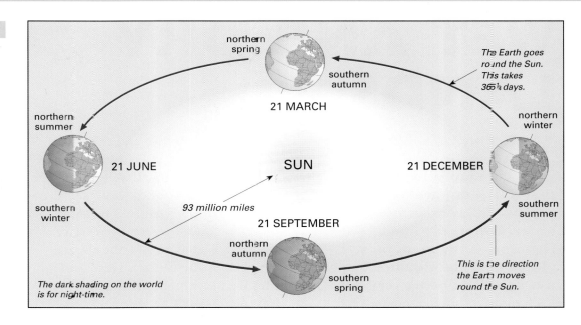

The dark shading on the world
is for night-time.

The Earth goes round the Sun. This takes 365¼ days.

21 MARCH — northern spring / southern autumn

21 JUNE — northern summer / southern winter

SUN — 93 million miles

21 SEPTEMBER — northern autumn / southern spring

21 DECEMBER — northern winter / southern summer

This is the direction the Earth moves round the Sun.

The seasons are different north and south of the Equator. In June it is summer in North America, Europe and Asia. The sun is overhead at the Tropic of Cancer. The North Pole is tilted toward the sun, and the Arctic enjoys 24 hours of daylight. Notice that Antarctica is in total darkness.

By December, the Earth has traveled half way round the sun. The sun is overhead at the Tropic of Capricorn. Antarctica now has 24 hours of daylight.

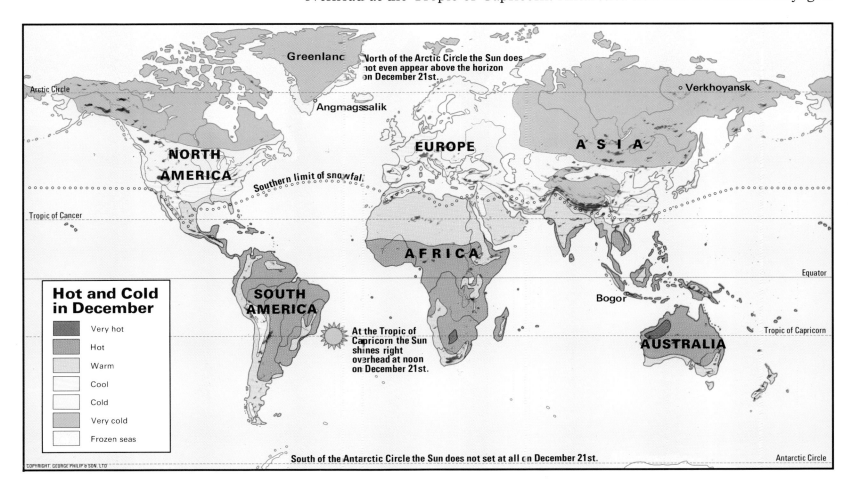

Hot and Cold in December

- Very hot
- Hot
- Warm
- Cool
- Cold
- Very cold
- Frozen seas

Arctic Circle

Greenland

North of the Arctic Circle the Sun does not even appear above the horizon on December 21st.

Angmagssalik

Verkhoyansk

NORTH AMERICA

EUROPE

ASIA

Southern limit of snowfall

Tropic of Cancer

AFRICA

Equator

SOUTH AMERICA

Bogor

At the Tropic of Capricorn the Sun shines right overhead at noon on December 21st.

Tropic of Capricorn

AUSTRALIA

South of the Antarctic Circle the Sun does not set at all on December 21st.

Antarctic Circle

COPYRIGHT GEORGE PHILIP & SON, LTD

WET AND DRY LANDS

Water is needed by all living things. The map below shows that different parts of the world receive different amounts of water. Follow the line of the Equator on the map: most places near the Equator are very wet as well as being very hot.

The map on the opposite page shows that near the Equator there are large areas of thick forest. Here, it rains almost every day. Now follow the Tropic of Cancer and the Tropic of Capricorn on both maps. The Tropics cross areas of desert, where it is dry all year.

Between the desert and the forest is an area of tall grass and bushes called the savanna. People here talk about the "wet" and "dry" seasons. For part of the year it is as rainy as at the Equator; for the rest of the year it is as dry as the desert.

North of the Sahara Desert is the Mediterranean Sea. Places around this sea have lovely hot, dry summers, but they do have rain in winter. There are areas near other deserts with a similar climate, such as California in North America and central Chile in South America, and around the Cape of Good Hope in the far south of Africa.

Forest and mountains in Alberta, Canada. *The coniferous trees can survive Canada's bitterly cold winters. In the high mountains, trees cannot grow: it is too cold and the soil is too thin.*

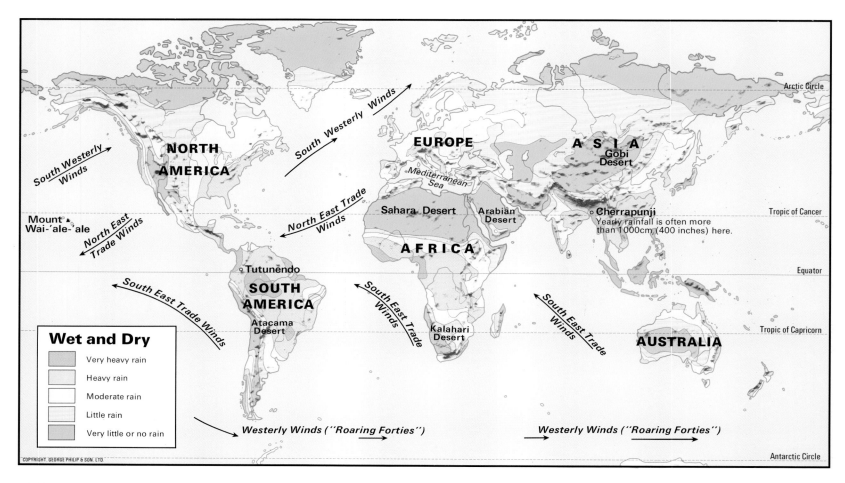

Wet and Dry

- Very heavy rain
- Heavy rain
- Moderate rain
- Little rain
- Very little or no rain

COPYRIGHT. GEORGE PHILIP & SON. LTD.

Burning the savanna, in northern Ghana, West Africa. *At the end of the long dry season, farmers burn the bush (long grass and small trees). The land will be ready for planting crops when it rains.*

In the temperate lands, many places have some rain all through the year. Damp winds from the sea bring plenty of rain to the coastal areas, and trees grow well. Far inland, near the center of the continents, and where high mountains cut off the sea winds, it is much drier. Here, there are vast grasslands, like the prairies of North America and the steppes of Russia. In the center of Asia, there is a desert with very cold winters.

Temperate forests stretch right across North America, Europe and Asia – except where they have been cleared for farmland and towns.

In the far north there is "tundra" which is snow-covered for many months in winter, and marshy in the short summer.

Finally, Greenland and Antarctica are mostly snow and ice.

Sand dunes in the desert in Namibia, southern Africa. *The Namib Desert has given its name to the country of Namibia. It is a very dry area, west of the Kalahari Desert.*

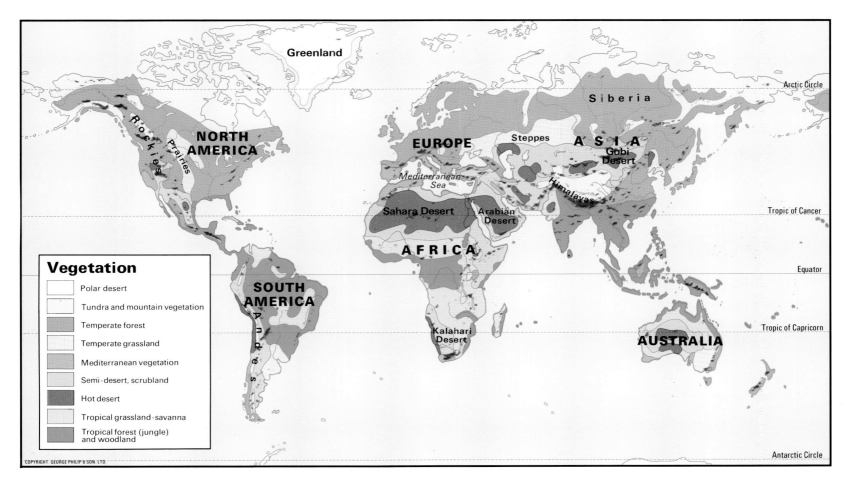

Vegetation

- Polar desert
- Tundra and mountain vegetation
- Temperate forest
- Temperate grassland
- Mediterranean vegetation
- Semi-desert, scrubland
- Hot desert
- Tropical grassland-savanna
- Tropical forest (jungle) and woodland

Greenland

Arctic Circle

Siberia

ROCKIES

NORTH AMERICA

Prairies

EUROPE

Steppes

A S I A

Gobi Desert

Mediterranean Sea

Himalayas

Tropic of Cancer

Sahara Desert

Arabian Desert

A F R I C A

Equator

SOUTH AMERICA

Andes

Kalahari Desert

AUSTRALIA

Tropic of Capricorn

Antarctic Circle

ENJOYING MAPS

The world is round, so the best possible model is a globe. It is impossible to draw a really accurate map of the round world on a flat piece of paper. The world maps on pages 6 to 9 and 11 to 15 have the right shape for the land, but the size of northern lands is too big. The map on page 10 has the wrong shapes but the size is right: it is an "equal-area" map.

The area maps (pages 18 to 89) show the continents and countries of the world. Each map has a key, with information that will help you to "read" the map. Use your imagination to "see" what the land is like in each part of the world that you visit through these pages. The photos and text will make your picture clearer.

These two pages explain the key to all the maps. The country

of Ghana is used as an example. Ghana is in square B2 of the map (right). Find 🅱 at the top of the map with one finger, and ➋ at the side of the map with another finger. Move each finger in the direction of the arrows; Ghana is where they meet.

The capital city of each country is underlined on the maps. The rulers of the country live in the capital city, and it is the biggest city in most countries. But not all capital cities are big. On this map, you can see three sizes of city. The biggest ones are marked by a square; they have over one million people. Middle-sized cities have a big circle, and smaller cities have a small circle. Small towns and villages are not shown on maps of this scale, but some have been included in this atlas because they are mentioned in the text.

The border between Ghana and Burkina Faso. *The red lines on the map show the boundaries between countries. When traveling from one country to another, you have to stop at the border. These children live in Ghana and their flag flies on their side of the border.*

"BYE-BYE SAFE JOURNEY" is the message on the arch. In Ghana, most officials speak English. In Burkina Faso officials speak French.

POSTAGE STAMPS ... are on many pages of this atlas

You can learn so much from stamps! The map shows you that Ghana is a country; the stamps tell you the official language of Ghana, and show you Ghana's flag.

The map tells you that Ghana has a coastline; the 10Np stamp tells you the name of Ghana's main port, and shows you the big modern cranes there.

The map shows that this port is very near to Accra, which is the capital city of Ghana.

The map tells you the name of Ghana's biggest lake (man-made). The 6Np stamp shows you the dam and its name.

You can see that they chose the narrowest part of the valley to build the dam. On page 57, there is a picture of a ferry on the lake.

COINS OF THE WORLD

The Ghana coin (left) shows cocoa pods growing on the branches of a cocoa tree. Cocoa is a major export from Ghana. Another Ghana coin (right) shows traditional drums.

Other countries also picture familiar items on their coins. **Nigeria** has a palm tree on its coins; **The Gambia** has a sailing ship on one of its coins (see page 53).

But don't believe everything you find on coins: there is a LION on the 10p UK coin!

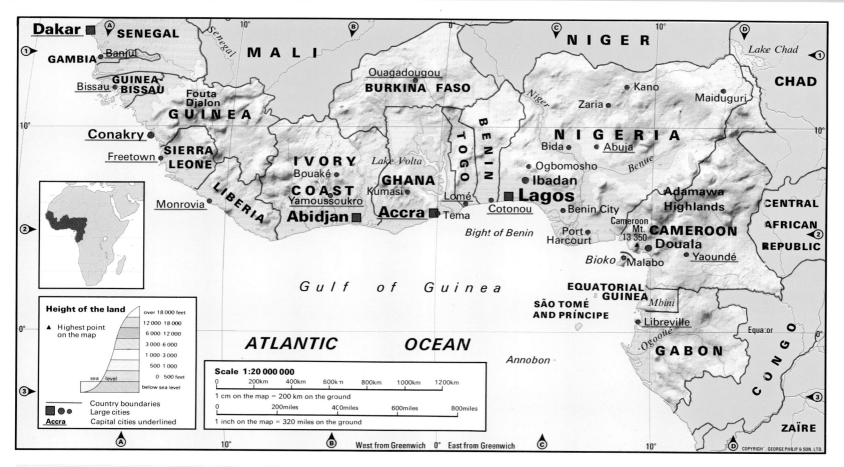

HEIGHT OF THE LAND

The countries of West Africa are colored so that you can tell the height of the land. Green shows the lowest land. Often the real land will not look green – in the dry season the grass is brown. The higher land is colored brown, even though some parts are covered with thick green forest! The highest point in West Africa is shown with a small black triangle – find it in square C2 – but the mountains are not high enough to be shown in mauve or white: look for these on page 45. And to find land below sea level, try page 25. In West Africa, Cameroon has some dramatic mountains, but elsewhere the change from lowland to highland is often quite gentle. The "shadows" on the map help you to see which mountains have steep slopes.

Water features – the ocean, big rivers and lakes – are in blue, and their names are in *italic print*.

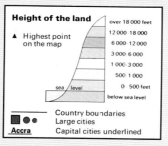

SCALE

This box shows the scale of the map. The scale can be written in different ways. The map is drawn to a scale of 1:20,000,000, which means that the distance between two places on the ground is exactly 20 million times bigger than it is on this page! Other maps in this atlas are drawn to different scales: little Belgium (page 25) is drawn at a scale of 1:2 million, while the largest country in the world is drawn at a scale of 1:45 million (Russia, page 41). Another way of writing the scale of this map is to say that 1 inch on the map is equal to 320 miles on the ground in West Africa.

You can use the scale line to make your own scale ruler. Put the straight edge of a strip of paper against the scale line and mark the position of 200, 400, 600 miles, etc. (Or use the scale in kilometers if you prefer.) Carefully number each mark. Now move your scale ruler over the map to see how far it is between places. For example, Accra to Abidjan is 250 miles.

EUROPE

The map shows the great North European Plain that stretches from the Atlantic Ocean to Russia. This plain has most of Europe's best farmland, and many of the biggest cities.

To the north of the plain are the snowy mountains of Scandinavia. To the south are even higher mountains: the Pyrenees, the Alps and Carpathians, and the Caucasus Mountains. Southern Europe has hills and mountains by the Mediterranean Sea. The small areas of lowland are carefully farmed.

PUZZLE

The most important building in Europe?
● *Where is it found?*
(Answer on page 96.)

EUROPE FACTS

AREA 4,066,019 sq miles (including European Russia). Europe is the smallest continent.
HIGHEST POINT Mt Elbrus (Russia), 18,481 feet
LOWEST POINT By Caspian Sea, minus 125 feet
LONGEST RIVER Volga (Russia), 2293 miles
LARGEST LAKE Caspian Sea*, 139,266 sq miles
BIGGEST COUNTRY Russia*, 6,592,800 sq miles (total area – Europe and Asia)
BIGGEST ALL-EUROPEAN COUNTRY Ukraine, 233,100 sq miles
SMALLEST COUNTRY Vatican City* (in Rome, Italy), less than one fifth of a square mile!
MOST CROWDED COUNTRY Malta
LEAST CROWDED COUNTRY Iceland
* A world record as well as a European record

Height of the land
▲ Highest point on the map

over 18 000 feet
12 000-18 000
6 000-12 000
3 000-6 000
1 000-3 000
500-1 000
0-500 feet
below sea level

sea level
Deeper blue – deeper sea

Scale 1:30 000 000
0 — 300km — 600km — 900km — 1200km — 1500km
1 cm on the map = 300 km on the ground
0 — 300miles — 600miles — 900miles
1 inch on the map = 480 miles on the ground

COPYRIGHT GEORGE PHILIP & SON, LTD.

SF
B
L
DK
F
D
NL
I
E

Northern Europe: Iceland. *Lake Jokulsarlon has many small icebergs which break off the glacier that comes from the ice cap. Ice melts to make the lake.*

Central Europe: Austria. *The Dachstein Mountains are part of the Alps. They are high enough to have patches of snow even in summer. The valley floors are farmed.*

Southern Europe: Sardinia. *The island of Sardinia is part of Italy and is in the Mediterranean. It is very hot and dry in the summer. It is a popular vacation destination.*

S

IRL

A

GB

P

GR

These license plates are from the 15 countries of the European Union. Can you name them? (Answers on page 96.)

Europe in the World

KEY
A. = Andorra
LI. = Liechtenstein
LUX. = Luxembourg
M. = Monaco
S.M. = San Marino
V.C. = Vatican City

Scale 1:30 000 000

| 0 | 300km | 600km | 900km | 1200km | 1500km |

1 cm on the map = 300 km on the ground

| 0 | 300miles | 600miles | 900miles |

1 inch on the map = 480 miles on the ground

COPYRIGHT GEORGE PHILIP & SON LTD.

The countries of Georgia, Armenia and Azerbaijan are really in Asia but are also included on this map and on page 37 because they are at a larger scale.

SCANDINAVIA

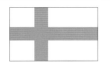

AREA 130,552 sq miles
POPULATION 5,125,000
MONEY Markka

DENMARK

AREA 16,629 sq miles
POPULATION 5,229,000
MONEY Krone

The five countries that make up Scandinavia are rich and successful, yet the people live further north than in almost any other part of the world.

The total population of each of these countries is small, and very few people live in the far north. Most people live in towns and cities, with excellent central heating in their houses and apartments.

Farming is difficult this far north because the winters are long and cold. Scandinavia has hardly any minerals except for iron ore in Sweden and oil under the North Sea. The mountains of Norway make travel difficult, but there are good train and boat services.

Geiranger fjord, Norway, is one of many long, narrow inlets of the sea along the Norwegian coast. Glaciers dug these deep, steep valleys. The village is on the flat land at the head of the fjord. The steep mountains mean that the best way to travel is often by boat.

LEGOLAND MODEL VILLAGE

Legoland is a model village beside the Lego factory in Denmark. Everything in the village is made of Lego! There are models of famous buildings as well as ordinary houses from different parts of the world. The photograph shows the model of a typical fishing village in the Lofoten Islands, which are off the northern coast of Norway. The Lego man and his friends can be found in shops all over the world!

Lake Saimaa, Finland, is one of hundreds of lakes in the southern part of that country. Only the largest are shown on the map. During the Ice Age, ice sheets scraped hollows in the rock which filled with water after the ice melted.

AREA 125,050 sq miles
POPULATION 4,361,000
MONEY Krone

SWEDEN

AREA 173,730 sq miles
POPULATION 8,893,000
MONEY Swedish krona

Reindeer in Lapland. Lapland is the northern part of Norway, Sweden and Finland, where the Lapps live. They keep reindeer for their milk, meat and leather, and also to pull sledges. Notice the warm and colorful clothes the Lapps wear. In winter, it is dark here even at midday, but in summer it is light at midnight.

The mountains of Iceland and Norway are high and rugged. There are large ice sheets and glaciers even today.

Denmark and southern Sweden are low-lying. The soil is formed from sand, gravel and clay brought by ice sheets in the Ice Age.

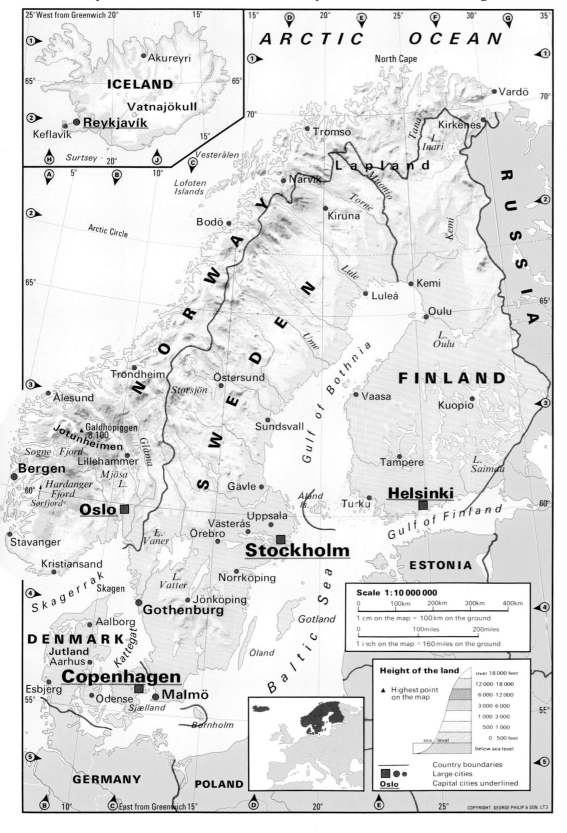

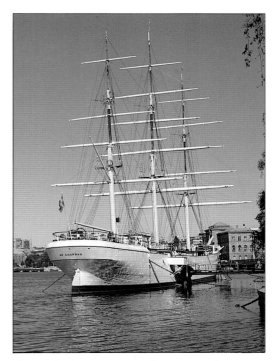

Stockholm harbor, Sweden: *this fine nineteenth-century sailing ship is now a Youth Hostel for visitors to the Swedish capital. Stockholm is built on lots of islands around a large harbor. It is fun to explore the city by boat.*

LAND OF ICE AND FIRE

Iceland has many volcanoes. *Most are quiet and peaceful (above left). But… sometimes a great volcanic eruption lights up the night sky and the light is reflected in the sea (above right).*

Only 260,000 people live in Iceland. It is near the Arctic Circle and there is ice on the mountains, in glaciers and ice sheets. A warm Atlantic current keeps the sea ice-free and it is full of fish. Iceland has an important fishing fleet.

THE UK AND IRELAND

AREA 94,202 sq miles
POPULATION 58,306,000
MONEY Pound sterling
CAPITAL London
FLAG Union Jack

The United Kingdom is made up of Great Britain (England, Wales and Scotland) and Northern Ireland. The UK was the most important country in the world 150 years ago. Many old factories and coal mines have now closed down, and several million people have no jobs.

Much of the UK is still quiet and beautiful, with very varied scenery. The north and west of Great Britain are made of old, hard rocks. This area is higher and wetter than the south and east, and has pasture for cattle and sheep. Most of the arable farming is in the lower, drier and flatter south and east.

Bodiam Castle is in the county of Sussex, south of London. It was built over 600 years ago against a possible French invasion. Today it is a ruin surrounded by a fine moat and its "invaders" are tourists. The tourist industry is very important for the UK, and visitors come from all over the world to visit historic places.

Ireland: Long ago, horses were used for plowing the fields – a skilled job. But today, "horsepower" means gasoline and machines.

IRELAND

AREA 27,135 sq miles
POPULATION 3,589,000
MONEY Irish pound
CAPITAL Dublin

Rugby football was invented last century by a schoolboy at an English private school at Rugby. It is very popular in Wales – the hosts of the Rugby World Cup competition in 1999.

STAMP

Can you spot 8 famous London landmarks on this stamp? (Answers on page 96.)

Dublin, capital of the Republic of Ireland, is built beside the River Liffey. These fine old houses overlooking the river are now carefully preserved. A quarter of the country's population lives in Dublin and its suburbs.

The Somerset Levels, south of Bristol in southwest England. The foreground was marshland which has been drained – it is below the level of high tides.

The Republic of Ireland is a completely separate country from the UK. There were twice as many people in Ireland 150 years ago as there are today. Farming is still important, but new factories have been built in many towns. Even so, many Irish people have moved to the UK or to the USA to find work.

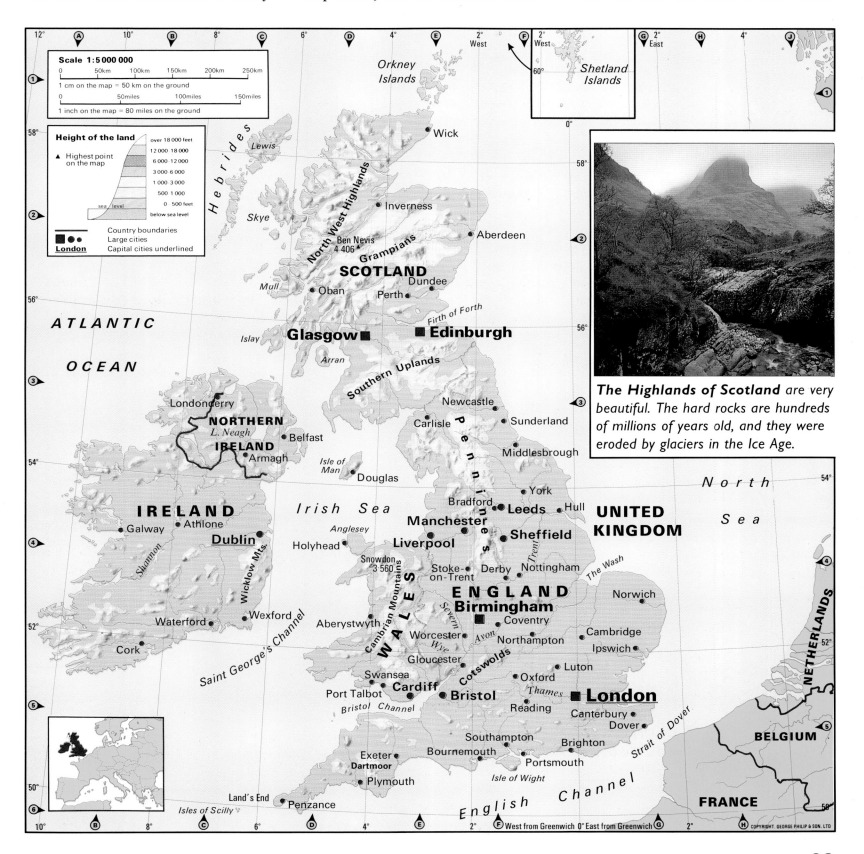

Scale 1:5 000 000

| 0 | 50km | 100km | 150km | 200km | 250km |

1 cm on the map = 50 km on the ground

| 0 | 50miles | 100miles | 150miles |

1 inch on the map = 80 miles on the ground

Height of the land

over 18 000 feet
12 000–18 000
6 000–12 000
3 000–6 000
1 000–3 000
500–1 000
0–500 feet
below sea level

▲ Highest point on the map

sea level

Country boundaries
Large cities
Capital cities underlined
London

Orkney Islands

Shetland Islands

Wick

Lewis

Hebrides

Skye

North West Highlands

Inverness

Aberdeen

Mull

Ben Nevis 4 406 ▲

Grampians

SCOTLAND

Dundee

Oban

Perth

Firth of Forth

Islay

Glasgow ■

■ **Edinburgh**

Arran

Southern Uplands

ATLANTIC

OCEAN

Newcastle

Londonderry

NORTHERN

L. Neagh

● Belfast

IRELAND

Armagh

Carlisle

Sunderland

Middlesbrough

Pennines

Isle of Man

Douglas

York

IRELAND

Irish Sea

Bradford

Leeds

Hull

UNITED

KINGDOM

Galway

Athlone

Anglesey

Manchester

Sheffield

Shannon

Dublin

Holyhead

Liverpool

Wicklow Mts.

Snowdon 3 560

Stoke-on-Trent

Derby

Nottingham

Trent

The Wash

North

Sea

E N G L A N D

Norwich

Wexford

Cambrian Mountains

Birmingham

Coventry

Cambridge

Waterford

Aberystwyth

Worcester

Avon

Northampton

Ipswich

Severn

Wye

Cork

Gloucester

Cotswolds

Luton

W A L E S

Swansea

Cardiff

● Oxford

Saint George's Channel

Port Talbot

Bristol

Thames

■ **London**

Bristol Channel

Reading

Canterbury

Dover

BELGIUM

Southampton

Brighton

Strait of Dover

Exeter

Bournemouth

Portsmouth

Dartmoor

Isle of Wight

Plymouth

English *Channel*

FRANCE

Land's End

Penzance

Isles of Scilly

NETHERLANDS

West from Greenwich 0° East from Greenwich

COPYRIGHT. GEORGE PHILIP & SON. LTD

The Highlands of Scotland are very beautiful. The hard rocks are hundreds of millions of years old, and they were eroded by glaciers in the Ice Age.

23

BENELUX

NETHERLANDS

AREA 16,033 sq miles
POPULATION 15,495,000
MONEY Guilder

BELGIUM

AREA 11,780 sq miles
POPULATION 10,140,000
MONEY Belgian franc

Benelux is a word made up from BElgium, NEtherlands and LUXembourg. Fortunately, the first two letters of each name are the same in most languages, so everyone can understand the word. These three countries agreed to cooperate soon after World War 2. But they still have their very own King (of Belgium), Queen (of the Netherlands), and Grand Duke (of Luxembourg).

The Benelux countries are all small and are the most crowded in mainland Europe, but there is plenty of countryside too. Most of the land is low and flat, so they are sometimes called the Low Countries.

LUXEMBOURG

AREA 1,000 sq miles
POPULATION 408,000
MONEY Luxembourg franc

Are these windmills? Most Dutch "windmills" are really wind pumps. They were used to pump water up from the fields into rivers and canals. The river is higher than the land! These are at Kinderdijk, east of Rotterdam.

GAINING LAND

The map shows that a large part of the Netherlands is below sea level. For over 1000 years, the Dutch have built dykes (embankments) to keep out the sea and rivers. Then the water is pumped out. Once they used wind pumps; today they use diesel or electric pumps. The rich farmland grows vegetables and flowers.

Bruges is a historic town in Belgium. These old houses have survived many wars. Canals run through the town. The houses have no back door or garden – but they get a lovely view!

SPOT THE DIFFERENCE

What is the difference between these two coins from Belgium? And why is there a difference? (Answers on page 96.)

Europort, Rotterdam. Rotterdam is by far the biggest port in the whole world. Ships come from all over the world, and barges travel along the River Rhine and the canals of Europe to reach the port. Whole families live on the barges; sometimes they even take their car with them!

PUZZLE

A puzzle from the Netherlands:
● What are these yellow objects?
● What are they made of?
● Why are they for sale?
(Answers on page 96.)

Luxembourg and eastern Belgium have pleasant wooded hills called the Ardennes. Once, there was a flourishing steel industry using coal from Belgium and iron ore from Luxembourg. Today, most of the coal mines have closed and central Belgium is a problem area.

The eastern part of the Netherlands has large areas of heath and forest. But the best-known landscape is the "polders" of the west.

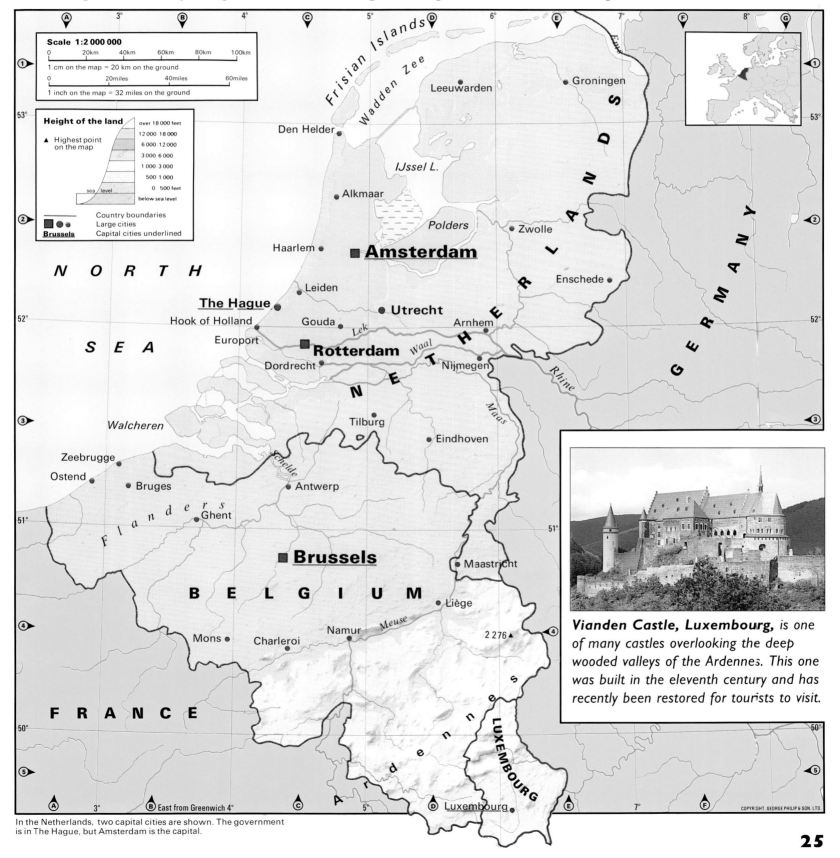

Scale 1:2 000 000

| 0 | 20km | 40km | 60km | 80km | 100km |

1 cm on the map = 20 km on the ground

| 0 | 20miles | 40miles | 60miles |

1 inch on the map = 32 miles on the ground

Height of the land

over 18 000 feet
12 000 · 18 000
6 000 · 12 000
3 000 · 6 000
1 000 · 3 000
500 · 1 000
0 · 500 feet
below sea level

▲ Highest point on the map

sea level

Country boundaries
Large cities
Brussels Capital cities underlined

Frisian Islands

Wadden Zee

Leeuwarden • Groningen

Den Helder

IJssel L.

Alkmaar

Polders • Zwolle

Haarlem • ■ **Amsterdam**

Enschede •

N O R T H

Leiden

The Hague • Utrecht

Hook of Holland Gouda Lek Arnhem

Europort ■ Rotterdam Waal

S E A Dordrecht Nijmegen

N E T H E R L A N D S

Rhine

G E R M A N Y

Maas

Walcheren Tilburg

Eindhoven

Zeebrugge

Ostend • Bruges Scheldt • Antwerp

F l a n d e r s • Ghent

B E L G I U M Maastricht

■ **Brussels**

• Liège

Mons • Charleroi Namur Meuse 2 276 ▲

F R A N C E

A r d e n n e s LUXEMBOURG

Luxembourg

Vianden Castle, Luxembourg, *is one of many castles overlooking the deep wooded valleys of the Ardennes. This one was built in the eleventh century and has recently been restored for tourists to visit.*

In the Netherlands, two capital cities are shown. The government is in The Hague, but Amsterdam is the capital.

25

FRANCE

*These Majorette
models are made in
France. They include
a Renault van, a
Michelin truck, an Air
France bus and a Paris
bus. The most popular
French cars are:*

RENAULT

CITROËN

PEUGEOT

*What else can you
find in your home that
is made in France?
In our home we have:
BIC ballpoint pens,
LE CREUSET frying
pans and saucepans,
ARCOROC glassware,
ARCOPOL cups,
a **MOULINEX** mixer,
and lots and lots of
MAJORETTE cars!*

France is a country with three coastlines: can you see which these are? It is hot in summer in the south, but usually cool in the mountains and in the north. France is the biggest country in Western Europe, so there are big contrasts between north and south.

The highest mountains are the Alps in the southeast and the Pyrenees in the southwest. They are popular for skiing in winter and for summer holidays too. More than half the country is lowland, and farming is very important. Besides fruit, vegetables and wine, France is famous for its many different cheeses and wines.

Mont Blanc. *The "White Mountain" is the
highest mountain in Western Europe. It is 15,771
feet high. Even in summer (as here) it is covered
in snow. Cable cars take tourists and skiers up
the mountain, and there is a road tunnel through
Mont Blanc to Italy.*

The Eiffel Tower
*was built in Paris in
1889. It was designed
by Monsieur Eiffel,
an engineer. It is
984 feet high and
weighs 9550 tons!*

FRENCH WINE

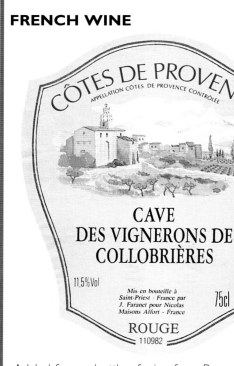

A label from a bottle of wine from Provence, in the
south of France. It shows a village in Provence, with
fruit trees and long, straight rows of vines.

AREA 212,934 sq miles
POPULATION 58,286,000
MONEY Franc

Market at Grasse.
*Which fruit can you
recognize on this stall?
(Answers on page 96.)
Every town in France
has a good market
with fresh fruit and
vegetables.*

France is changing fast. The number of people living in villages is going down, and the population of the cities is growing – partly swelled by Arabs from North Africa who have come to live in France. The biggest city is Paris, which is also the capital. Ten million people live in the Paris region, and five big new towns have been built around Paris. "Disneyland Paris" brings many more tourists to the area.

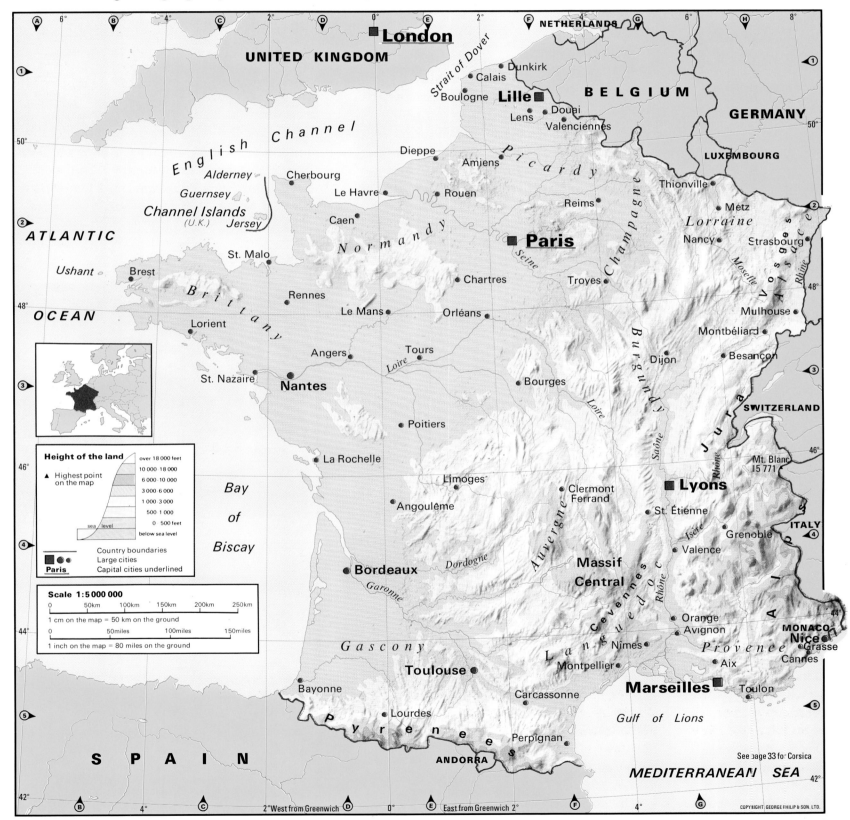

Height of the land

▲ Highest point on the map	over 18 000 feet
	10 000–18 000
	6 000–10 000
	3 000–6 000
	1 000–3 000
	500–1 000
sea level	0–500 feet
	below sea level

Country boundaries
Large cities
Paris Capital cities underlined

Scale 1:5 000 000

0   50km   100km   150km   200km   250km

1 cm on the map = 50 km on the ground

0   50miles   100miles   150miles

1 inch on the map = 80 miles on the ground

See page 33 for Corsica

COPYRIGHT. GEORGE PHILIP & SON. LTD.

GERMANY AND AUSTRIA

GERMANY

AREA 137,803 sq miles
POPULATION 82,000,000
MONEY Deutschmark

AUSTRIA

AREA 32,374 sq miles
POPULATION 8,004,000
MONEY Schilling

Berlin: this ruined tower, next to the new tower of the Memorial Church, is left as a reminder of the destruction caused by war. It is in the city center. Berlin is no longer divided and is once again the capital of a united Germany.

Germany has more people than any other European country apart from Russia. Most of the 82 million Germans live in towns and cities. Several million people called "guest workers" have come from southern Europe and Turkey to work in Germany's factories. But nowadays there is unemployment in Germany, as in other European countries, and many "guest workers" have returned home. Among the many different goods made in Germany there are excellent cars: BMW, Ford, Mercedes, Opel, Porsche and Volkswagen.

There is also plenty of beautiful and uncrowded countryside. The north is mostly lowland. Parts of the south, such as the Black Forest, are mountainous and popular for vacations.

Germany was one country from 1870 to 1945. In 1990 it became one country again. From 1945 until 1990, it was divided into West Germany and East Germany, and there was a border fence between the two. In Berlin, the high wall that divided the city into east and west was knocked down in 1989.

Edelweiss are flowers that grow high in the Alps. They can survive in thin soil on steep slopes, and do not mind being buried by snow all winter. They are a national symbol in Austria.

The Rhine Gorge, in western Germany. Castles once guarded this important river route. The River Rhine flows from Switzerland, through Germany to the Netherlands. Big barges travel between the ports and factories beside the river.

TRANSPORT

Germany has excellent railways. This train (above) hangs from one rail. This monorail is built over the River Wupper (near the River Ruhr) to save space.

These three stamps show a diesel engine (top left), a model of a "hover train" (right), and a double-decker car transporter (left). Germany's fastest trains are labeled ICE: "Inter-City Express."

AUSTRIA: Until 1918, Austria and Hungary were linked, and together ruled a great empire which included much of Central Europe and Slovenia, Croatia and Bosnia (see page 34). But now Austria is a small, peaceful country.

In the west of Austria are the high Alps, and many tourists come to enjoy the beautiful scenery and winter sports. Busy freeways and electric railways cross the Austrian Alps to link Germany with Italy.

Most Austrians live in the lower eastern part of the country. The capital, Vienna, was once at the center of the Austrian Empire; now it is in a corner of the country.

Hallstatt, Austria, is built on steep slopes which are part of the Dachstein Mountains in the eastern Alps, southeast of Salzburg. It lies beside a deep blue lake with the same name. Prehistoric remains have been found near here.

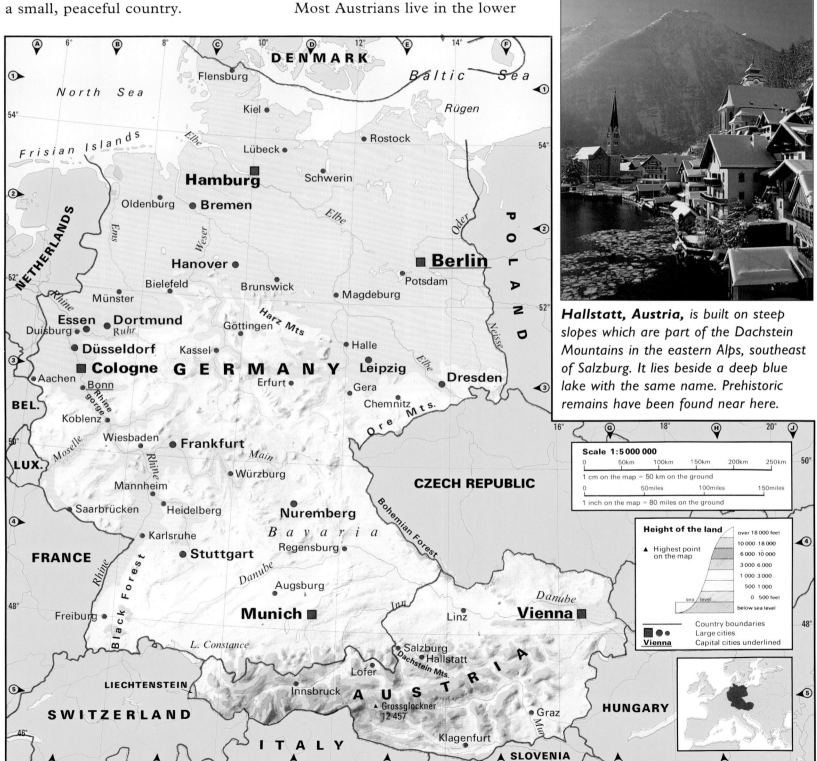

Scale 1:5 000 000

1 cm on the map = 50 km on the ground

1 inch on the map = 80 miles on the ground

Height of the land

over 18 000 feet
10 000 - 18 000
6 000 - 10 000
3 000 - 6 000
1 000 - 3 000
500 - 1 000
0 - 500 feet
below sea level

▲ Highest point on the map

Country boundaries
Large cities
Vienna Capital cities underlined

Germany is shown with two capital cities. Berlin is the capital, but the seat of government is in Bonn.

29

SPAIN AND PORTUGAL

SPAIN

AREA 194,896 sq miles
POPULATION 39,664,000
MONEY Peseta

PORTUGAL

AREA 35,670 sq miles
POPULATION 10,600,000
MONEY Escudo

Spain and Portugal are separated from the rest of Europe by the high Pyrenees Mountains. Most people traveling by land from the north reach Spain along the Atlantic or Mediterranean coasts.

The Meseta is the high plateau of central Spain. Winters are very cold, and summers are very hot. Olives and grapes are the main crops, and both Spain and Portugal export famous wines such as sherry and port. Cars are the biggest export from Spain nowadays. Both Spain and Portugal have fine cities with great churches and cathedrals, built when they were the richest countries in the world.

Christopher Columbus' ship in Barcelona, Spain. *Beyond the palm trees and the plaza (square) is a replica of the ship in which Columbus sailed across the Atlantic Ocean in 1492 to discover the "New World" of the Americas. The voyage was paid for by the Queen of Spain.*

Portuguese fishermen *mending their nets at Tavira, on the Algarve. They continue to land sardines and other fish, but the town relies on the tourist trade for most of its income.*

DID YOU KNOW?

Gibraltar is still a British colony, but it is only about 2½ square miles in area. Spain still owns two towns in Morocco: *Ceuta* and *Melilla*. Spain wants Gibraltar – and Morocco wants Ceuta and Melilla. The argument has been going on for nearly 300 years....

THE ALHAMBRA PALACE

The Alhambra Palace, Granada. This beautiful palace was built by the Moors (Arabs from North Africa). The Moors ruled southern Spain for hundreds of years, until 1492. The Arabs brought new crops and new ideas to Europe, such as oranges, rice and sugarcane, which are still grown in Spain today.

The photo (left) of the Court of Lions shows the stone lions carved 600 years ago by Arab craftsmen.

Village in southern Spain. *The old houses crowd closely together, and roads are very narrow: wide enough for a donkey, but not for trucks. People whitewash their houses to reflect the rays of the hot sun. Some of the roofs are used as balconies.*

Spain is popular for vacations: the Costa Brava (Rugged Coast), Costa del Sol (Coast of the Sun) and Balearic Islands are crowded in summer. The Canary Islands belong to Spain, although they are over 700 miles away, off the coast of Africa (see map page 55: square B2).

In Portugal, the Algarve coast is the most popular vacation area, along with Madeira which is far out in the Atlantic (see map page 55: B1).

Scale 1:5 000 000

0   50km   100km   150km   200km   250km

1 cm on the map = 50 km on the ground

0   50miles   100miles   150miles

1 inch on the map = 80 miles on the ground

Bay   of   Biscay

FRANCE

Height of the land

	over 18 000 feet
	10 000–18 000
▲ Highest point on the map	6 000–10 000
	3 000–6 000
	1 000–3 000
	500–1 000
	0–500 feet
sea level	below sea level

Country boundaries
Large cities
Madrid Capital cities underlined

West from Greenwich 0° East from Greenwich

COPYRIGHT. GEORGE PHILIP & SON. LTD.

31

SWITZERLAND AND ITALY

SWITZERLAND

AREA 15,942 sq miles
POPULATION 7,268,000
MONEY Swiss franc

The Matterhorn
in the Swiss Alps is
14,691 ft high. Glaciers
helped carve its shape.
Zermatt is the ski
resort which gives good
views of the peak.

Italy is shaped like a boot: its toe seems to be kicking Sicily! The shape is caused by the long range of fold mountains called the Apennines. The great Roman Empire was centered on Italy, and there are many Roman ruins. Yet Italy was only united as a country less than 150 years ago. Italy has lots of big factories. The Fiat car plant in Turin is one of the largest and most modern in the world.

The south of Italy and the islands of Sicily and Sardinia have hot, dry summers. These areas are much less rich than the north. Many people have moved to the north to find work. But government projects are bringing factories and better roads.

In Switzerland, most people live in cities north of the Alps. Switzerland is one of the world's richest countries, with modern banks, offices and factories. Rivers, dams and waterfalls in the Alps are used for making hydroelectric power: trains, factories and homes in Switzerland all run on cheap electricity. Cable cars powered by electricity take skiers and tourists high into the beautiful mountains. Switzerland holds some amazing world records (see below).

Venice, in northeast Italy, is a city built in the sea. Everywhere in the old town has to be reached by boat, or on foot, because the "roads" are canals.

ITALIAN FOOD

Large plum tomatoes are tinned (above). Many kinds of fruit are dried and used in cakes (right).

Pasta (above) is made from Italian wheat. Spaghetti, macaroni and ravioli are pastas.

SWISS RECORD BREAKERS!

- The longest road tunnel is the St Gotthard tunnel (10.14 miles).
- The longest stairway is beside the Niesenbahn mountain railway, near Spiez. It has 11,674 steps!
- The steepest railway goes up Mount Pilatus. It has a gradient of 48%.
- Switzerland has been at peace with everyone since 1815. That's quite a record!

Celano, in the Abruzzo region. This is in the Apennine Mountains in central Italy. The old hill town with its castle was a safe place to live. The new town spreads over flat land which was once a lake.

ITALY

AREA 116,320 sq miles
POPULATION 58,181,000
MONEY Lira

Other countries on this map:
VATICAN CITY in Rome,
SAN MARINO within Italy,
MALTA, an island country south of Italy.

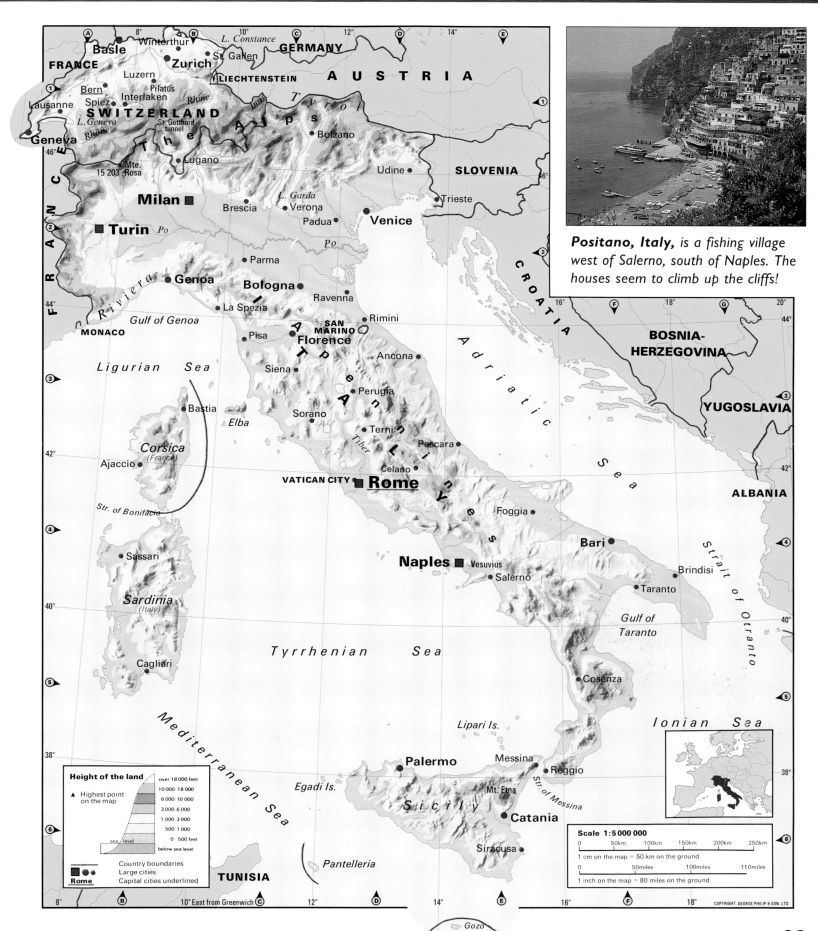

Positano, Italy, *is a fishing village west of Salerno, south of Naples. The houses seem to climb up the cliffs!*

GERMANY

FRANCE

Basle
Winterthur
St. Gallen
Zurich
Luzern
LIECHTENSTEIN

AUSTRIA

Bern
Spiez
Pilatus
Interlaken
Lausanne
SWITZERLAND
L. Geneva
Geneva
Rhone
Rhine
St. Gotthard tunnel
Mte.
15 203 Rosa
Lugano
Bolzano

SLOVENIA

Udine

L. Garda
Brescia
Verona
Padua
Venice
Trieste

Milan

Turin
Po
Po

Parma

Genoa
Bologna
Ravenna

Riviera
La Spezia
Rimini
SAN MARINO
MONACO
Pisa
Florence

CROATIA

Gulf of Genoa

Ligurian Sea
Siena
Ancona

Bastia
Perugia
Elba
Sorano

Corsica
(France)
Terni
Pescara

Ajaccio
Tiber
Celano

VATICAN CITY **Rome**

BOSNIA-HERZEGOVINA

YUGOSLAVIA

ALBANIA

Foggia

Bari

Sassari

Naples
Vesuvius
Salerno
Brindisi
Taranto

Sardinia
(Italy)

Gulf of Taranto

Cagliari

Tyrrhenian Sea

Cosenza

Mediterranean Sea

Lipari Is.

Ionian Sea

Palermo
Messina
Reggio

Egadi Is.
Mt. Etna
Str. of Messina

Sicily
Catania

Siracusa

Pantelleria

Str. of Bonifacio

Str. of Otranto

Adriatic Sea

Apennines

The Alps
Tyrol
Inn
Rhine

Height of the land
▲ Highest point on the map
over 18 000 feet
10 000-18 000
6 000-10 000
3 000-6 000
1 000-3 000
500-1 000
0 - 500 feet
sea level
below sea level

Country boundaries
Large cities
Rome Capital cities underlined

Scale 1:5 000 000
0 50km 100km 150km 200km 250km
1 cm on the map = 50 km on the ground
0 50miles 100miles 150miles
1 inch on the map = 80 miles on the ground

TUNISIA

8° 10° East from Greenwich 12° 14° 16° 18°

COPYRIGHT. GEORGE PHILIP & SON. LTD

MALTA Gozo Valletta

SOUTHEAST EUROPE

GREECE

AREA 50,961 sq miles
POPULATION 10,510,000
MONEY Drachma

BULGARIA

AREA 42,822 sq miles
POPULATION 9,020,000
MONEY Lev

ALBANIA

AREA 11,100 sq miles
POPULATION 3,458,000
MONEY Lek

Most of southeast Europe is very mountainous, except near the River Danube. Farmers keep sheep and goats in the mountains and grow grain, vines and sunflowers on the lower land.

The coastlines are popular with tourists. There are many vacation resorts beside the Aegean Sea (**Greece** and **Turkey**) and the Black Sea (**Romania** and **Bulgaria**). The Romanians are building new ski villages in their mountains. All these countries are trying to develop new industries, but this is still one of the poorest parts of Europe.

Albania is the least-known country in all Europe: very few people visit it. No railways crossed the frontier of Albania until 1985.

Yugoslavia was 1 country with 2 alphabets (Latin and Cyrillic), 3 religious groups (Roman Catholic, Orthodox and Muslim), 4 languages and 6 republics. No wonder there are now problems! **Slovenia**, **Croatia**, **Macedonia** and **Bosnia-Herzegovina** are now independent countries.

The town of Korcula, in Croatia, is built on an island – also called Korcula – in the Adriatic Sea, northwest of Dubrovnik. In the distance are the limestone mountains of the mainland. Until 1991, Croatia was part of Yugoslavia, but after some fighting it became independent.

THE CORINTH CANAL

A passenger liner being towed through the Corinth Canal in southern Greece. The canal was cut in 1893 and is 4 miles long. It links the Gulf of Corinth with the Aegean Sea.

THE DANUBE

This stamp shows a boat at the gorge on the River Danube called the Iron Gates, on the southern border of Romania. The Danube flows from Germany to a marshy delta beside the Black Sea.

Harvest time in Romania. The tomato harvest is being gathered by hand on a hot summer day. The horse-drawn cart will take the full boxes back to the village for distribution.

ΑΒΓΔΕΖΗΘΙΚΛΜΝΞΟΠΡΣΤΥΦΧΨΩ
A V/B G D E Z E TH I K L M N X O P R S T Y F CH PS O

The Greek alphabet. *The Greeks developed their alphabet before the Romans, and they still use it. Some letters are the same as ours (A, B . . .), and some look the same but have a different sound (P, H . . .). The other letters are completely different. Some Greek letters appear in the Cyrillic alphabet, which is used in Bulgaria, Yugoslavia and Russia (see page 41). The word "alphabet" is formed from the first two Greek letters: alpha and beta. The Greek letter for D is called "delta."*

Mikonos, Greece, *used to be a quiet village on a quiet island in the Aegean Sea. The journey from Athens was 7 hours by boat. Today, airplanes bring over half a million tourists to the island every year. They love the sunshine, the beaches and the boating.*

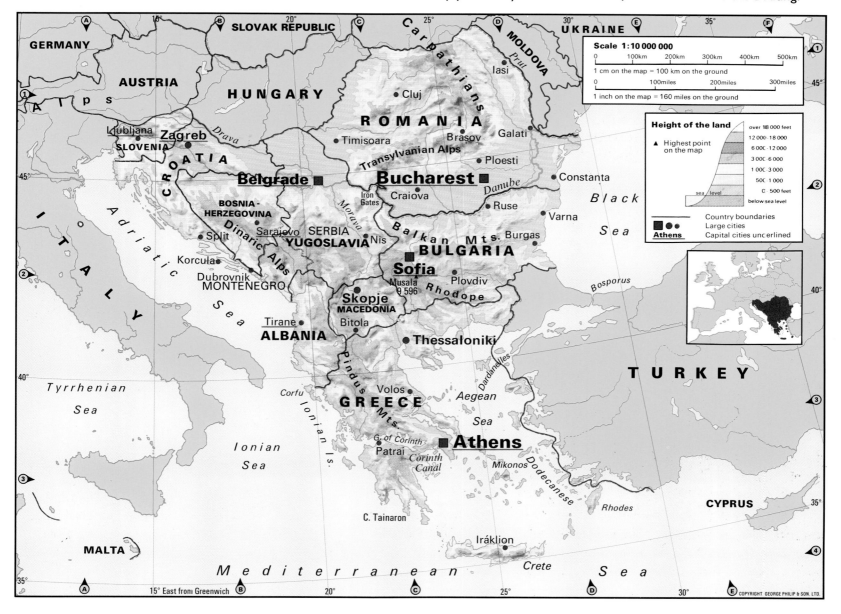

Scale 1:10 000 000

0   100km   200km   300km   400km   500km

1 cm on the map = 100 km on the ground

0   100miles   200miles   300miles

1 inch on the map = 160 miles on the ground

Height of the land

| | over 18 000 feet |
| | 12 000-18 000 |
▲ Highest point | 6 000-12 000 |
on the map | 3 000-6 000 |
	1 000-3 000
	500-1 000
	0-500 feet
sea level | below sea level |

■ ● ● Country boundaries / Large cities

Athens Capital cities underlined

GERMANY · SLOVAK REPUBLIC · UKRAINE · MOLDOVA · AUSTRIA · HUNGARY · Carpathians · Iasi · Prut · Cluj · ROMANIA · Ljubljana · Zagreb · SLOVENIA · Drava · Timisoara · Brasov · Galati · Transylvanian Alps · Ploesti · CROATIA · Belgrade · Bucharest · Constanta · BOSNIA-HERZEGOVINA · Iron Gates · Craiova · Danube · Black · Split · Sarajevo · SERBIA · Morava · Ruse · Varna · Sea · Dinaric Alps · YUGOSLAVIA · Nis · Balkan Mts. · Burgas · Korcula · BULGARIA · Dubrovnik · MONTENEGRO · Sofia · Plovdiv · Bosporus · Musala 9 596 · Skopje · Rhodope · MACEDONIA · Bitola · Tirane · Thessaloniki · ALBANIA · TURKEY · ITALY · Adriatic Sea · Dardanelles · Pindus Mts. · Volos · Aegean · 40° · Tyrrhenian Sea · Corfu · GREECE · Sea · G. of Corinth · Athens · Ionian Is. · Patrai · Corinth Canal · Mikonos · Dodecanese · Ionian Sea · CYPRUS · Rhodes · C. Tainaron · MALTA · Iráklion · Crete · Mediterranean Sea

15° East from Greenwich   COPYRIGHT GEORGE PHILIP & SON. LTD.

EASTERN EUROPE

AREA 120,726 sq miles
POPULATION 38,587,000
MONEY Zloty

AREA 35,919 sq miles
POPULATION 10,500,000
MONEY Forint

AREA 233,100 sq miles
POPULATION 52,027,000
MONEY Hryvna

Poland has a coastline on the Baltic Sea. There are huge shipbuilding factories at Gdansk. There are big factories in the towns in the south, too, where there is plenty of coal. Most of the country is flat farmland, but there are magnificent mountains in the far south which are being "rediscovered" by tourists from Western Europe.

Czechoslovakia split into two countries in 1993. The Czech Republic is west of the Slovak Republic. Both countries have beautiful hills and mountains, with fine pine trees. Skoda cars come from the Czech Republic. Further south is Hungary, which is a small, flat country. Mostly it is farmland, but Hungary also has the biggest bus factory in the world.

Polish, Czech and Slovak are all Slavic languages. Hungarian is a totally different language; it came from central Asia. Some Hungarian speakers also live in Slovakia and Romania.

Town square in Telc, Czech Republic. *The historic centers of towns are carefully preserved in Eastern Europe. Some have been totally rebuilt in the old style, after wartime bombing.*

Church in a lake! *Europe's longest river is the Volga in Russia. Dams have been built on this river, so lakes have formed behind the dams — and whole villages have vanished beneath the water. That is why there is now a church in a lake. Sadly, the dams also trap polluted water.*

Church in Ukraine, *where many people are Orthodox Christians. The churches are beautiful, and the services are often very long. The Ukraine is Europe's biggest country, apart from Russia. The population is nearly as big as the UK or France.*

AREA 80,154 sq miles
POPULATION 10,500,000
MONEY Rouble

Budapest, on the River Danube. *Buda and Pest were twin cities on either side of the River Danube. Now they have become Budapest, capital of Hungary. This picture shows old buildings on the hills of Buda.*

Eleven countries on this map were part of the USSR until 1991. The three Baltic Republics broke away first (see box, right). Belarus (meaning "White Russia") and little Moldova are landlocked countries. Ukraine, the largest country completely in Europe, has large areas of fertile farmland. There is plenty of coal for its steelworks. The three countries east of the Black Sea have had local wars since independence.

Harvest time in Poland. You can still see "horsepower" in action, though there are now far more tractors than horses. The wheat is tied into "stooks" to dry.

THREE "REBORN" COUNTRIES

Estonia, Latvia and Lithuania became independent countries once more in 1991. They were also independent from 1918 to 1940. They proudly show their flags on their stamps. These three countries are called "The Baltic Republics". because they all have a coastline on the Baltic Sea. Their land is low-lying with large areas of forest. Each country is very small, and has a small population – much smaller than the population of Paris or London.

The border of Poland (right) and the Slovak Republic (left) runs along a high ridge of the Tatra Mountains. It is marked by small posts beside the footpath. The steep slopes were shaped by ice. A cable car can take you to the border for a walk, or for skiing in winter.

ASIA

The world's largest continent is Asia, which stretches from the cold Arctic Ocean in the north to the warm Indian Ocean in the tropical south. Mainland Asia nearly reaches the Equator in Malaysia. Several Asian islands are on the Equator: Sumatra, Borneo and Sulawesi. In the west, Asia reaches Europe and the Mediterranean, and in the east Asia reaches the Pacific Ocean. In the center are the high, empty plateaus of Tibet and Mongolia.

Two countries cover over half of Asia: Russia and China. India looks quite small – yet it is over ten times as big as Italy or the UK! But some of Asia's important countries are very small indeed, such as Lebanon and Israel in southwest Asia (Middle East); Singapore and Brunei in southeast Asia (Far East).

Over half the world's population lives in Asia. The coastal areas of south and east Asia are the most crowded parts. Seven of the "top ten" most populated countries in the world are in Asia: China, India, Indonesia, Russia, Japan, Bangladesh and Pakistan (see page 9).

This Buddhist shrine is like many found in Nepal. It has been decorated with prayer flags and painted eyes.

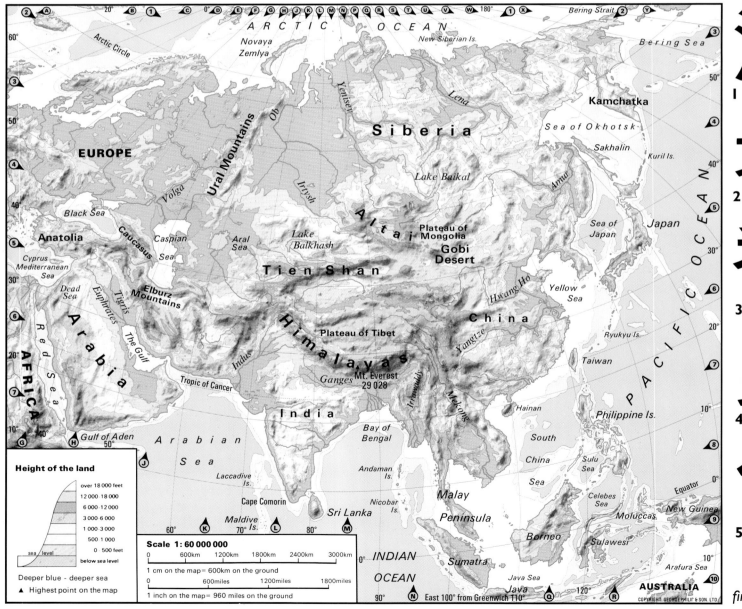

Height of the land

over 18 000 feet
12 000 - 18 000
6 000 - 12 000
3 000 - 6 000
1 000 - 3 000
500 - 1 000
0 - 500 feet
sea level
below sea level

Deeper blue - deeper sea

▲ Highest point on the map

Scale 1: 60 000 000

| 0 | 600km | 1200km | 1800km | 2400km | 3000km |

1 cm on the map = 600km on the ground

| 0 | 600miles | 1200miles | 1800miles |

1 inch on the map = 960 miles on the ground

East 100° from Greenwich 110°

COPYRIGHT. GEORGE PHILIP & SON. LTD.

澳埃香美台

Turn to page 96 to find out which

ASIA FACTS

AREA 17,137,820 sq miles (including Asiatic Russia)

HIGHEST POINT Mount Everest (Nepal/China), 29,028 ft (A *world record* as well as an Asian record.)

LOWEST POINT Shores of Dead Sea (Israel/Jordan), 1312 feet below sea level (A *world record* as well as an Asian record.)

LONGEST RIVERS Yangtze (China), 3960 miles; Yenisey (Russia), 3442 miles

BIGGEST COUNTRY Russia, 6,592,800 sq miles (A *world record* as well as an Asian record.)

SMALLEST COUNTRY The Maldives, 115 sq miles

LARGEST LAKE Caspian Sea 139,266 sq miles (A *world record* as well as an Asian record.) The Caspian Sea is shared by five countries – which are they? (Answers on page 96.)

Himalayan Mountains, Nepal. *The photograph shows the peaks of the Annapurnas rising above the cloud. Annapurna I is 26,502 feet high and was first climbed in 1950. The other four peaks in the group are over 24,500 feet high. The Himalayas are the world's highest mountain range, with all the world's "top ten" highest peaks, including Mount Everest.*

洲及港國灣

countries are in Chinese script here.

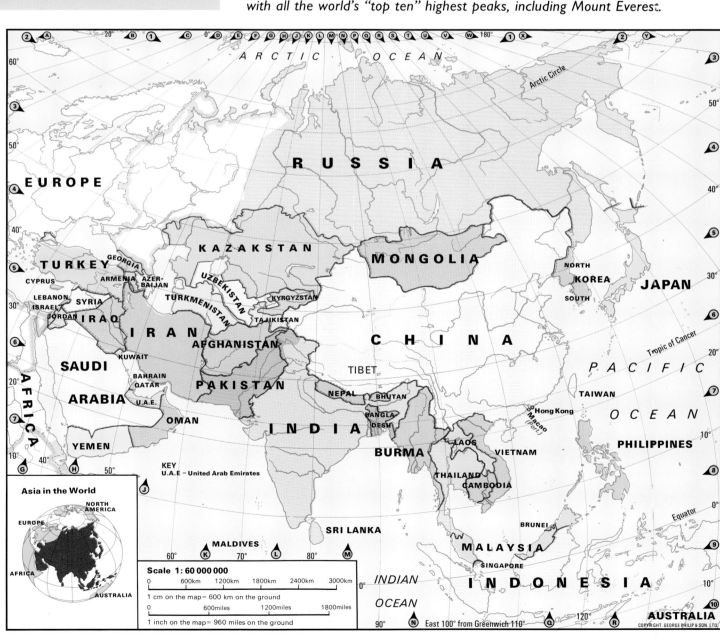

KEY
U.A.E = United Arab Emirates

Asia in the World

Scale 1 : 60 000 000

1 cm on the map = 600 km on the ground

1 inch on the map = 960 miles on the ground

COPYRIGHT. GEORGE PHILIP & SON. LTD

RUSSIA AND NEIGHBORS

RUSSIA

AREA 6,592,800 sq miles
POPULATION 148,385,000
MONEY Rouble

UZBEKISTAN

AREA 172,740 sq miles
POPULATION 22,833,000
MONEY Som

TURKMENISTAN

AREA 188,450 sq miles
POPULATION 4,100,000
MONEY Manat

Russia stretches across two continents, Europe and Asia. Most of the people live in the European part, west of the Ural Mountains. Some people have moved east to new towns in Siberia.

Because Russia is so huge, there are many different climates and almost all crops can be grown. The far north is snow-covered for most of the year (see page 88). Further south is the largest forest in the world – a vast area of coniferous trees stretching from the Baltic Sea to the Sea of Okhotsk in the far east. Grassy plains, called the steppes, are found south of the forest. In some parts, grain is grown on huge farms. Russia also has huge deposits of many different minerals and can supply most of the needs of its many different factories.

The republics of central Asia are mostly in a desert area – hot in summer but bitterly cold in winter. With irrigation, crops such as sugarcane and cotton grow well.

St Basil's cathedral, Moscow, is at one end of Red Square. It is famous for its brightly colored domes: each one is different. In the background are the domes and towers of buildings inside the Kremlin walls. "Kremlin" means "fortress." The Moscow Kremlin has a cathedral and offices of the government of Russia.

In Uzbekistan, people still use traditional looms like this one, for weaving silk, cotton and wool – but there is modern industry as well. Uzbekistan is one of the 15 "new" countries created when the USSR broke up in 1991. Can you name them? (Page 37 will help; answers on page 96.)

THE ARAL SEA . . .

. . . is getting smaller. These ships were once in the Aral Sea, but are now on dry land. This salty lake is drying up because rivers do not refill it with enough water. The water is used to irrigate fields instead.

Siberia has the world's largest forest. It stretches from the Ural Mountains to the far east of Russia. Most of the trees are conifers. They can survive the Siberian winters, which are long and extremely cold.

А	Б	В	Г	Д	Е	Ё	Ж	З	И	Й	К	Л	М	Н	О	П	Р	С	Т	У	Ф	Х	Ц	Ч	Ш	Щ	Ю	Я
A	B	V	G	D	E	YO	ZH	Z	I	Y	K	L	M	N	O	P	R	S	T	U	F	KH	TS	CH	SH	SHCH	YU	YA

The Cyrillic alphabet. *Russian is written in the Cyrillic alphabet. This is partly based on Latin letters (the same as English letters) and partly on Greek letters (see page 35).*

The alphabet was invented centuries ago by St Cyril, so that the Russian church could show it was separate from both the Roman and the Greek churches. In Cyrillic, R is written P, and S is written C. So the Metro is written МЕТРО.

Can you understand this message? Use the key above: **Х А Б А Р О В С К** *(square S4) is on the River* **А М У Р** *(see square R3 on the map).*

Now can you write Volga (the river) in Russian? Check your answer with the postage stamp on page 36. Now work out what the sign on the railway carriage (right) says. It's not as hard as it looks!

TRANS-SIBERIAN RAILWAY

It takes a week to cross Russia by train, and you must change your watch seven times. Here is the distance chart and timetable (only the main stops are shown).

МОСКВА-ВЛАДИВОСТОК

This is the plate on the side of the train. The translation is on page 96. This is one of the world's most exciting train journeys.

DISTANCE (IN MILES)	TOWN	TIME (IN MOSCOW)	DAY
0	Moscow	15:05	1
595	Kirov	04:00	2
1130	Yekaterinburg	16:25	2
1688	Omsk	03:13	3
2077	Novosibirsk	10:44	3
2550	Krasnoyarsk	22:31	3
3221	Irkutsk	16:23	4
3509	Ulan Ude	00:02	5
3855	Chita	09:23	5
4544	Skovorodino	05:20	6
5301	Khabarovsk	01:10	7
5777	Vladivostok	13:30*	7

* This is 20:30 local time in Vladivostok.

At these stations, there is time for a quick walk – and some bartering. But don't forget to allow another week to come back!

More details of European Russia are shown on page 37

MIDDLE EAST

SAUDI ARABIA

AREA 829,995 sq miles
POPULATION 18,395,000
MONEY Saudi riyal

JORDAN

AREA 34,444 sq miles
POPULATION 5,547,000
MONEY Jordan dinar

IRAN

AREA 636,293 sq miles
POPULATION 68,885,000
MONEY Rial

The "Middle East" is another name for "southwest Asia." It is the part of Asia which is closest to Europe and Africa. In fact, it is the only place where three continents meet. Turkey is partly in Europe and mostly in Asia. Of all the countries on this map, Turkey and Iran have the most people.

Most of the Middle East is semi-desert or desert. Yet many great civilizations have existed here, such as the Assyrian, the Babylonian and the Persian. Their monuments are found in the fertile valleys of the largest rivers, the Tigris and the Euphrates.

Scarce water is used to irrigate crops in some places. In others, herds of sheep and goats are kept. Dates from Iraq come from desert oases; oranges come from irrigated land in Israel. So much water is being taken from the River Jordan that the Dead Sea is getting smaller. Some countries make fresh water from salt water, but it is expensive.

Craft stall in Istanbul. *Craft industries still thrive in Turkey, and throughout the Middle East. The metal plates and pots were hammered out and decorated by hand. Europe and Asia meet at Istanbul, which used to be called Constantinople.*

IRAQ

AREA 169,235 sq miles
POPULATION 20,184,000
MONEY Iraqi dinar

STAMPS

Progress in Qatar *is shown by the highways and high-rise office blocks being built with money from oil.*

HOLY CITIES OF THE MIDDLE EAST

Jerusalem: a Jewish boy's Bar Mitzvah ceremony at the West Wall ("Wailing Wall"). The huge stones (in the background, on the right) are all that remains of the Jewish temple. Jerusalem is a holy city for Jews, Christians and Muslims. People of all three religions live here and many pilgrims and tourists visit the city.

Mecca: crowds of pilgrims surround the Kaaba (the huge black stone, right) inside the Great Mosque. Mecca is the holiest city of Islam as it is where the prophet Mohammed was born. Muslims try to come to worship here at least once in their lifetime. But wherever they are, they face toward Mecca when they pray.

Yemen: *an Arab scribe makes beautiful writing into an art form on this stamp.*

The Middle East has changed dramatically in the last 50 years. Oil was found beneath the Arabian desert and around The Gulf. At the same time, oil was in great demand in Europe and all over the world. The sale of oil has made some countries very rich, especially Saudi Arabia, Kuwait and Qatar. Often the rulers have benefited most, but they have also used the money to build schools, hospitals, fine roads and office blocks (see Qatar stamp). The "oil boom" has meant that many foreign workers have come to these countries.

Muscat is the capital city and chief port of Oman. The city is surrounded by rock desert and dry mountains. The Sultan has his palace here.

Camels in the desert of the United Arab Emirates – a view that has not changed for centuries. Only camels can be kept in such dry conditions.

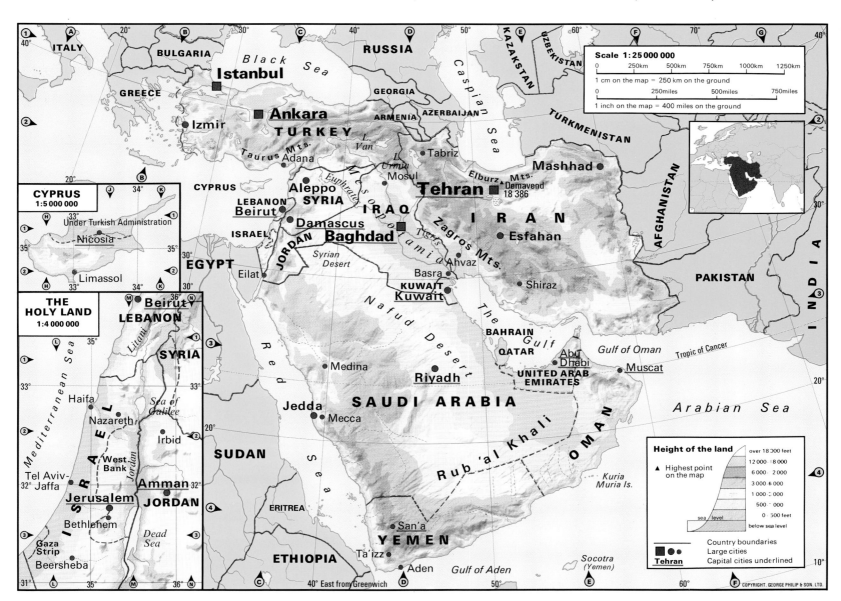

CYPRUS 1:5 000 000

Under Turkish Administration

Nicosia

Limassol

THE HOLY LAND 1:4 000 000

Beirut
LEBANON
SYRIA
Litani
Haifa
Sea of Galilee
Nazareth
Irbid
West Bank
Tel Aviv-Jaffa
Amman
Jerusalem
JORDAN
Bethlehem
Dead Sea
Gaza Strip
Beersheba
I S R A E L
Jordan
Mediterranean Sea

ITALY
BULGARIA
Black Sea
RUSSIA
KAZAKHSTAN
UZBEKISTAN
GREECE
Istanbul
Izmir
Ankara
T U R K E Y
GEORGIA
ARMENIA
AZERBAIJAN
Caspian Sea
TURKMENISTAN
Taurus Mts.
Adana
L. Van
L. Urmia
Tabriz
Mosul
Elburz Mts.
Demavend 18 386
Mashhad
Tehran
CYPRUS
Aleppo
SYRIA
LEBANON
Beirut
Damascus
ISRAEL
Baghdad
I R A Q
Mesopotamia
Tigris
Euphrates
Zagros Mts.
I R A N
Esfahan
AFGHANISTAN
EGYPT
Eilat
JORDAN
Syrian Desert
Ahvaz
Basra
KUWAIT
Kuwait
Shiraz
PAKISTAN
INDIA
Red Sea
Nafud Desert
BAHRAIN
QATAR
Gulf
Gulf of Oman
Tropic of Cancer
Abu Dhabi
Muscat
Medina
UNITED ARAB EMIRATES
Riyadh
Jedda
Mecca
SAUDI ARABIA
O M A N
Arabian Sea
SUDAN
D e s e r t
Rub 'al Khali
Kuria Muria Is.
ERITREA
San'a
Y E M E N
Ta'izz
ETHIOPIA
Aden
Gulf of Aden
Socotra (Yemen)

Scale 1:25 000 000
0 250km 500km 750km 1000km 1250km
1 cm on the map = 250 km on the ground
0 250miles 500miles 750miles
1 inch on the map = 400 miles on the ground

Height of the land
over 18 000 feet
▲ Highest point on the map
12 000–18 000
6 000–12 000
3 000–6 000
1 000–3 000
500–1 000
0–500 feet
sea level
below sea level

Country boundaries
Large cities
Tehran Capital cities underlined

40° East from Greenwich

COPYRIGHT. GEORGE PHILIP & SON. LTD.

43

SOUTH ASIA

INDIA

AREA 1,269,338 sq miles
POPULATION 942,989,000
MONEY Indian rupee
CAPITAL New Delhi

PAKISTAN

AREA 307,374 sq miles
POPULATION 143,595,000
MONEY Pakistan rupee
CAPITAL Islamabad

SRI LANKA

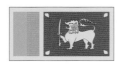

AREA 25,332 sq miles
POPULATION 18,359,000
MONEY Sri Lankan rupee

The world's highest mountains appear on this map, including Mount Everest. The Himalayas form a great mountain chain which joins on to other high mountain areas, such as the Hindu Kush.

More than 1200 million people live in south Asia. The deserts and mountains do not have many people, but the river valleys, plains and plateaus are crowded.

Afghanistan, **Bhutan** and **Nepal** are rugged, mountainous countries.

Bangladesh is very different: it is mostly flat, low-lying land where the great rivers Ganges and Brahmaputra reach the sea.

Pakistan is a desert country, but the River Indus is used to irrigate crops.

India is the largest country. It stretches 2050 miles from the Himalayas to Cape Comorin. Until 1947, Pakistan and Bangladesh were part of the Indian Empire, ruled by Britain.

Sri Lanka (formerly called Ceylon) is a mountainous island off the coast of India.

The Maldives are a chain of low, flat, coral islands in the Indian Ocean.

Wool for carpets. *This lady in northern India is winding wool which will be used to make carpets. She sits in the courtyard of her house, where the plows and pots and pans are also kept.*

TEA

Tea is an important crop in the hills of Sri Lanka where nights are cool, and there is plenty of rain. Women pick the new young leaves from the bushes (as shown on the stamp). The leaves are then dried and crushed, and packed into large tea chests for storage. "Ceylon Tea" is one of Sri Lanka's most important exports. Where does the tea you drink come from?

INDIAN FOOD
Most Indians are vegetarians. They like hot and spicy food. How many ingredients in this picture can you name?
(Answers on page 96.)

AFGHANISTAN

AREA 251,772 sq miles
POPULATION 19,509,000
MONEY Afghani

NEPAL

AREA 54,363 sq miles
POPULATION 21,953,000
MONEY Nepalese rupee

RELIGION is very important in the lives of people in south Asia.

Hinduism is the oldest religion, and most people in India and Nepal are Hindus.

Buddhism began in India, but only Sri Lanka and Bhutan are mainly Buddhist today.

Islam is the religion of the majority of people in Afghanistan, Pakistan and Bangladesh.

Many **Sikhs** live in northern India; there are also **Christian** groups in all these countries.

Rice is an important food crop in south Asia. It grows best where the land is flat, and where the weather is hot and wet. In a good year, rice grows in the wet fields and is ready for harvesting after four or five months. If the monsoon fails and there is a drought, the seedlings will shrivel up. If the rice crop fails, many people go hungry. Where irrigation is available, the farmer can control the water supply and may be able to grow two rice crops a year.

Planting rice, Kashmir, India. These men are planting out rice seedlings in the wet soil.

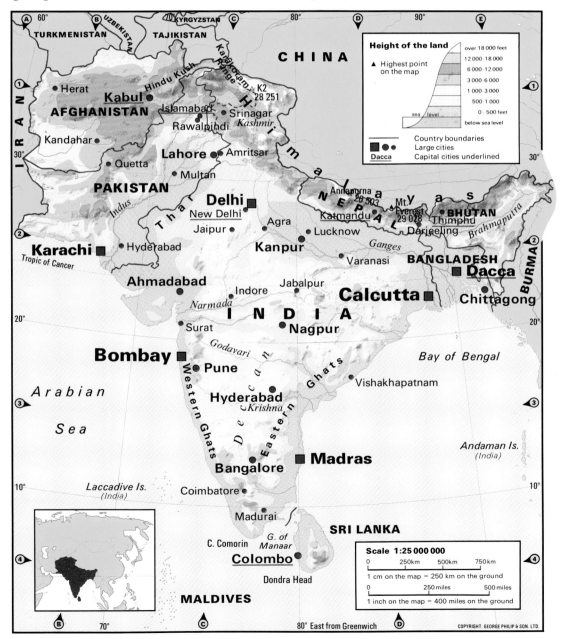

MOUNT EVEREST

Mount Everest is the world's highest mountain – 29,028 feet above sea level. It was not climbed until 1953.

Everest is on the border of Nepal and Tibet (now part of China) – find it on the map in square D2. It is called "Sagarmatha" in Nepalese, and in Chinese it is "Qomolangma" (Queen of Mountains).

The photograph shows a glacier below the icy summit, and the bare rock that climbers have to cross. At this height, the air has little oxygen, so climbing is very hard.

SOUTHEAST ASIA

PHILIPPINES

AREA 115,300 sq miles
POPULATION 67,167,000
MONEY Peso

THAILAND

AREA 198,116 sq miles
POPULATION 58,432,000
MONEY Baht

SINGAPORE

AREA 239 sq miles
POPULATION 2,990,000
MONEY Singapore dollar

Singapore is the world's most crowded country. Old houses (in the foreground) are being pulled down and new skyscrapers are replacing them.

The Equator crosses Southeast Asia, so it is always hot. Heavy tropical rainstorms are common. The mainland and most of the islands are very mountainous.

Indonesia is the biggest country. It used to be called the Dutch East Indies.

The Philippines is another large group of islands, south of China. They were Spanish until 1898.

Malaysia includes part of the mainland and most of northern Borneo.

Brunei is a very small but a very rich country on the island of Borneo.

Burma (Myanmar) was part of the Indian Empire. It became independent in 1948.

Vietnam, Laos and **Cambodia** were once called French Indochina.

Thailand has always been independent, and has a king.

Rice terraces, Bali. Rice grows on terraces cut into the mountainside in Bali. Each terrace is sown and harvested by hand. Bali is a small island east of Java. Some people claim that it is the most beautiful island of Indonesia, and in all the world!

GROWING RICE

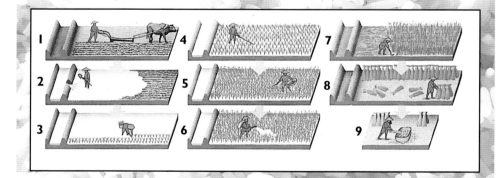

1 PLOWING	4 WEEDING	7 HARVESTING
2 IRRIGATION	5 FERTILIZING	8 DRYING
3 TRANSPLANTING	6 SPRAYING	9 THRESHING

Rice is the world's most important crop. The nine stages in growing rice are shown above. It is hot, hard work. Rice needs plenty of water as well as hot sunshine. New varieties of plants yield more rice, but they also need more fertilizer, more water and more care.

Floating market in Thailand. Farmers bring their fruit and vegetables by boat to a market at Damnoen Saduak, to the west of Bangkok. Fish are cooked on some of the boats and sold for lunch.

46

The mountains of Southeast Asia are covered with thick tropical forest (look at the stamp of Laos). These areas are very difficult to reach and have few people. The large rivers are important routes inland. Their valleys and deltas are very crowded indeed.

Java, Bali and Singapore are among the most crowded islands in the world – yet several bigger islands, such as Sulawesi and Borneo, have very small populations.

Laos. Elephants carry huge logs from the jungle. Laos was called Lanxang – "land of a million elephants."

Vietnam. These young children are learning to draw a map of their country.

Malaysia has a hot, wet climate. Pineapples grow well here. Some are tinned and exported.

Indonesia is mainly an Islamic country. The moon and star (seen here above a mosque) are traditional symbols of Islam.

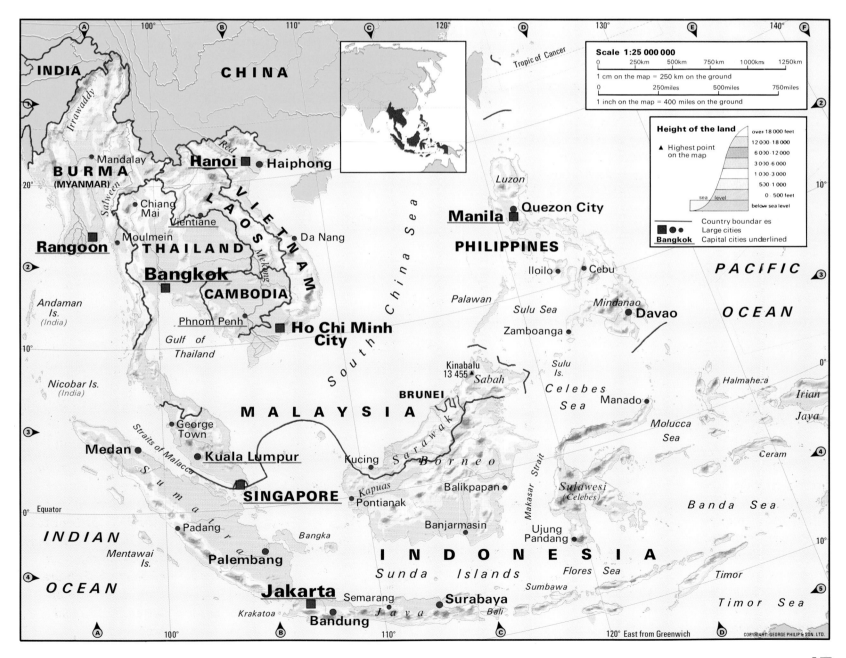

CHINA AND NEIGHBORS

CHINA

AREA 3,705,386 sq miles
POPULATION 1,226,944,000
MONEY Yuan

MONGOLIA

AREA 604,826 sq miles
POPULATION 2,408,000
MONEY Tugrik

China has over a billion people (1,226,944,000) – more than any other country in the world. The map shows that there are many high mountains in China, such as the huge plateau of Tibet and the rugged mountains of the southwest where the Giant Pandas live. Not many people live in these mountains, nor in the deserts of the north, near Mongolia.

So the lower land of eastern China is very crowded indeed. Rice grows well south of the River Yangtze. North of the Yangtze, where the winters are colder, wheat and maize are important food crops, but it is hard to grow enough.

North Korea is a Communist country. It separated from South Korea in the Korean War in 1953.

South Korea has over 44 million people – more than Canada and Australia put together!

Taiwan is an island country which used to be called Formosa, or Nationalist China. It is not Communist and is not part of China.

China's amazing mountains. The photograph shows the amazing shapes of the limestone mountains in southern China. The mountains that look "unreal" in Chinese paintings really are real! It is almost impossible to travel through this area except by boat. The rain has slowly dissolved the limestone to make these picturesque mountains. This is the River Li, a tributary of the Yangtze.

NORTH KOREA

AREA 46,540 sq miles
POPULATION 23,931,000
MONEY N. Korean won

SOUTH KOREA

AREA 38,232 sq miles
POPULATION 45,088,000
MONEY S. Korean won

Building a reservoir. *Everybody, male and female, pulls a heavy cart of rocks to make a new dam across a river. The dam will provide water for power and for irrigation – and it will control flooding too.*

STAMP

Mongolia *has its own language and script. It is a huge country with many deserts.*

The Great Wall of China *was over 3000 miles long (see map) – by far the longest man-made structure in the world. Building started 2000 years ago to keep China's enemies out. This section has been repaired recently.*

HONG KONG

Most of Hong Kong was part of China until 1898 and is Chinese again from 1997 onward. For 99 years the British ruled Hong Kong. These photographs show tall skyscrapers, which stand on hillsides. Nearly 6 million people live in this small, crowded territory. Travel is a problem. Double-deck trams and buses can carry lots of people.

FACT BOX

- One out of every five people in the world is Chinese.
- The Chinese invented the compass, paper and printing.
- The Chinese have been eating with chopsticks for 3000 years!
- The place furthest from the open sea is in China: the Dzungarian Desert, which is over 1500 miles from the sea.
- Tibet is the highest plateau in the world. Its average height is nearly 16,500 feet above sea level.

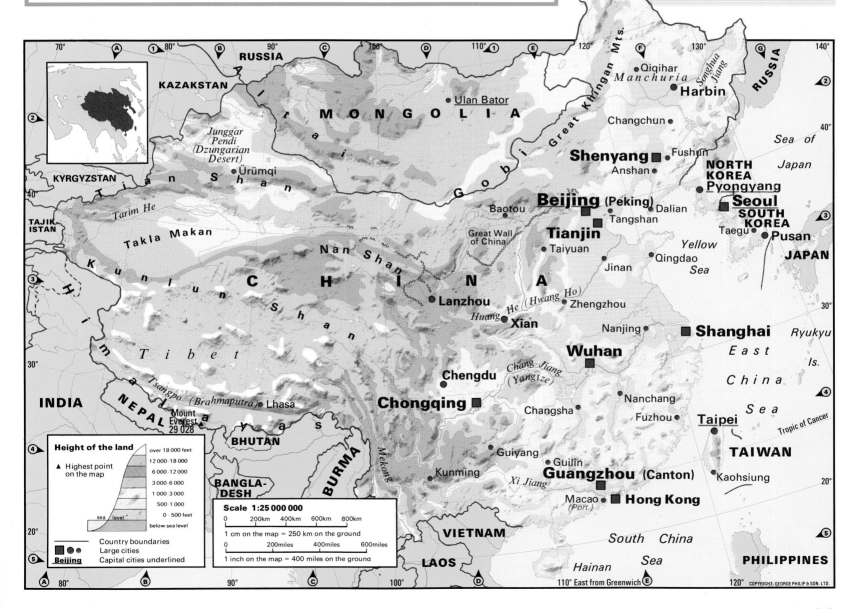

Scale 1:25 000 000

1 cm on the map = 250 km on the ground

1 inch on the map = 400 miles on the ground

Height of the land
- over 18 000 feet
- 12 000–18 000
- 6 000–12 000
- 3 000–6 000
- 1 000–3 000
- 500–1 000
- 0–500 feet
- below sea level
- ▲ Highest point on the map

Country boundaries
Large cities
Capital cities underlined

JAPAN

KANSAI AIRPORT

This new airport serves Osaka and Kobe. The runway and terminal are on land reclaimed from the sea, as flat land is scarce in Japan.

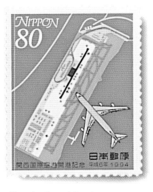

Osaka's old airport was in the city. The new airport is just over half a mile offshore. Fast expressways link it to the city. Can you match the photo and the map on the stamp? (HINT: look at one upside down!)

Japan is quite a small country: it is smaller than France or Spain. Canada is 27 times as big as Japan! But Japan has a big population – about 125,000,000. This is over twice as many people as France, and five times as many as Canada.

People talk of the "Japanese miracle." This small country is mostly mountains, has very few mines and hardly any oil, yet it has become the world's biggest producer of televisions, radios, stereo hi-fis, cameras, trucks, ships and many other things. Japanese cars and computers are admired throughout the world.

There are booming cities in the south of Japan, with highly skilled, hard-working people. Many of them live in the city suburbs and travel to work in overcrowded trains. Most Japanese families have small, space-saving homes. The main room is usually a living room by day, then the beds are unrolled for the night and packed away next morning. But away from the cities, most of Japan is still beautiful and peaceful.

Mount Fuji, with tea fields in the foreground. *Mount Fuji (Fuji-san) is Japan's most famous mountain. It is an old volcano, 12,388 feet high. In winter, the upper slopes are covered with snow. Tea is important in Japan. It is usually drunk as "green tea" and often with great ceremony.*

JAPAN

AREA 145,869 sq miles
POPULATION 125,156,000
MONEY Yen
CAPITAL Tokyo
MAIN ISLAND Honshu

Cherry blossom time at a garden in Nagano, *in the center of Honshu Island. Japan has many gardens which are especially beautiful in spring.*

STAMP

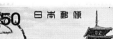

Horyu Temple, at Nara. *The beautiful temple on the right is called a pagoda. Japanese pagodas are carefully preserved. Their unusual shape originally came partly from Indian and partly from Chinese temples.*

Bullet train. *Japan's "bullet trains" go like a bullet from a gun! The trains run on new tracks with no sharp curves to slow them down. They provide a superb service except when there is an earthquake warning. When that happens, the trains have to go more slowly, to be safe.*

Most Japanese live on Honshu, the largest island. Hokkaido, the northernmost island, is much less crowded. Winters are very cold and even the summers are too cold for growing rice. But in the south of Japan, rice is the main food crop. Some of the hillsides look like giant steps, because they are terraced to make flat fields. Many mountains in Japan are volcanoes: 54 are active and there are over 100 others.

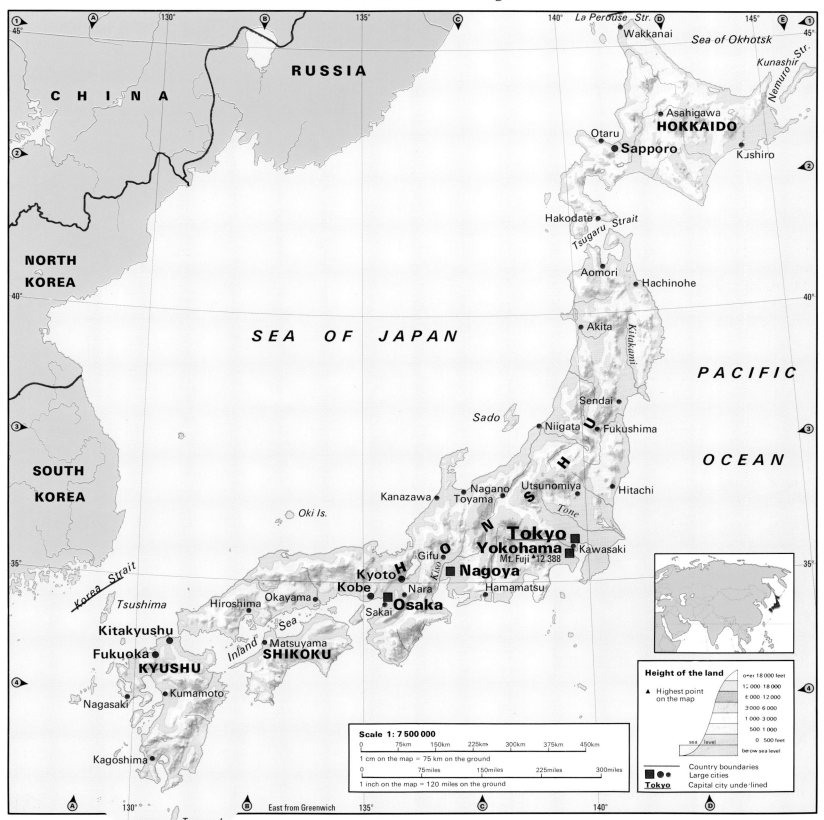

Height of the land

over 18 000 feet	
12 000-18 000	
6 000-12 000	
3 000-6 000	
1 000-3 000	
500-1 000	
0-500 feet	

▲ Highest point on the map

below sea level

Country boundaries
Large cities
Tokyo Capital city underlined

Scale 1: 7 500 000

0   75km   150km   225km   300km   375km   450km

1 cm on the map = 75 km on the ground

0   75miles   150miles   225miles   300miles

1 inch on the map = 120 miles on the ground

East from Greenwich

AFRICA

Most of the countries of Africa have quite small populations – except for Nigeria and Egypt. But everywhere the population is growing fast. It is difficult to provide enough schools and clinics for all the children and there are not enough good jobs.

Imagine traveling southward across Africa, along the 20°E line of longitude. You start in Libya. Your first 600 miles will be across the great Sahara Desert (where you must travel in winter) – sand, rock and the high rugged Tibesti Mountains. Then you reach thorn bushes, in the semi-desert Sahel area of Chad.

By 15°N you are into savanna – very long grass and scattered trees. You cross the country known as CAR for short. The land becomes greener and at about 5°N you reach the equatorial rain forest . . a real jungle! You are now in Zaïre.

Then the same story happens in reverse – savanna in Angola; then semi-desert (the Kalahari and the Karoo). Finally, you reach the coast of South Africa – a journey of nearly 5000 miles.

Railways are vital for exports from Africa – especially for the "landlocked" countries.

Children in Ghana. *Everywhere in Africa, there are lots of children. The fathers of these children are fishermen: in the background you can see nets drying and big dugout canoes. The canoes are made from the huge trees of the rain forest, and can cope with big waves in the Gulf of Guinea.*

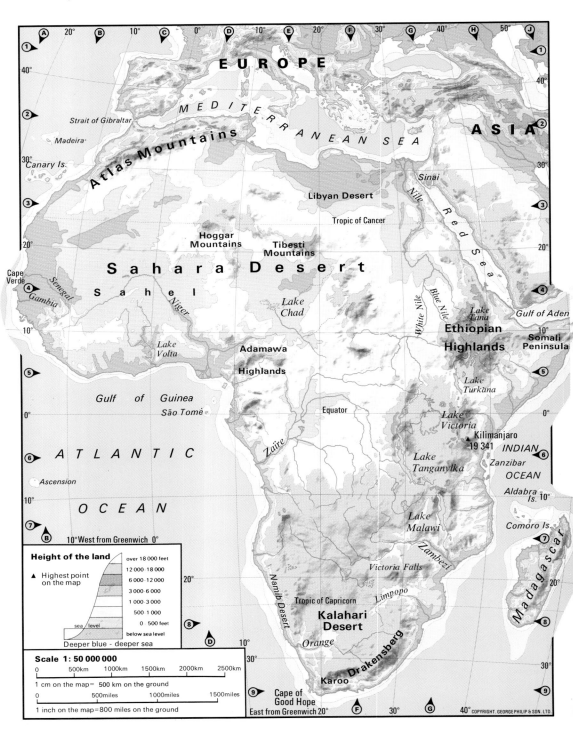

Height of the land

▲ Highest point on the map

over 18 000 feet	
12 000-18 000	
6 000-12 000	
3 000-6 000	
1 000-3 000	
500-1 000	
sea level	0 - 500 feet
	below sea level

Deeper blue - deeper sea

Scale 1: 50 000 000

0   500km   1000km   1500km   2000km   2500km

1 cm on the map= 500 km on the ground

0   500miles   1000miles   1500miles

1 inch on the map=800 miles on the ground

ORIGIN OF COUNTRY NAMES

CHAD Named from Lake Chad
GAMBIA, NIGER, NIGERIA From big rivers
GHANA, BENIN, MALI Names of great
  empires in West Africa a long time ago
IVORY COAST Ivory, from the tusks of
  elephants, was traded along this coast
NAMIBIA From the Namib Desert
SIERRA LEONE "Lion Mountain" (Portuguese)
TANZANIA From *Tanganyika* (the
  mainland) and the island of *Zanzibar*

The pyramids of Egypt are tombs
built by slaves over 4000 years ago. The
picture shows the largest, which are at
Giza, near Cairo. They are still the largest
buildings in the whole of Africa. They are
near the River Nile, in the Sahara Desert.

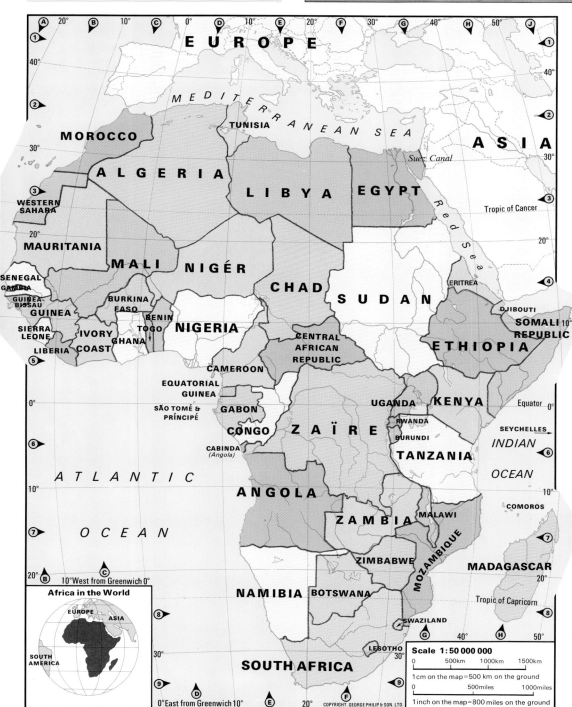

COINS OF AFRICA

All the 55 countries
of Africa have their
own banknotes
and stamps. Most
countries have coins
as well. Pictures
on the coins usually
show something about
the country. The 5 Bututs coin from The
Gambia (above) shows
a fine sailing ship.
There is Arabic
writing because
many people
are Muslims. The
10 Kobo coin from
Nigeria shows palm trees.

AFRICAN FACTS

AREA 11,706,165 sq miles
HIGHEST POINT Mount Kilimanjaro
  (Tanzania), 19,341 feet
LOWEST POINT Shores of Lake Assal
  (Djibouti), 508 feet below sea level
LONGEST RIVER Nile, 4145 miles
  (also a world record)
LARGEST LAKE Lake Victoria
  (East Africa), 26,828 sq miles
BIGGEST COUNTRY Sudan, 967,493 sq miles
SMALLEST COUNTRIES
  Mainland: Gambia, 4,363 sq miles;
  Islands: Seychelles, 176 sq miles (see page 9)

Scale 1:50 000 000

Africa in the World

1cm on the map=500 km on the ground

1 inch on the map=800 miles on the ground

COPYRIGHT. GEORGE PHILIP & SON. LTD.

* At the time of going to press, the government of Zaïre had been overthrown by rebels who planned to rename the country "The Democratic Republic of the Congo."

NORTH AFRICA

EGYPT

AREA 386,660 sq miles
POPULATION 64,100,000
MONEY Egyptian pound

MOROCCO

AREA 172,413 sq miles
POPULATION 26,857,000
MONEY Moroccan dirham

MALI

AREA 478,837 sq miles
POPULATION 10,700,000
MONEY CFA franc

Most of North Africa is desert – but not all. The coastlines and mountains of northwest Africa get winter rain: good crops are grown and the coasts of Tunisia and Morocco are popular with tourists.

All these countries are Islamic. Morocco has the oldest university in the world: the Islamic University in Fez. The largest country in Africa is the Sudan. A civil war has continued for years because the people of the far south do not want to be ruled by the Islamic north.

People can live in the desert if there is water. Some modern settlements have been built deep in the desert where there are valuable minerals, and water is pumped from underground. These minerals are the main reason why some countries are richer than others. Algeria and Libya have plenty of oil beneath the desert. But the countries in the southern part of the Sahara are among the poorest in the world. They had severe famines in the 1970s and 1980s.

A market near Timbuktu, in Mali, is a place to meet as well as to trade. People bring the goods they hope to sell in locally made baskets or in reused cartons which they balance on their heads.

SUDAN

AREA 967,493 sq miles
POPULATION 29,980,000
MONEY Sudanese dinar

A tall story! Trees can be very useful in so many ways – this man is looking for the only giraffes in North and West Africa. They were brought to Niger by a German who thought the local people could look after the giraffes and make money from tourists!

SUEZ CANAL

This old print shows the procession of ships through the Suez Canal at its opening in December 1869. The canal links the Mediterranean with the Red Sea (see map: G1). It was dug in 1859–69 by Arabs, organized by a Frenchman, Ferdinand de Lesseps. Before the canal opened, the route by sea from Europe to India and the Far East was around the whole of Africa.

Oasis near Lake Djerid, Tunisia. Water is just below the ground, so date palms can grow well. But in the background, great sand dunes loom on the skyline. If they advance, they may cover the oasis.

Egypt has the biggest population of any North African country. Its capital, Cairo, is one of the biggest cities in the world. The River Nile brings water to the valley and delta. The land is carefully farmed (with irrigation) and crowded with people; the rest of Egypt is almost empty. The world population map on page 10 makes the contrast very clear. The map below shows that part of the desert is below sea level.

The lack of rain has helped to preserve many of the marvellous monuments, palaces and tombs built by the ancient Egyptians. The pyramids at Giza, near Cairo, are 4500 years old (see page 53). They are the only one of the Seven Wonders of the ancient world still surviving.

THE SAHARA DESERT

The Sahara is the biggest desert in the world. It is over 3 million sq miles in size. From west to east it is over 3100 miles; from north to south it extends about 1200 miles and it is still growing.

THE HOTTEST SHADE TEMPERATURE ever recorded, 136.4°F, was in Al Aziziyah, Libya, in 1922.

THE SUNNIEST PLACE in the world, over 4300 hours of sunshine per year, is in the eastern Sahara.

THE HIGHEST SAND DUNES in the world, 1400 feet high, are in central Algeria (see below).

THE LONGEST RIVER in the world is the River Nile, 4145 miles long.

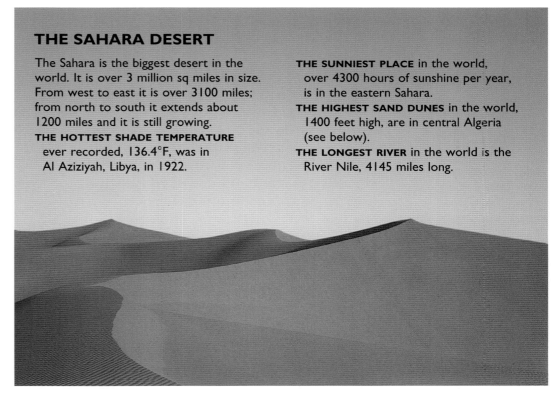

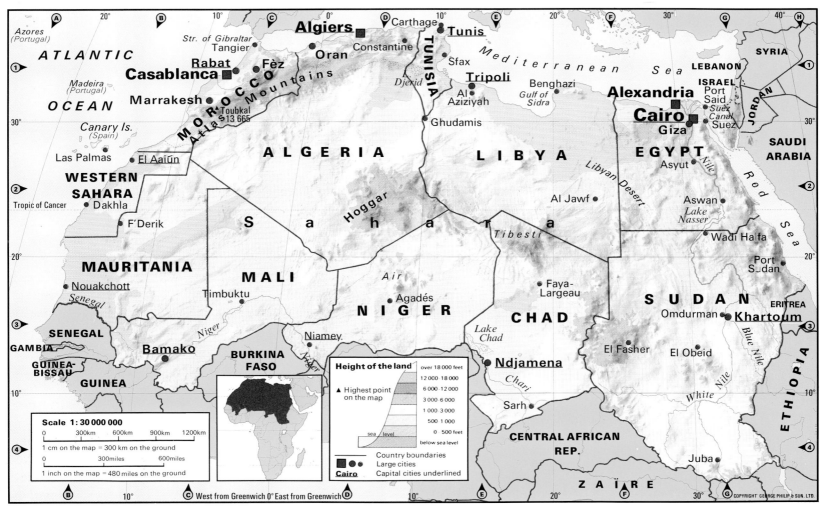

Scale 1:30 000 000

0   300km 600km 900km 1200km

1 cm on the map = 300 km on the ground

0   300miles   600miles

1 inch on the map = 480 miles on the ground

Height of the land

over 18 000 feet
12 000-18 000
6 000-12 000
3 000-6 000
1 000-3 000
500-1 000
0 500 feet
below sea level

▲ Highest point on the map

sea level

Country boundaries
Large cities
Cairo Capital cities underlined

West from Greenwich 0° East from Greenwich

COPYRIGHT GEORGE PHILIP & SON. LTD.

WEST AFRICA

NIGERIA

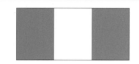

AREA 356,668 sq miles
POPULATION 88,515,000
MONEY Naira

THE GAMBIA

AREA 4,363 sq miles
POPULATION 1,144,000
MONEY Dalasi

IVORY COAST

AREA 124,502 sq miles
POPULATION 14,271,000
MONEY CFA franc

There are lots of countries in West Africa. In the last 300 years, European countries grabbed parts of the coastline and later they took over the inland areas as well. Now, all the countries are independent, but still use the language of those who once ruled them. English, French, Spanish or Portuguese is spoken. Many Africans speak a European language as well as one or more African languages.

Nigeria is the largest and most important country in West Africa. It has over 88 million people – more than any other African country. Although English is the official language, there are about 240 others in Nigeria!

In many parts of West Africa, there is rapid progress. Most children now go to primary school, and the main cities have television and airports. But many people are still very poor. Civil war has made poverty much worse in some countries – for example, in Sierra Leone and Liberia.

Village in Cameroon: *building houses with mud for the walls and tall grass for thatch. These materials are free and the homes are less hot than those with imported corrugated iron roofs.*

SIERRA LEONE

AREA 27,699 sq miles
POPULATION 4,467,000
MONEY Leone

Market day, Nigeria. *Red peppers for sale in Benin City, in southern Nigeria. Red peppers are very popular in West Africa – they give a strong flavor in cooking. Markets are important in both towns and villages throughout Africa.*

BIRDS

West Africa has many brightly colored birds which live in the forest and savanna. These stamps show a Grey Headed Bush-Shrike (left) and a Variable Sunbird (below).

West Africa is also home for part of the year to many birds that are familiar in Europe. Swallows, warblers, swifts and many others migrate to Africa during the European winter.

Women pounding yams, Benin. *They use a large wooden bowl and long pestles (pounding sticks) to break up and mash the yams. These root crops are eaten at most meals. It is very hard work: much easier if it is shared! They are probably singing to help keep a rhythm for using the pestles. The baby will love this!*

The southern part of West Africa, near the Equator, is forested. The tall trees are being felled for their hardwood. Many crops are grown in the forest area and sold overseas: cocoa (for chocolate-making); coffee, pineapples and bananas; rubber (for car and truck tires). The main food crops are root crops, such as cassava and yams.

Further north, the trees thin out and there is savanna. The tall grass with some trees is suitable for cattle farming. There are big herds of cattle, and beautiful leather goods are on sale in the markets. Cotton and groundnuts (peanuts) are grown in the savanna lands. The main food crops are grass-like: rice, maize and millet. In the far north of West Africa there is semi-desert: the Sahara is advancing southward.

Palm-oil harvest, Ghana. These people are carrying heavy baskets full of oil-palm fruit. The oil palm grows in the hot, wet climate of the tropical forest. The fruits grow in bunches, with as many as 3000 bright-red palm fruits in a bunch. The fruit and the kernels are crushed in a factory to obtain oils. These oils are very useful for cooking and in making soap.

Yeji ferry, Ghana. This big ferry carries trucks, cars, people and their heavy loads across Lake Volta. This man-made lake flooded Ghana's main road to the north. As the water rose in the new lake, the trees and much of the wildlife died. A fifteenth of all Ghana's land was "lost" under the lake, and new villages had to be built.

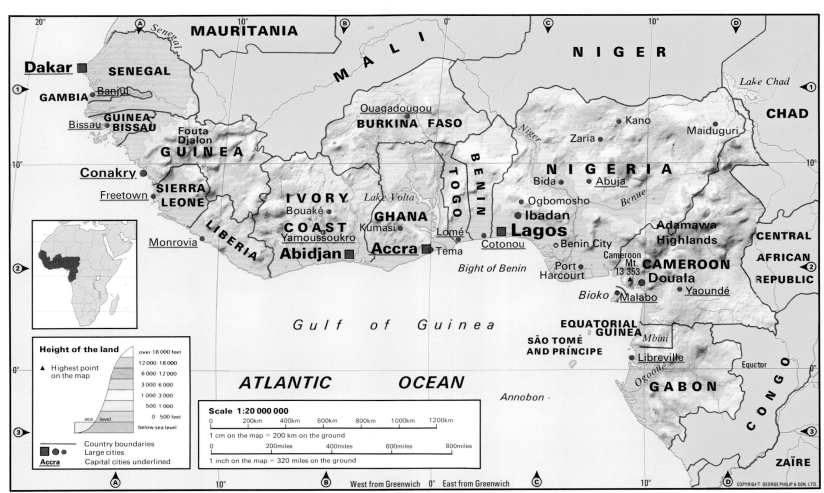

Height of the land

▲ Highest point on the map

over 18 000 feet
12 000 - 18 000
6 000 - 12 000
3 000 - 6 000
1 000 - 3 000
500 - 1 000
0 - 500 feet
sea level
below sea level

Country boundaries
Large cities
Accra Capital cities underlined

Scale 1:20 000 000

0   200km   400km   600km   800km   1000km   1200km
1 cm on the map = 200 km on the ground
0   200miles   400miles   600miles   800miles
1 inch on the map = 320 miles on the ground

West from Greenwich 0° East from Greenwich

COPYRIGHT GEORGE PHILIP & SON. LTD.

57

CENTRAL AND EAST AFRICA

Central Africa is mostly lowland, with magnificent trees in the tropical rain forest in Zaïre and Congo. Some timber is used for buildings and canoes (see photograph right); some is exported. The cleared land can grow many tropical crops.

East Africa is mostly high savanna land with long grass, and scattered trees. Some parts are reserved for wild animals; in other parts, there are large farms for export crops such as coffee and tea. But in most of East Africa, the people keep cattle and grow crops for their own needs.

The Somali Republic, Djibouti and Eritrea are desert areas, but the mountain areas of Ethiopia get plenty of rain. There have been terrible wars and famines in Ethiopia, Eritrea and Somalia.

In 1994 and 1995, a civil war in Rwanda led to a million deaths and more than a million refugees traveling to Zaïre and Tanzania. Wars like this damage people, the animals, and the environment (see below).

The River Zaïre at Mbandaka. *Children who live near the river learn to paddle a dugout canoe from an early age. The boats are hollowed out of a single tree with an axe. The River Zaïre is an important transport route. Mbandaka is a river port about four days by steamer from Kinshasa.*

MINERALS OF TANZANIA

Africa is mostly made of old, hard rocks. There are valuable minerals such as sapphires (top stamp) and diamonds (bottom stamp) in these rocks in some areas. They are cut and polished to become lovely gems. Despite its mineral wealth, Tanzania is one of the world's poorest countries.

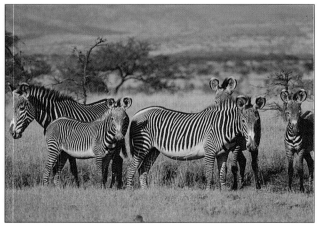

In a game reserve in Kenya, *a group of Grevy's Zebra graze the savanna grassland. In the dry season, the grass is brown, but in the rainy season it is tall and green. The game reserves are carefully managed and people come from all over the world to see the wildlife.*

Gorillas in Rwanda. *These gorillas live high up in the forested mountains. They are at risk because of the 1994–5 civil war.*

Buses in the center of Nairobi, Kenya. *This modern capital city has many high-rise buildings – yet only 100 years ago there was no town here.*

In all these countries, there is much poverty and people are moving to the cities. But there are many signs of development: new farm projects, new ports and roads, new clinics and schools.

The population of this area is growing fast. It has doubled in less than 25 years. Some of these countries have the world's highest population growth rates.

Mount Kilimanjaro, Tanzania. *Africa's highest mountain is the beautiful cone of an old volcano. It is near the Equator, but high enough to have snow all year.*

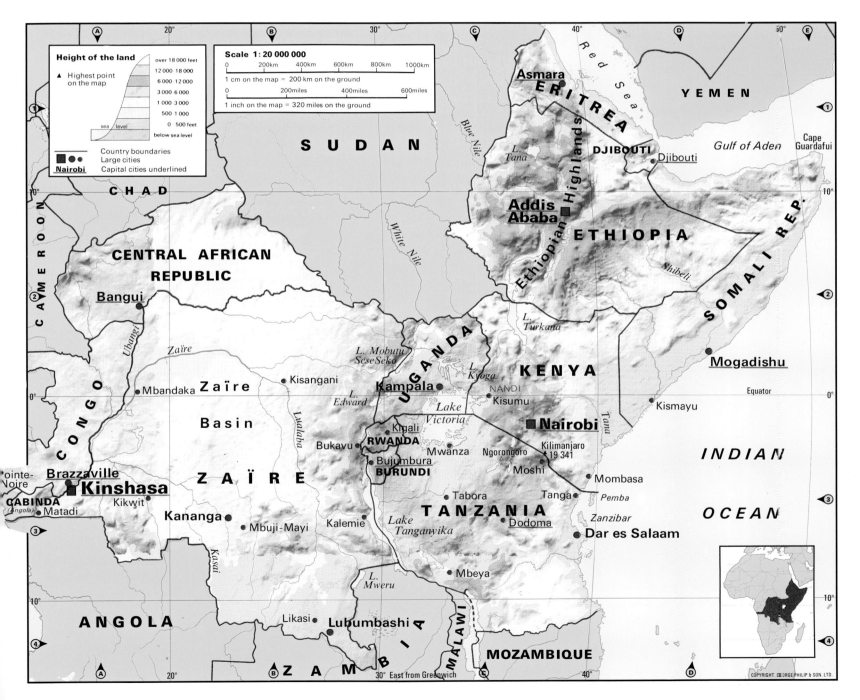

Height of the land

▲ Highest point on the map

	over 18 000 feet
	12 000 · 18 000
	6 000 · 12 000
	3 000 · 6 000
	1 000 · 3 000
	500 · 1 000
	0 · 500 feet
sea level	
	below sea level

■ ● ● Country boundaries
Large cities
Nairobi Capital cities underlined

Scale 1: 20 000 000

0   200km   400km   600km   800km   1000km

1 cm on the map = 200 km on the ground

0   200miles   400miles   600miles

1 inch on the map = 320 miles on the ground

SUDAN

YEMEN

Red Sea

ERITREA

Asmara

DJIBOUTI

Gulf of Aden

Cape Guardafui

Blue Nile

L. Tana

CHAD

Addis Ababa

Ethiopian Highlands

ETHIOPIA

SOMALI REP.

CENTRAL AFRICAN REPUBLIC

White Nile

Shibeli

CAMEROON

Bangui

Ubangi

Zaïre

Kisangani

Mbandaka

Zaïre

L. Mobutu Sese Seko

UGANDA

L. Edward

Kampala

L. Kyoga

KENYA

NANDI

Kisumu

L. Turkana

Mogadishu

Kismayu

Equator

Tana

CONGO

Basin

Lualaba

Kigali

Bukavu

RWANDA

Bujumbura

BURUNDI

Lake Victoria

Mwanza

Ngorongoro

Nairobi

Kilimanjaro 19 341

Moshi

Mombasa

Pemba

INDIAN

Pointe-Noire

Brazzaville

Kinshasa

Kikwit

CABINDA (Angola)

Matadi

Kanganga

Mbuji-Mayi

ZAÏRE

Kalemie

Lake Tanganyika

Tabora

TANZANIA

Dodoma

Tanga

Zanzibar

Dar es Salaam

OCEAN

Kasai

Kananga

L. Mweru

Mbeya

MALAWI

ANGOLA

Likasi

Lubumbashi

ZAMBIA

MOZAMBIQUE

30° East from Greenwich

COPYRIGHT GEORGE PHILIP & SON. LTD.

59

SOUTHERN AFRICA

AREA 470,566 sq miles
POPULATION 44,000,000
MONEY Rand

ANGOLA

AREA 481,351 sq miles
POPULATION 10,844,000
MONEY Kwanza

BOTSWANA

AREA 224,606 sq miles
POPULATION 1,481,000
MONEY Pula

Most of southern Africa is a high, flat plateau. The rivers cannot be used by ships because of big waterfalls like the Victoria Falls (see photograph right). But the rivers can be useful. Two huge dams have been built on the River Zambezi – at Kariba (in Zambia) and at Cabora Bassa (in Mozambique). The map shows the lakes behind each dam. The power of the falling water is used to make electricity.

Angola and **Mozambique** used to be Portuguese colonies, and Portuguese is still their official language – though many different African languages are spoken, too. Most of the other countries shown on the map have English as their official language.

The map shows you that many southern African countries are landlocked: they have no coastline. The railways leading to the ports in neighboring countries are very important. Copper from **Zambia** and **Botswana** is sent abroad in this way.

The Victoria Falls are on the River Zambezi, at the border of Zambia and Zimbabwe. Africans call the falls Mosi-oi-tunya – "the smoke that thunders." They were named after the English Queen Victoria by the explorer David Livingstone. The falls are more than half a mile wide and over 330 feet high. The dense forest in the foreground relies on the spray from the falls.

MOZAMBIQUE

AREA 309,494 sq miles
POPULATION 17,800,000
MONEY Metical

Cape Town, South Africa. The flat-topped mountain is called "Table Mountain." It looks as flat as a table. When cloud covers it, it is called "the tablecloth"! Cape Town is near the Cape of Good Hope, the most southerly point in Africa.

A VILLAGE IN ZAMBIA

A Zambian girl drew this picture of her village during a lesson at her school. Her village is close to the River Zambezi in the west of Zambia. Look for a well, a man hoeing, a fisherman and a man looking after cattle. On the road there is a bus, a car and a van.

Ring-tailed Lemur, Madagascar. The island of Madagascar has wonderful forests and some of its wildlife is unique. But several species are under threat of extinction.

The **Republic of South Africa** is the wealthiest country in Africa. It has the richest gold mine in the world, and also the world's deepest mine. It is 12,392 feet deep! South Africa was home to the world's largest diamond – found in 1905.

Most of the black people are still very poor. For many years, they were kept apart from the rich white people who used to rule the country. In 1994 they gained the vote and could share in their country's government.

Namibia and **Botswana** are dry areas, with small numbers of people. Some of the rivers in this area never reach the sea. The map on this page shows big swamps and "salt pans": these are the places where the river water evaporates. **Lesotho** is a small mountainous country, completely surrounded by the Republic of South Africa.

Madagascar is the fourth largest island in the world. The people and their language are a mixture of African and Indonesian.

Children in Mozambique hope for a better future after many years of war. Their country is the poorest in Africa, and has also suffered from both disastrous floods and drought.

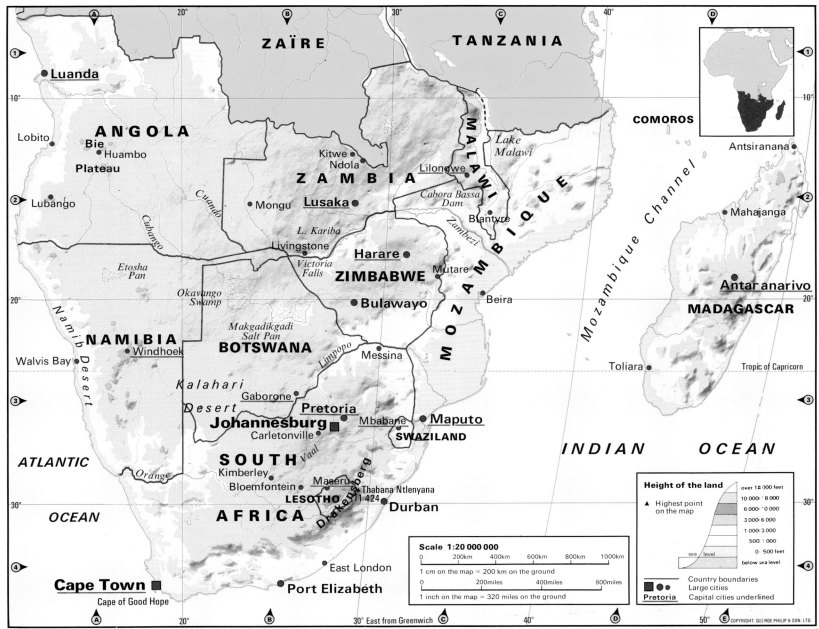

Scale 1:20 000 000
| 0 | 200km | 400km | 600km | 800km | 1000km |

1 cm on the map = 200 km on the ground

| 0 | 200miles | 400miles | 600miles |

1 inch on the map = 320 miles on the ground

Height of the land
- over 15 000 feet
- 10 000–15 000
- 6 000–10 000
- 3 000–6 000
- 1 000–3 000
- 500–1 000
- 0–500 feet
- below sea level

▲ Highest point on the map

Country boundaries
Large cities
Pretoria Capital cities underlined

COPYRIGHT GEORGE PHILIP & SON. LTD.

In South Africa, Pretoria is shown as the capital but the parliament meets in Cape Town.

THE PACIFIC

This map shows half the world. Guess which place is furthest from a continent: it is to be found somewhere in the south Pacific. The Pacific Ocean also includes the deepest place in the world: the Mariana Trench (36,050 feet deep). It would take over an hour for a steel ball weighing one and a quarter pounds to fall to the bottom!

There are thousands of islands in the Pacific. Some are volcanic mountains, while many others are low, flat coral islands. Coral also grows around the volcanoes.

A few islands have valuable minerals – for example Bougainville (copper) and Nauru (phosphates).

Coral reef in French Polynesia, *from the air. Coral BELOW sea level is ALIVE! A reef is built up from the shells of dead coral. Gradually plants colonize parts of the reef.*

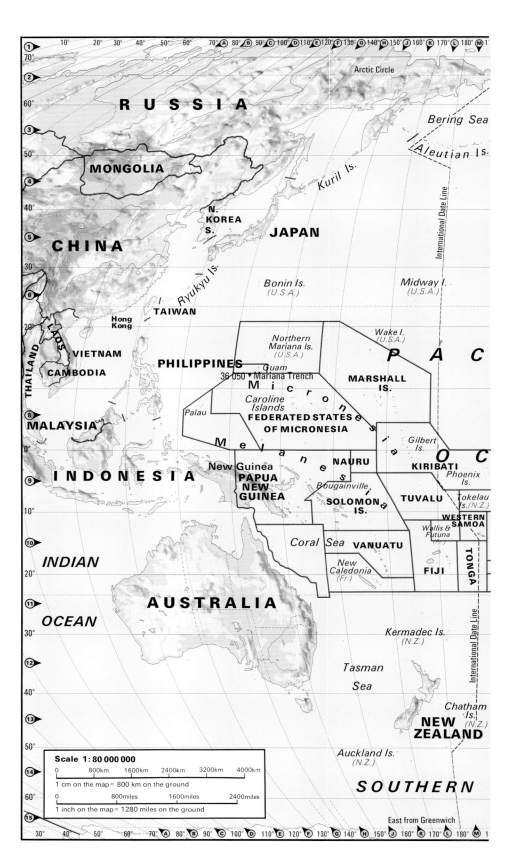

Scale 1 : 80 000 000

1 cm on the map = 800 km on the ground

1 inch on the map = 1280 miles on the ground

East from Greenwich

Most islanders are occupied in farming. Many tropical crops grow well; sugarcane, bananas and pineapples are important exports.

Islands big enough for a full-sized airport, such as Fiji, the Samoan islands, Tahiti, and Hawaii (see page 72), now get many tourists.

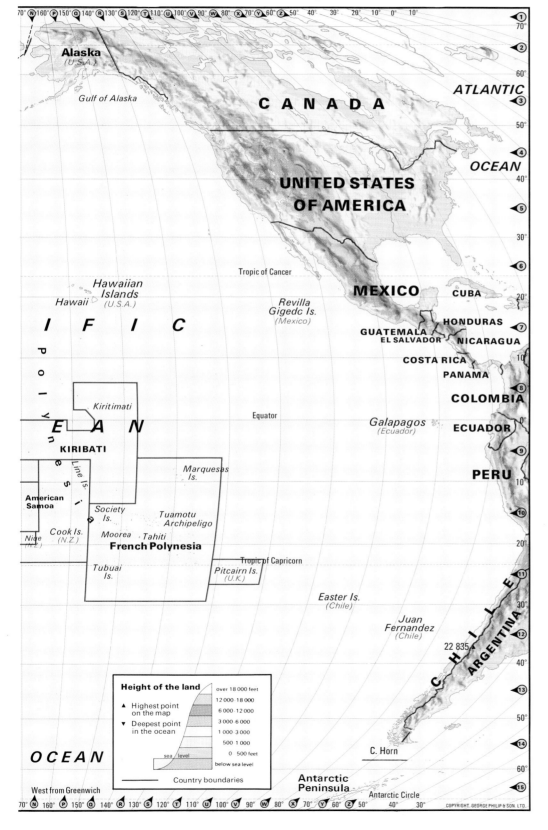

Height of the land

- ▲ Highest point on the map
- ▼ Deepest point in the ocean

	over 18 000 feet
	12 000-18 000
	6 000-12 000
	3 000-6 000
	1 000-3 000
	500-1 000
sea level	0-500 feet
	below sea level

— Country boundaries

West from Greenwich

COPYRIGHT. GEORGE PHILIP & SON. LTD.

Easter Island, South Pacific. These huge stone sculptures each weigh about 50 tons! They were cut long ago with simple stone axes, and lifted with ropes and ramps – an amazing achievement for people who had no metal, no wheels and no machines. Look for Easter Island on the map (in square U11): it is one of the most remote places in the world. It is now owned by Chile, 2399 miles away in South America.

PACIFIC FACTS

OCEAN AREA 69,356,000 sq miles – the world's biggest ocean

HIGHEST POINT Mount Wilhelm (Papua New Guinea), 14,790 feet

LOWEST POINT ON LAND Lake Eyre (Australia), 53 feet below sea level

DEEPEST PART OF OCEAN Mariana Trench, 36,050 feet below surface. This is the deepest place on Earth.

LONGEST RIVER Murray–Darling (Australia), 2330 miles

LARGEST LAKE Lake Eyre (Australia), 3400 sq miles

BIGGEST COUNTRY Australia, 2,967,893 sq miles

SMALLEST COUNTRY Nauru, 8 sq miles

Most Pacific countries are large groups of small islands. Their boundaries are cut at sea – just lines on a map. For example, Kiribati is 33 small coral atolls spread over 2,000,000 square miles of ocean.

AUSTRALIA

AUSTRALIA

AREA 2,967,893 sq miles
POPULATION 18,107,000
MONEY Australian dollar

THE GREAT BARRIER REEF

The Great Barrier Reef is the world's largest living thing! It is an area of coral over 1240 miles long, which grows in the warm sea near the coast of Queensland.

The reef is also home to colorful fish that swim among the coral. They can be seen from glass-bottomed boats.

Australia is the world's largest island, but the world's smallest continent. It is the sixth-largest country in the world, smaller than the USA or Canada, but more than twice the size of India. Yet Australia has only about 18 million people. Most Australians are descended from people who came from Europe in the past 150 years.

Only a few people live in the mountains or in the outback – the enormous area of semi-desert and desert that makes up most of the country. The few outback people live on huge sheep and cattle farms, in mining towns, or on special reserves for the original Australians – the Aborigines.

The Flying Doctor can visit remote farms in the outback by air. The airplane is designed to be an ambulance, too. People in the outback use two-way radios to get medical advice, to call the doctor, and also to receive school lessons.

Ayers Rock rises steeply out of the dry plains in central Australia. It is 1142 feet high. The sides have deep gullies and strange caves. For the Aborigines, it is a holy place called Uluru. Many tourists come for the hard climb or to watch the rock glow deep red at sunset.

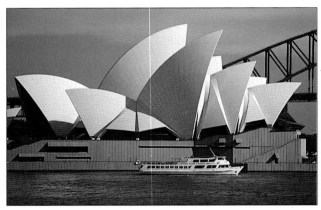

Sydney Opera House cost millions of dollars to build and has become the new symbol of Sydney. It is by the harbor, below the famous harbor bridge (in the background) which was built in Newcastle, UK!

AUSTRALIAN ANIMALS

Australia is not joined to any other continent. It has been a separate island for millions of years, and has developed its own unique wildlife. Most of the world's marsupials live in Australia.

Australia 50c
Leadbeater's Possum
Endangered Species

Australia 30c
Nailtailed Wallaby
Endangered Species

Australia 5c
Queensland Hairy-nosed Wombat
Endangered Species

The map shows that all the state capitals are on the coast. Canberra is a planned city built inland which became the national capital in 1927. Most Australians live near the coast and most live in towns. Even so, large areas of coast are almost uninhabited.

*TRICK QUESTION: Which was the biggest island in the world, before Australia was discovered? Think hard – then turn to page 96.

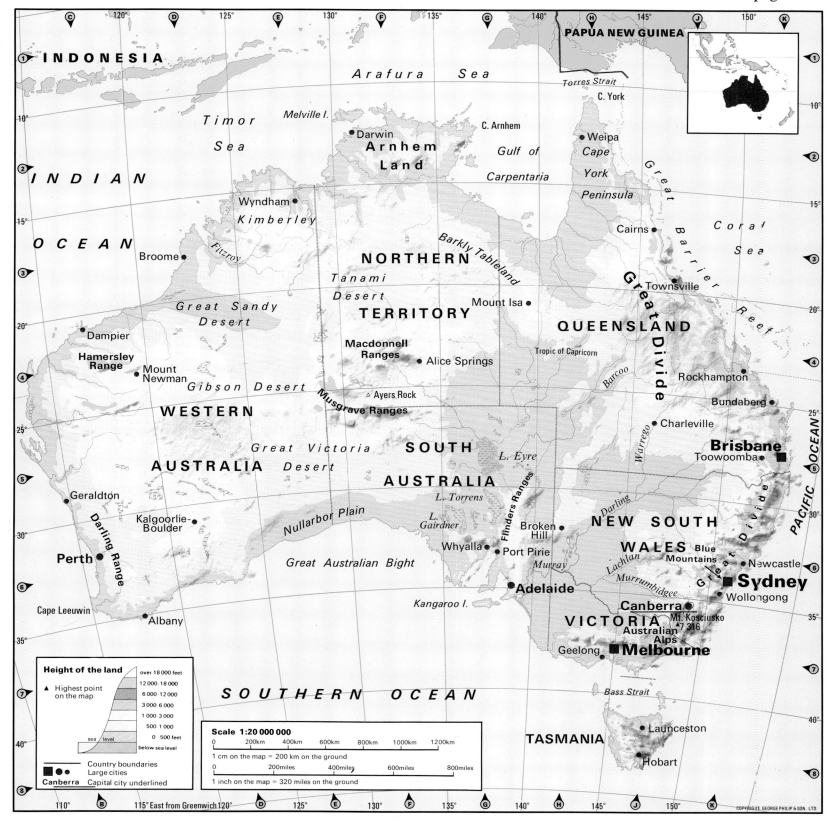

Height of the land
▲ Highest point on the map

over 18 000 feet
12 000-18 000
6 000-12 000
3 000-6 000
1 000-3 000
500-1 000
0 - 500 feet
sea level
below sea level

Country boundaries
Large cities
Canberra Capital city underlined

Scale 1:20 000 000
0 200km 400km 600km 800km 1000km 1200km
1 cm on the map = 200 km on the ground
0 200miles 400miles 600miles 800miles
1 inch on the map = 320 miles on the ground

COPYRIGHT GEORGE PHILIP & SON. LTD.

65

NEW ZEALAND

New Zealand is on the opposite side of the Earth from Europe. This "double map" is printed as if you were looking right through a transparent globe. It shows that the far north of New Zealand is at the same latitude as North Africa, and that the far south of New Zealand is at the same latitude as the center of France.

The two main islands that make up New Zealand are 1240 miles east of Australia. Only 3½ million people live in the whole country. The capital is Wellington, near the center of New Zealand, but the largest city is Auckland in the north.

The original inhabitants were the Maoris, but now they are only about 8 per cent of the population. Some place names are Maori words, such as Rotorua, Whangarei and Wanganui.

South Island is the largest island, but has fewer people than North Island. There are more sheep than people! Mount Cook, the highest point in New Zealand (12,313 feet) is in the spectacular Southern Alps. Tourists visit the far south to see the glaciers and fjords. The fast-flowing rivers are used for hydroelectricity.

Auckland is sometimes called "the city of sails" because so many people own or sail a yacht here. The city center (background) looks out over two huge natural harbors that are ideal for sailing. To the north is Waitemara Harbor and to the south is the shallow Manukau Harbor. Auckland is New Zealand's biggest city, and also an important port for huge container ships.

NEW ZEALAND

AREA 103,737 sq miles
POPULATION 3,567,000
CURRENCY Dollar

KIWI FRUIT . . .

. . . were known as "Chinese Gooseberries" until New Zealanders (nicknamed "Kiwis") improved them, renamed them, and promoted them. Now they are a successful export crop for farmers, and many other countries also grow them — it is interesting to find out where YOUR kiwi fruit comes from.

The Maoris lived in New Zealand before the Europeans came. Today, most live in North Island and many of their traditions have become part of New Zealand life. Perhaps you have seen the "haka" on TV before an "All Blacks" rugby game?

The Southern Alps stretch the length of South Island. The fine scenery attracts tourists, and the grassland is used for sheep grazing.

North Island has a warmer climate than South Island. In some places you can see hot springs and boiling mud pools and there are also volcanoes. Fine trees and giant ferns grow in the forests, but much of the forest has been cleared for farming. Cattle are kept on the rich grasslands for meat and milk. Many different kinds of fruit grow well, including apples, kiwi fruit and pears, which are exported.

GEOTHERMAL POWER

Geothermal power station, north of Lake Taupo, North Island. In this volcanic area, there is very hot water underground. When drilled, it gushes out as steam. This can be piped to a power station (above) to generate electricity. Hot steam gushing out of a natural hole is called a geyser (below).

Map labels:
C. Maria van Diemen
Dargaville
Whangarei
Great Barrier I.
Coromandel Peninsula
Auckland
Hamilton
North Island
Bay of Plenty
Rotorua
TASMAN
L. Taupo
Gisborne
New Plymouth
Mt. Taranaki Kaimanawa
C. Egmont (Mt. Egmont) Mts.
8 261
Napier
Hastings
SEA
Wanganui
Palmerston North
C. Farewell
Tasman Bay
Lower Hutt
Nelson
Wellington
Blenheim
Spenser Mts.
Kaikoura Ra.
Greymouth
South Island
Westland Bight
Southern Alps
Pegasus Bay
Christchurch
Banks Peninsula
Mt. Cook 12 313
Canterbury Plains
Timaru
Canterbury Bight
L. Wanaka
Waitaki
PACIFIC
Queenstown
Oamaru
L. Te Anau
L. Manapouri
Clutha
OCEAN
Dunedin
Invercargill
Foveaux Strait
Stewart I.

168° East from Greenwich 170°
Cook Strait
Waikato

Height of the land

over 18 000 feet	
12 000 - 18 000	
6 000 - 12 000	
3 000 - 6 000	
1 000 - 3 000	
500 - 1 000	
0 - 500 feet	
below sea level	

▲ Highest point on the map
sea level

■ ● ● Large cities
Wellington Capital city underlined

Scale 1:7 500 000
0   75km   150km   225km   300km   375km
1 cm on the map = 75 km on the ground
0   75miles   150miles   225miles
1 inch on the map = 120 miles on the ground

COPYRIGHT GEORGE PHILIP & SON, LTD.

NORTH AMERICA

North America includes many Arctic islands, a huge mainland area (quite narrow in Central America) and the islands in the Caribbean Sea. The map shows the great mountain ranges, including the Rockies, which are the most impressive feature of this continent.

Almost all of the west is high and mountainous, yet Death Valley is *below* sea level. The rocks have been folded into mountain ranges, but the highest peaks are volcanoes. The Appalachian Mountains in the east are also fold mountains. And the island chains of the northwest (the Aleutian Islands) and the southeast (the West Indies) are the tops of underwater ranges divided by shallow seas.

The political map of North America is quite a simple one. The boundary between Canada and the USA is mostly at exactly 49°N. Four of the five Great Lakes have one shore in Canada and one shore in the USA★. Canada's two biggest cities, Toronto and Montreal, are south of the 49° line! Find them on the map on page 71.

Greenland used to be a colony of Denmark, but now it is self-governing. Most of Greenland is covered by ice all year. See page 88 for more about Greenland.

★ Which ones? Answers on page 96.

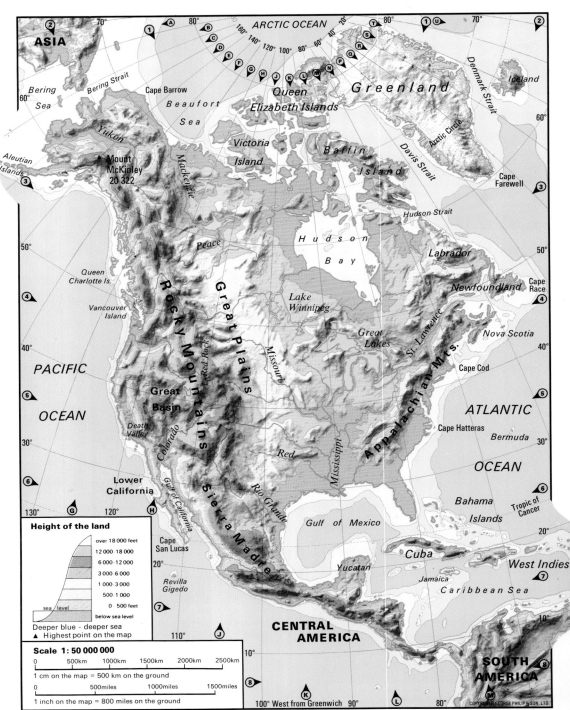

Flyovers, Los Angeles. *There are three levels of road at this road junction in Los Angeles; sometimes there are traffic jams as well! In 1994, a huge earthquake destroyed many road bridges.*

Height of the land

over 18 000 feet
12 000-18 000
6 000-12 000
3 000-6 000
1 000-3 000
500-1 000
0-500 feet
below sea level
Deeper blue - deeper sea
▲ Highest point on the map

Scale 1 : 50 000 000

0   500km   1000km   1500km   2000km   2500km
1 cm on the map = 500 km on the ground
0   500miles   1000miles   1500miles
1 inch on the map = 800 miles on the ground

The eight countries of **Central America** have more complicated boundaries. Six of these countries have two coastlines. The map shows that one country has a coastline only on the Pacific Ocean, and one has a coastline only on the Caribbean Sea*. These countries are Spanish-speaking: in fact there are more Spanish speakers here than in Spain.

The **West Indies** are made up of islands; there are lots of countries too. One island has TWO countries on it*. They are shown in more detail on page 81. This area is often called "The Caribbean." Some West Indians have emigrated to the USA, Britain and France.

* Which ones? Answers on page 96.

Market in St George's, Grenada.
The West Indies have hot sunshine and plenty of rain. This is an ideal climate for growing vegetables and fruit. These stalls are stacked high with local produce. Many islands have volcanic soil which is rich in minerals and very fertile.

Grenada is an island country which grows and exports bananas and nutmeg.

NORTH AMERICA FACTS

AREA 9,362,538 sq miles
HIGHEST POINT Mount McKinley (Alaska), 20,322 feet
LOWEST POINT Death Valley (California), 282 feet below sea level
LONGEST RIVERS
 Red Rock–Missouri–Mississippi, 3710 miles
 Mackenzie–Peace, 2630 miles
LARGEST LAKE Lake Superior*, 31,795 sq miles
BIGGEST COUNTRY
 Canada, 3,851,788 sq miles
SMALLEST COUNTRY Grenada (West Indies), 133 sq miles
RICHEST COUNTRY USA
POOREST COUNTRY Haiti
MOST CROWDED COUNTRY Barbados
LEAST CROWDED COUNTRY Canada

* The world's largest freshwater lake

CANADA

CANADA

AREA 3,851,788 sq miles
POPULATION 29,972,000
MONEY Canadian dollar
CAPITAL Ottawa
NATIONAL DAY 1 July

STAMPS

This stamp is an air-picture of the prairies of central Canada. The huge flat fields of grain reach to the far horizon, and beyond.

In western Canada, the Rocky Mountains are high and jagged. There are glaciers among the peaks. The Rockies stretch for 3000 miles through both Canada and the USA. They were a great barrier to the early explorers and to the early settlers and railway engineers.

Only one country in the world is bigger than Canada*, but 30 countries have more people than Canada. Most of Canada is almost empty: very few people live on the islands of the north, or in the Northwest Territories, or in the western mountains, or near Hudson Bay. The farmland of the prairies (see the top stamp) is uncrowded too. So . . . where do Canadians live?

The answer is that more Canadians live in cities than in the countryside. The map shows where the biggest cities are – all of them are in the southern part of Canada, and none are as far north as Norway or Sweden in Europe.

These photographs show Canada in summer. In winter, it is very cold indeed in both central and northern Canada. Children go to school even when it is 40° below zero. The mildest winters are in the southwest, around Vancouver.

* Which country? See page 9.

The Niagara Falls *are between Lake Erie and Lake Ontario, on the border of the USA (in the distance) and Canada. One part is called the Horseshoe Falls: can you see why? Ships have to use a canal with locks to get past the falls. The falling water is used to generate hydroelectricity.*

Quebec City. *The Chateau Frontenac (seen on the left) is built in the style of a French chateau (castle). This part of Canada was once owned by the French, and the people still speak French. On the right is the port beside the River St Lawrence. Large ocean-going ships can dock here.*

A long-distance train *travels through a pass in the Rocky Mountains. The trans-Canada railway helped unite Canada as one country 110 years ago.*

LANGUAGES IN CANADA

Canada has two official languages: French and English. So Canadian stamps say "Postes/Postage," instead of only "Postage." Most of the French-speaking Canadians live in the province of Quebec.

The biggest city in Quebec is Montreal: it is four times as big as Ottawa, the capital of Canada.

***Vancouver, British Columbia:** the biggest city in the west of Canada.*

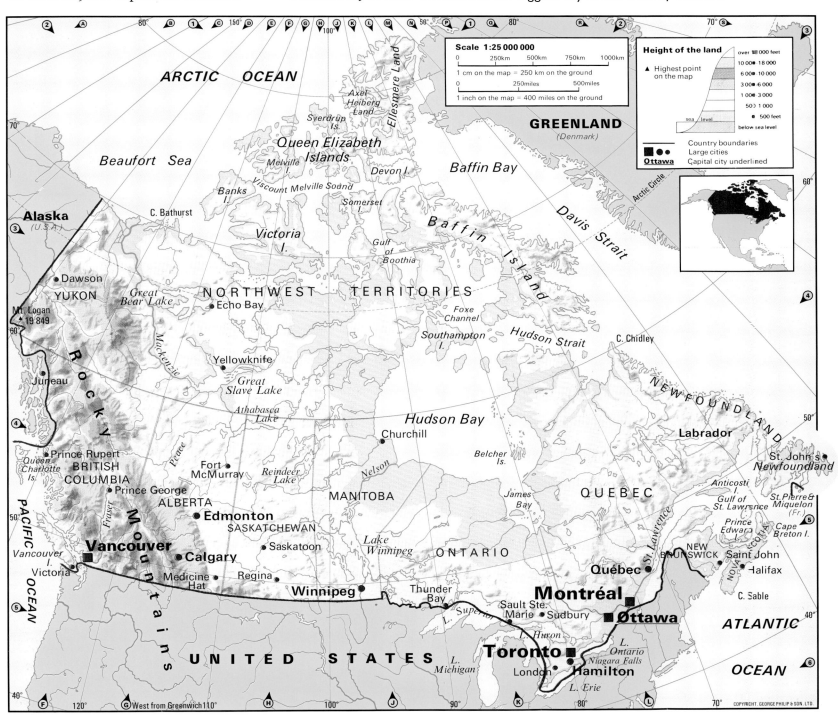

Scale 1:25 000 000

1 cm on the map = 250 km on the ground

1 inch on the map = 400 miles on the ground

Height of the land

over 18 000 feet
10 000–18 000
6 000–10 000
3 000–6 000
1 000–3 000
500–1 000
sea level
below sea level

▲ Highest point on the map

Country boundaries
Large cities
Ottawa Capital city underlined

USA

Who are "the Americans"? Of every 100 people in the USA, over 80 have ancestors from Europe. The first colonists came from Britain, France and Spain, but later on, people came from almost all parts of Europe to the USA.

About 12 people out of every 100 came from West Africa, brought to the USA as slaves to work in the southern states. By 1865, the slaves were free. Many black Americans now live in the northeast. More recently, many Spanish-speaking people have arrived from Mexico and Puerto Rico.

There are now fewer than one million American Indians in the USA, some of whom live on special reservations.

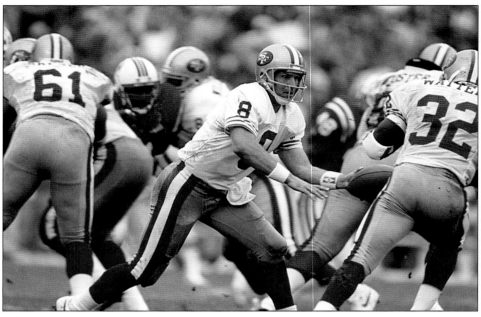

American football: the San Francisco 49ers, from California. The teams often have to travel many thousands of miles for each game. The players travel by air – it takes three days to cross the USA by train!

STARS AND STRIPES

United States 13c

In 1776 there were only 13 states in the USA: so the US flag had 13 stars and 13 stripes. As more and more states joined

the USA, more stars were added to the flag. Now there are 50 states, and 50 stars.

HAWAII

Hawaii is the newest state in the USA: it became a state in 1959. The picture shows Waikiki beach in Honolulu, the biggest city. Honolulu is on Oahu island. These faraway Pacific islands are the tops of volcanoes, over 1800 miles from mainland USA (see map page 63). If the height of Mauna Kea is measured from the seabed, it is 32,883 feet: the world's highest mountain. The islands are the most southerly part of the USA.

STAMP

First Moon Landing, 1969

An American was the first man on the Moon. The astronaut is holding the USA flag. Above his head is the Earth, half in darkness.

USA

AREA 3,618,765 sq miles
POPULATION 263,563,000
MONEY US dollar
CAPITAL Washington, DC

The map shows the 50 states of the USA. The first 13 states were on the east coast, settled by Europeans who had sailed across the Atlantic. As the Americans moved westward, so more and more states were formed. The western states are bigger than the states in the east. You can see their straight boundaries on the map.

DISTANCE CHART

Read the chart just like a tables-chart, or a graph. The distance chart shows how big the USA is. How far is it from Seattle to Miami? Or from New Orleans to Chicago? (Answers on page 96.)

Road distances in miles

	New York	Miami	Chicago	New Orleans	Seattle
Miami	1329				
Chicago	836	1365			
New Orleans	1324	873	925		
Seattle	2867	3384	2043	2617	
San Francisco	3014	3054	2174	2251	840

ALASKA

Alaska is the biggest state of the USA – but it has the fewest people. It was bought from Russia in 1867 for $7 million: the best bargain ever, particularly as oil was discovered a hundred years later. Oil has helped Alaska to become rich. Timber and fish are the other main products. Much of Alaska is mountainous or covered in forest. In the north, there is darkness all day in December, and months of ice-cold weather. But in the short summer, visitors love the long days and short nights. Farming is not possible in most of Alaska – except in the far south.

These are 48 of the 50 states. The other two are Alaska (map above) and Hawaii (map opposite)
★ State capital

ABBREVIATIONS

VT. = Vermont
N.H. = New Hampshire
MASS. = Massachusetts
CONN. = Connecticut
D.C. = District of Columbia

EASTERN USA

Washington, DC, is the capital city. The tall pillar is a monument to George Washington, who became the first President of the USA in 1776. The city is named after him. The building with the tall dome is the Capitol.

The map shows only half the USA, but over three-quarters of the population live in this half of the country.

The great cities of the northeast were the first big industrial areas in America. Pittsburgh's American football team is still called the Pittsburgh Steelers, even though many of the steelworks have closed down.

In recent years, many people have moved from the "snowbelt" of the north to the "sunbelt" of the south. New industries are booming in the south, where once there was much poverty. And many older people retire to Florida, where even midwinter feels almost like summer.

In the south of the USA it is hot enough for cotton, tobacco and peanuts to be successful crops. The palm tree on the flag of South Carolina (below, right) suggests that the climate of this part of America is nearly tropical.

The Appalachian Mountains are beautiful, especially in the fall (autumn), when the leaves of the trees turn red. But this area is the poorest part of the USA. Coal mines have closed and farmland is poor. The good farmland is west of the Appalachians, where you can drive for hundreds of miles past wheat and sweetcorn.

Canterbury Church, New Hampshire.
The northeast corner of the USA is called New England and was settled by English colonists. This church by the village green is very like old England! The settlers named their towns and villages after places they had known in England.

WHICH US CITY IS MOST IMPORTANT?

Washington, DC, is the capital city, where the President lives. But New York has far more people and industries than Washington. So *both* are the most important city – but in different ways.

Manhattan Island, New York. The world's first skyscrapers were built on Manhattan Island: the hard granite rock gave good foundations. The older skyscrapers each have a different shape; the newer ones are flat-topped.

Every US state has its own flag: six state flags are on the page opposite. Several states were named after kings and queens of England – in the days when these states were English colonies. For example, CAROLina (North and South) use the Latin name for King Charles I; MARYland is named after his wife, Queen Mary, and GEORGia is named after King George II. But LOUISiana is named after King Louis XIV of France because France colonized the Mississippi.

GREAT LAKES

Try using the first letters of the Great Lakes to make a sentence:

Superior	**S**uper
Michigan	**M**an
Huron	**H**elps
Erie	**E**very
Ontario	**O**ne

Now you'll *never* forget the west-to-east order of the Great Lakes!

THE MISSISSIPPI

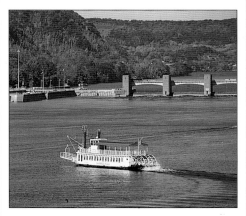

The Mississippi River was known as the "Great River Road" because it was an important route into the heart of the USA. "Stern-wheeler" paddle-steamers traveled the river with cargoes. It is still an important river today. Dams (above) and locks make it easier for big barges to use the river. The dams also help to reduce the risk of floods.

GREAT RIVER ROAD

U.S. POSTAGE 5c

Oak Alley Plantation, Louisiana.
The cotton planters in the south lived in fine mansions like this one. Their wealth was based on slavery. The slaves lived in very different homes. No wonder the slaves wanted to be free! In 1865, slavery was abolished in the USA.

75

WESTERN USA

CALIFORNIA

COLORADO

SOUTH DAKOTA

Many parts of the western USA have hardly any people. The Rocky Mountains are beautiful for holidays, but it is hard to make a living there.

The only big city on the high plateaus west of the Rockies is Salt Lake City, Utah. Some former mining towns are now "ghost towns": when the mines closed, all the people left. The toughest area of all is the desert land of Arizona in the southwest. The mountains and deserts were a great problem to the pioneers, but today the spectacular scenery and wildlife is preserved in large national parks.

The "Wild West." Scenes like this one are rare now, except when they are put on for the many tourists who visit the area. But in the days of the "Wild West," 100 years or more ago, the skills of cowboys were vital. Look carefully – this picture shows a cowgirl *rounding up horses!*

Wheat harvest, USA. A huge combine harvester moves across a field of wheat. Up to 150 years ago, this land was covered in grass and grazed by buffaloes. Much of this wheat will go abroad.

WHAT DO THE NAMES MEAN?

The Spanish were the first settlers in the western USA, and they have left us many Spanish names. Can you match the name and its meaning? (Answers on page 96.)

Amarillo (Texas)	The pass
Colorado	Yellow
El Paso (Texas)	The angels
Los Angeles	St Francis
San José	Colored
San Francisco	St Joseph

STAMP

Energy conservation. A great idea! Americans use more energy than anyone else.

WYOMING

ARIZONA

NEW MEXICO

NEBRASKA

OKLAHOMA

TEXAS

Grand Canyon, Arizona. The Colorado River has cut a huge canyon a mile deep and several miles wide in this desert area of the USA. The mountains slowly rose, while the river kept carving a deeper valley.

The Great Plains east of the Rocky Mountains are flat but high. Denver has the "Mile-high Stadium"! These dry plains have enormous cattle ranches. Where there is enough rain, crops of wheat and sweetcorn (maize) stretch to the horizon.

The Pacific coastlands of the northwest have plenty of rain and the climate is quite like northwest Europe. The mountains and valleys are thickly forested and timber is an important product.

CALIFORNIA

California now has more people in it than any other state. It has many advantages. In the Central Valley, the climate is right for many crops: oranges from California are well known, and grapes grow well and are made into wine. The desert of the south is attractive to retired people – many people migrate here from all over the USA.

A street car in San Francisco.
Street cars still climb the steep hills in San Francisco, California. A moving cable runs beneath the street. The car is fixed to the cable and starts with a jerk! In the background you can see an inlet of the Pacific and Alcatraz – once a top-security prison island.

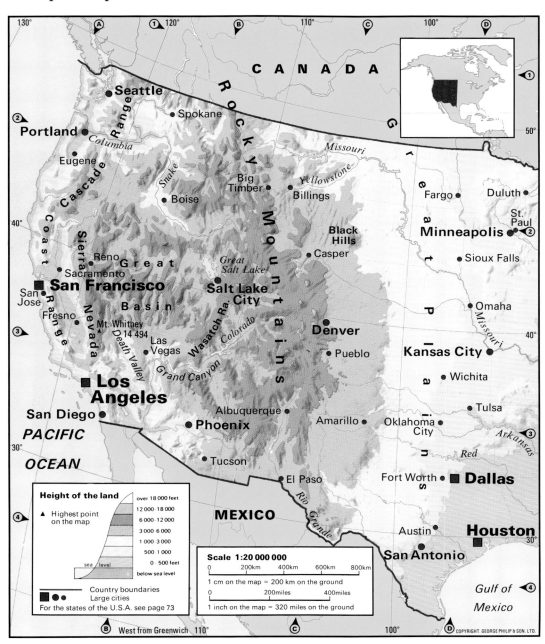

Height of the land
- over 18 000 feet
- 12 000-18 000
- 6 000-12 000
- 3 000-6 000
- 1 000-3 000
- 500-1 000
- 0-500 feet
- below sea level

▲ Highest point on the map

sea level

■ ● ● Country boundaries
Large cities
For the states of the U.S.A. see page 73

Scale 1:20 000 000

0 200km 400km 600km 800km
1 cm on the map = 200 km on the ground

0 200miles 400miles
1 inch on the map = 320 miles on the ground

West from Greenwich 110°

COPYRIGHT GEORGE PHILIP & SON. LTD.

Hollywood *is a suburb of Los Angeles. Rich film stars live here in expensive houses. The clear blue skies and lack of rain were helpful to film makers. But now, Los Angeles has so many cars there is more smog from pollution than clear skies.*

77

CENTRAL AMERICA

MEXICO

AREA 756,061 sq miles
POPULATION 93,342,000
MONEY New peso

PANAMA

AREA 29,761 sq miles
POPULATION 2,629,000
MONEY Balboa

GUATEMALA

AREA 42,042 sq miles
POPULATION 10,624,000
MONEY Quetzal

Mexico is by far the most important country on this map. Over 91 million people live in Mexico – more than in any country in Europe. Mexico City has a population of about 19 million: it is one of the biggest cities in the world. A major earthquake did much damage there in 1985.

Most Mexicans live on the high plateau of central Mexico. Industries are growing fast in Mexico City and near the border with the USA. There are very few people in the northern desert, in Lower California in the northwest, in the southern jungle, or in Yucatan in the east.

The other seven countries on this map are quite small. None of them has as many people as Mexico City!

Once ruled by Spain, these countries have been independent since the 1820s. Civil wars have caused many problems in Central America. But the climate is good for growing many tropical crops.

Ruins at Chichen Itza, Mexico. *Great temples were built by the people known as Mayas over a thousand years ago. These amazing ruins are in Yucatan, the most easterly part of Mexico. The tourists look tiny, which shows you how HUGE the pyramid is. Today, this is an area of jungle.*

BELIZE

AREA 8,865 sq miles
POPULATION 216,000
MONEY Belize dollar

TORTILLAS – A RECIPE FOR YOU TO COOK

Ingredients
8 ounces of maize flour (sweetcorn flour)
salt and water

Method
1 Mix the maize flour, salt and water into a soft dough.
2 Pat into round shapes about ¼ inch thick, and 4½ inches across.
3 Melt a little margarine in a frying pan.
4 Place the tortillas in the hot frying pan.
5 For best results, turn the tortillas over.
6 Serve at once!
You have now cooked one of the most important meals of Central America. Maize (sweetcorn) was developed as a crop in the Americas, and is now grown in many parts of the world. You eat maize often as cornflakes.

The Toucan is sometimes called the "banana-beak bird," for an obvious reason! It eats fruit and lives in the forest, nesting in a hole in a tree. If the forest is cleared, it will have nowhere to live.

THE PANAMA CANAL

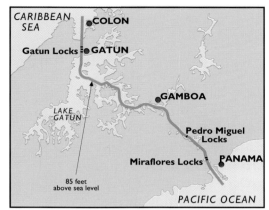

CARIBBEAN SEA
COLON
Gatun Locks GATUN

LAKE GATUN

GAMBOA

Pedro Miguel Locks

Miraflores Locks   PANAMA

85 feet above sea level

PACIFIC OCEAN

The **Panama Canal** links the Caribbean Sea with the Pacific Ocean. It was opened in 1914. Many workers died of fever while digging the canal through the jungle. It is 50 miles long, and the deepest cutting is 269 feet deep – the world's biggest "ditch"!

There are six locks along the route of the canal. The photograph (left) shows two ships traveling through the canal. The map and diagram show that part of the route is through Lake Gatun, at 85 feet above sea level. So the ships have to pass through three locks at each end.

Over 15,000 ships use the canal each year, and sometimes there are "traffic jams" at the locks: it is the busiest big-ship canal in the world. Before the Panama Canal was built, the only sea route from the Pacific to the Atlantic was round South America.

In which direction are ships traveling from the Caribbean to the Pacific? Does this surprise you? Look at the map below.

PANAMA CANAL CROSS-SECTION

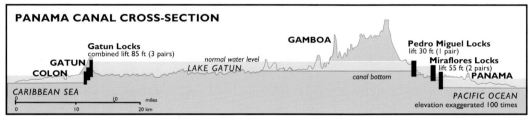

Gatun Locks
combined lift 85 ft (3 pairs)

GAMBOA

Pedro Miguel Locks
lift 30 ft (1 pair)

Miraflores Locks
lift 55 ft (2 pairs)

GATUN
COLON

normal water level
LAKE GATUN

canal bottom

PANAMA

CARIBBEAN SEA

PACIFIC OCEAN
elevation exaggerated 100 times

10   miles
0   10   20 km

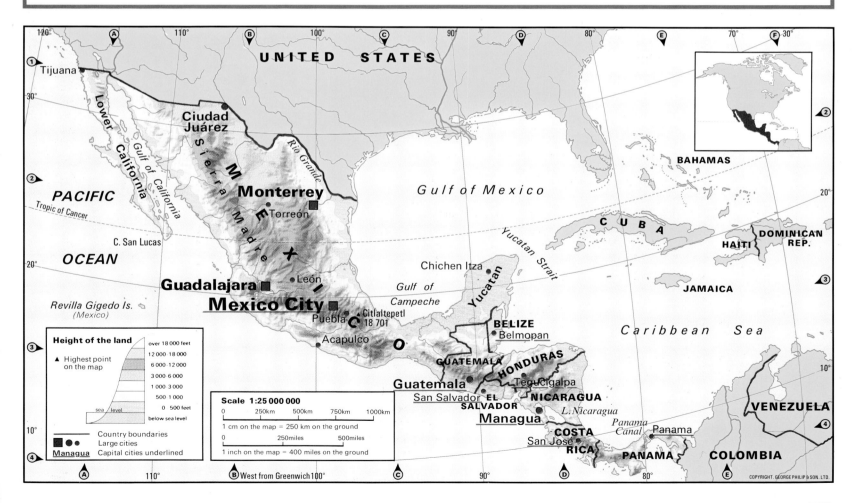

Height of the land

▲ Highest point on the map

over 18 000 feet
12 000-18 000
6 000-12 000
3 000-6 000
1 000-3 000
500-1 000
0-500 feet
sea level
below sea level

■ ● ● Country boundaries
Large cities
Managua Capital cities underlined

Scale 1:25 000 000

0   250km   500km   750km   1000km

1 cm on the map = 250 km on the ground

0   250miles   500miles

1 inch on the map = 400 miles on the ground

UNITED STATES

Tijuana

Lower California

Gulf of California

Ciudad Juárez

Rio Grande

Sierra Madre

Monterrey
Torreón

C. San Lucas

PACIFIC OCEAN

Tropic of Cancer

Revilla Gigedo Is. (Mexico)

Guadalajara   León
Mexico City
Puebla Citlaltepetl 18 701
Acapulco

Gulf of Mexico

Chichen Itza

Yucatan Strait

Gulf of Campeche

Yucatan

BELIZE
Belmopan

GUATEMALA HONDURAS
Guatemala   Tegucigalpa
San Salvador EL NICARAGUA
SALVADOR
Managua   L. Nicaragua
COSTA   Panama
San José RICA   Canal Panama
PANAMA

CUBA

HAITI DOMINICAN REP.

JAMAICA

Caribbean Sea

BAHAMAS

VENEZUELA

COLOMBIA

COPYRIGHT. GEORGE PHILIP & SON. LTD.

A 110°   B West from Greenwich 100°   C   90°   D   80°   E

WEST INDIES

JAMAICA

AREA 4,243 sq miles
POPULATION 2,700,000
MONEY Jamaican dollar

CUBA

AREA 42,803 sq miles
POPULATION 11,050,000
MONEY Cuban peso

HAITI

AREA 10,714 sq miles
POPULATION 7,180,000
MONEY Gourde

The West Indies are a large group of islands in the Caribbean Sea. Some islands are high and volcanic, others are low coral islands – but all of them are beautiful. Most West Indians have African ancestors: they were brought from West Africa as slaves, to work in the sugar and tobacco fields. And in Trinidad, workers came from India as well.

Most of the islands are now independent countries – and tourism is more important than farming in many places. Winter is the best time to visit; summer is very hot and humid, with the risk of hurricanes. In recent years, many West Indians have emigrated to the UK from Commonwealth islands, to France from Guadeloupe and Martinique, and to the USA from Puerto Rico. The most important crops for export are bananas and other fruit, sugar and tobacco. A few islands have developed their minerals, for example bauxite in Jamaica and oil in Trinidad.

Coconut palms and beach, Barbados.
It is beautiful – but beware! The tropical sun can quickly burn your skin. And if you seek shade under the coconut palms, you might get hit by a big coconut! Even so, the West Indies are very popular with tourists – especially Americans escaping from cold winters.

Dutch colonial houses, Curaçao. *The island of Curaçao has been Dutch for many years. The colonists came from the Netherlands, and tried to build houses just like the ones at home. Several other small West Indian islands still have European connections.*

TOURISM – GOOD & BAD NEWS

Tourism is GOOD news because it brings money and jobs to many West Indian islands. The sunny weather means tourists come all year round. There is work in the hotels and restaurants. Farmers can sell more vegetables and a great variety of delicious fruit (right). Beautiful scenery is looked after so that tourists will come and visit – waterfalls, hot springs, old forts and churches as well as coral reefs and lovely beaches. But tourism can also be BAD news . . .

pollution; noise; waste of water; and many local people do not want to be stared at and photographed by rich tourists who may not treat them as equals.

The flag of Jamaica (far left) has a meaning: GOLD stands for sunshine and natural resources; GREEN for farming and future hope; BLACK for hardships, past and present.

The West Indies used to be colonies of European countries. Today, most of the islands are independent, but still have close links with Europe. Look at the map; can you spot*:

● An island that is part of France?
● An island that is owned by the Netherlands?
● An island owned by the UK?
● A group of islands – half are owned by the UK; half by the USA?

(* Answers on page 96.)

Beware of the hurricane season! *What a contrast to the peaceful beach (see picture, left)! Violent tropical storms are a danger every summer. Strong winds can reach over 180 miles per hour, with torrential rain. They uproot trees and wreck boats and buildings; floods damage crops.*

Loading bananas, Dominica. *Bananas are the main export of several islands. Here women are carrying heavy loads of bananas on their heads to the small boats which take the bananas to the Geest banana ship. The bananas travel to Europe in this refrigerated ship. Loading the ship is easier in deep-water harbors.*

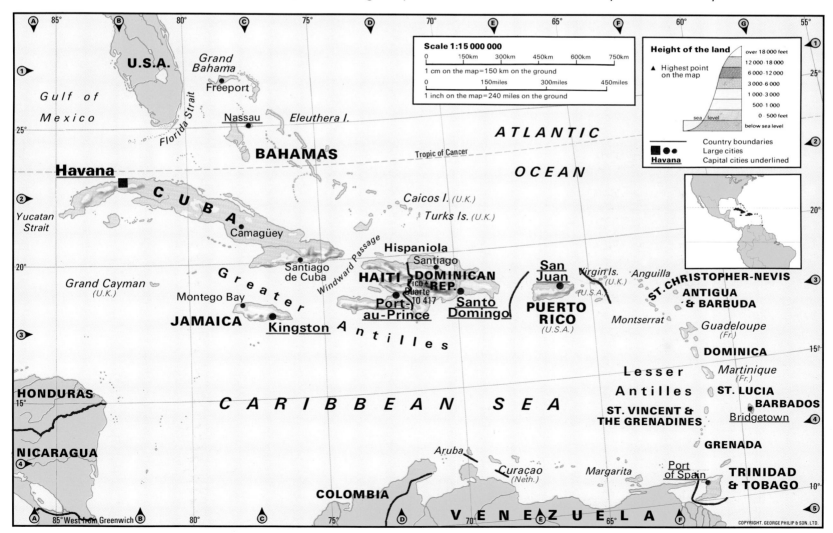

SOUTH AMERICA

A tour of South America would be very exciting. At the Equator are the hot steamy jungles of the Amazon lowlands. To the west comes the great climb up to the Andes Mountains. The peaks are so high that even the volcanoes are snow-capped all year. Travelers on buses and trains are offered extra oxygen to breathe, because the air is so thin.

Squeezed between the Andes and the Pacific Ocean in Peru and northern Chile is the world's driest desert – the Atacama Desert, which stretches southward from the border with Peru for nearly 1000 miles.

Further south in Chile are more wet forests – but these forests are cool. The monkey-puzzle tree originates here. But eastward, in Argentina, there is less rain and more grass. Cattle on the Pampas are rounded up by cowboys, and further south is the very cold and dry area called Patagonia where sheep farming is important.

Reed boats on Lake Titicaca, the highest navigable lake in the world. It is high in the Andes, at 12,503 feet above sea level. Totora reeds grow around the shores, and the Indians tie bundles of reeds together to make fishing boats. The picture shows the reed shelters they use while they make the boats and go fishing. In the background you can see a mountain rising from the plateau.

Lake Titicaca is shared between Peru and Bolivia. A steam-powered ferry boat travels the length of the lake.

Why is Lake Titicaca the only stretch of water available for the Bolivian navy? (Check the map!)

Height of the land

over 18 000 feet	
12 000 - 18 000	
▲ Highest point on the map	6 000 - 12 000
	3 000 - 6 000
	1 000 - 3 000
	500 - 1 000
sea level	0 - 500 feet
	below sea level

Deeper blue - deeper sea

Scale 1 : 40 000 000

0 — 400km — 800km — 1200km — 1600km — 2000km

1 cm on the map = 400 km on the ground

0 — 400miles — 800miles — 1200miles

1 inch on the map = 640 miles on the ground

COPYRIGHT. GEORGE PHILIP & SON. LTD.

South America stretches further south than any other continent (apart from Antarctica). The cold and stormy tip of South America, Cape Horn, is only 620 miles from Antarctica.

In every South American country, the population is growing fast. Most of the farmland is owned by a few rich people, and many people are desperately poor. Young people are leaving the countryside for the cities, most of which are encircled by shanty towns. There is rapid progress in the big cities, but many people do not benefit.

ONE country occupies nearly half the total area of South America, and has over half the population of the whole continent: BRAZIL.

Brasília, Brazil. Brasília became the new capital of Brazil in 1960. It is a planned town, with tall office blocks and large open spaces. This is fine for car owners, but not for others as there are very few trees although the weather is very hot. Most Brazilians live near the coast, and Brasília was a brave attempt to get people to move inland. Over a million people now live there.

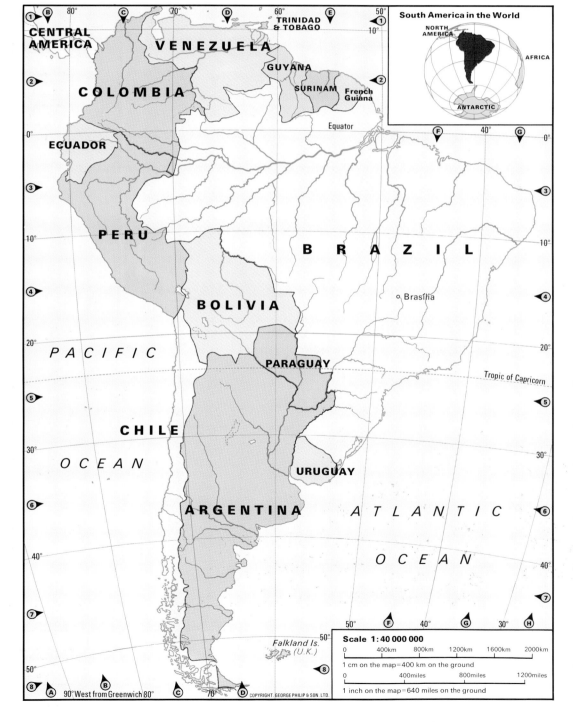

SOUTH AMERICA FACTS

AREA 6,795,360 sq miles
HIGHEST POINT Mount Aconcagua (Argentina), 22,835 feet
LOWEST POINT No land below sea level
LONGEST RIVER Amazon, 4006 miles
LARGEST LAKE Lake Titicaca (Bolivia and Peru), 3199 sq miles
BIGGEST COUNTRY Brazil, 3,286,472 sq miles
SMALLEST COUNTRY Surinam* 63,039 sq miles
RICHEST COUNTRY Venezuela
POOREST COUNTRY Guyana
MOST CROWDED COUNTRY Ecuador
LEAST CROWDED COUNTRY Surinam
HIGHEST WATERFALL Angel Falls, 3212 feet (a world record)
* French Guiana is smaller, but it is not independent

TROPICAL SOUTH AMERICA

BRAZIL

AREA 3,286,472 sq miles
POPULATION 161,416,000
MONEY Cruzeiro real

PERU

AREA 496,223 sq miles
POPULATION 23,588,000
MONEY Sol

COLOMBIA

AREA 439,733 sq miles
POPULATION 34,948,000
MONEY Peso

Brazil is by far the biggest country in South America, and has more people (about 161 million) than the rest of South America put together.

Most people still live near the coast. Parts of the Amazon forest are now being settled, but large areas inland are still almost empty. The poorest parts are in the northeast, where the rains often fail, and in the shanty towns around the cities. Modern industry is growing very fast, but there are still too few jobs. Brazil has pioneered fuel made from sugarcane for cars and trucks.

Colombia, Ecuador, Peru and Bolivia are known as the Andean states. Colombia is known for its coffee. Bananas and other tropical crops grow near the coast of Ecuador, but the capital city is high in the mountains. Peru relies on mountain rivers to bring water to the dry coastal area. Bolivia has the highest capital city in the world. It is the poorest country in South America: farming is difficult and even the tin mines hardly make a profit.

Machu Picchu, Peru, the lost city of the Incas, is perched on a mountainside 7800 feet above sea level. The last Inca emperor probably lived here in 1580. The ruins were rediscovered in 1911.

ECUADOR

AREA 109,483 sq miles
POPULATION 11,384,000
MONEY Sucre

Amazon jungle. The hot, wet jungle covers thousands of miles. There is no cool season, and the forest is always green. The trees can be 160 feet high. New roads and villages, mines and dams are being built in the Brazilian jungle, and parts of the forest are being destroyed.

THE GALAPAGOS ISLANDS

These volcanic islands belong to Ecuador but are 620 miles from the mainland. They have unique plants and animals because they have been isolated for so long. The giant tortoises are the most famous and spectacular "residents."

Going to market, Peru. This lady is a descendant of the Incas who lived in Peru before the Spanish arrived. She carries her baby on her back in a fine woven blanket. In most South American countries, the Indians are among the poorest people.

Venezuela is the richest country in South America because of its mineral wealth. Oil is pumped up from beneath Lake Maracaibo, and iron ore is mined from the plateau south of the River Orinoco. The world's highest waterfall, the Angel Falls, is in Venezuela.

In Guyana there are important deposits of bauxite, which is used to make aluminum. Guyana was once British and Surinam was once Dutch. But French Guiana is *still* French.

DID YOU KNOW?

Ecuador means *Equator*: the Equator (0°) crosses the country

Colombia is named after Christopher Columbus, who sailed from Europe to the Americas in 1492

Bolivia is named after Simon Bolivar, a hero of the country's war of independence in the 1820s

La Paz, in Bolivia, means *peace*

Cattle and cowboys. *To the south of the Amazon forest, there is c large area of dry woodland and grassland in Brazil called the Mato Grosso. Cattle are grazed here, and horses are still used to round them up.*

TEMPERATE SOUTH AMERICA

ARGENTINA

AREA 1,068,296 sq miles
POPULATION 34,663,000
MONEY Peso

CHILE

AREA 292,258 sq miles
POPULATION 14,271,000
MONEY Peso

URUGUAY

AREA 68,498 sq miles
POPULATION 3,186,000
MONEY Peso

Chile is 2600 miles long, but it is only about 125 miles wide, because it is sandwiched between the Andes and the Pacific.

In the north is the Atacama Desert, the driest in the world. In one place, there was no rain for 400 years! Fortunately, rivers from the Andes permit some irrigation. Chilean nitrates come from this area. Nitrates are salts in dried-up lakes; they are used to make fertilizers and explosives. Copper is mined high in the mountains.

In the center, the climate is like the Mediterranean area and California, with hot dry summers and warm wet winters with westerly winds. This is a lovely climate, and most Chileans live in this area.

In the south, Chile is wet, windy and cool. Thick forests which include the Chilean pine (monkey-puzzle tree) cover the steep hills. The reason for these contrasts is the wind. Winds bringing rain blow from the Pacific all year in the south; but only in winter in the center; and not at all in the north.

Geysers in the Andes, Chile. *Hot steam hisses into the cold air, 13,150 feet above sea level in the Andes of northern Chile. It shows there is still plenty of volcanic activity in the Andes.*

PARAGUAY

AREA 157,046 sq miles
POPULATION 4,979,000
MONEY Guarani

STAMP

Valparaiso is Chile's main port. It is on the coast near the capital. The city was founded in 1536 by the Spanish who arrived in the good ship Santiaguillo. Chile was ruled by the Spanish until 1818. Valparaiso means "valley of paradise" – which is not quite true!

THE ANDES

The Andes are over 4400 miles long, so they are the longest mountain range in the world. They are fold mountains, with a very steep western side, and a gentler eastern side. Most of the high peaks are volcanoes: they are the highest volcanoes in the world. Mount Aconcagua (22,835 feet) is extinct. Mount Guallatiri, in Chile, is the world's highest active volcano.

The higher you climb, the cooler it is. And the further you travel from the Equator, the cooler it is. Therefore, the snowline in southern Chile is much lower than in northern Chile.

Sheep farming in Patagonia, Argentina. *Southern Argentina has a cool, dry climate. Very few people live there – but lots of sheep roam the extensive grasslands. There are almost as many sheep in Argentina as there are people.*

Argentina means "silvery" in Spanish: some of the early settlers came to mine silver. But today, Argentina's most important product is cattle. Cool grasslands called the Pampas (see map below) are ideal for cattle grazing.

Argentina is a varied country: the northwest is hot and dry, and the south is cold and dry. The frontier with Chile runs high along the top of the Andes.

Buenos Aires, the capital city, is the biggest city in South America; it has 11 million people. The name means "good air," but gasoline fumes have now polluted the air.

Paraguay and **Uruguay** are two countries with small populations. Each country has under five million people. Nearly half the population of Uruguay lives in the capital city, Montevideo, which is on the coast. In contrast Paraguay is a landlocked country. Animal farming is the most important occupation in both these countries.

All these four countries – Chile, Argentina, Paraguay and Uruguay – have Spanish as their official language. Most of the people have European ancestors, except in Paraguay where there are a lot of South American Indians.

THE FALKLAND ISLANDS

Port Stanley, capital of the Falklands, looks similar to an English town. These islands are a British colony in the South Atlantic. They are about 300 miles east of Argentina, which claims them as the Islas Malvinas. Britain fought an Argentine invasion in 1982, and the military force is now as large as the population (only 2000). Sheep farming is the main occupation.

Santiago, capital of Chile, has a beautiful setting between the Andes and the coastal mountains. A third of Chile's people live in Santiago. Its name means "St James" – the patron saint of Spain, which once ruled Chile.

THE ARCTIC

The Arctic is an ocean, which is frozen all through the winter and still has lots of ice in summer. It is surrounded by the northernmost areas of three continents, but Greenland is the only truly Arctic country.

For most of the year the land is snow-covered. During the short summer, when the sun never sets, the snow and the frozen topsoil melt. But the deeper soil is still frozen, so the land is very marshy. This treeless landscape is called the tundra.

The reindeer and caribou can be herded or hunted, but farming is impossible. In recent years, rich mineral deposits have been found. Canada, the USA and Russia have military bases near the Arctic Ocean.

From the Atlantic Ocean, there is easy access to the Arctic Ocean. But from the Pacific Ocean, the only route to the Arctic Ocean is the narrow Bering Strait, between Siberia (Russia) and Alaska (USA).

ARCTIC FACTS

Fourth largest **ocean** – 5,439,000 sq miles
World record for least sunshine
Surrounded by cold **land**
North Pole **first reached** in 1909

The Inuit (Eskimo) village of Savissavik, near Thule in northern Greenland. The houses are mostly wooden and are well insulated against the cold. They are built on stilts to protect them from the effects of frost moving the ground in winter, and to stop the warmth of the houses melting the ground beneath.

Inuit (Eskimo) fishing for cod through a crack in the spring ice. He has traveled over the sea from his village by sledge. Fish are a good source of protein for families in the far north.

WILDLIFE IN GREENLAND

Land animals have to cope with very long winters. The Arctic fox turns white for camouflage.

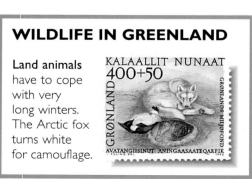

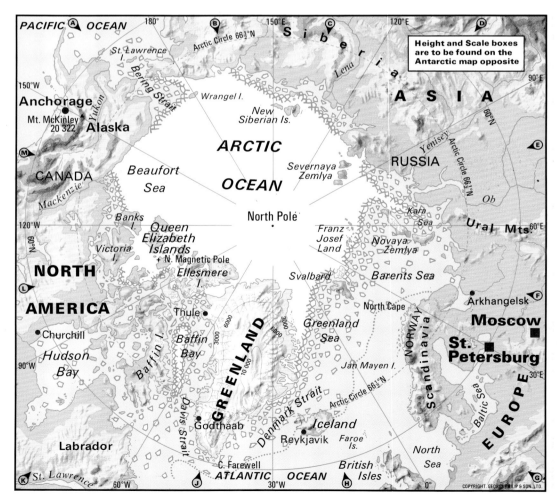

ANTARCTICA

Antarctica is the continent surrounding the South Pole. It is the coldest, windiest and iciest place in the world! It is also very isolated, as the map shows.

No people live in Antarctica permanently. Some scientists work in research stations. Everything that is needed has to be brought in during the short summer. From November to January, icebreakers can reach the land. But huge icebergs are always a danger. In winter (May to July) it is always dark, the sea is frozen, and people have to face extreme cold and dangerous blizzards.

No-one "owns" Antarctica. The Antarctic Treaty ensures that the continent should only be used for scientific research. This means it should remain peaceful for ever. The flags of the 32 nations that have signed the treaty stand in a ring round the South Pole, near the USA's Amundsen-Scott base. Even Antarctica has more and more tourists visiting the area every year.

ANTARCTICA FACTS

Fifth largest **continent** – 5,443,000 sq miles
World record for coldest temperature
Surrounded by cold **seas**
South Pole **first reached** in 1911

Rookery of Gentoo Penguins in Antarctica. *Penguins cannot fly, but they can swim very well. The parents use their feet to protect the eggs and chicks from the cold ice! No land animals live in Antarctica, but the ocean is full of fish, which provide food for penguins, seals and whales.*

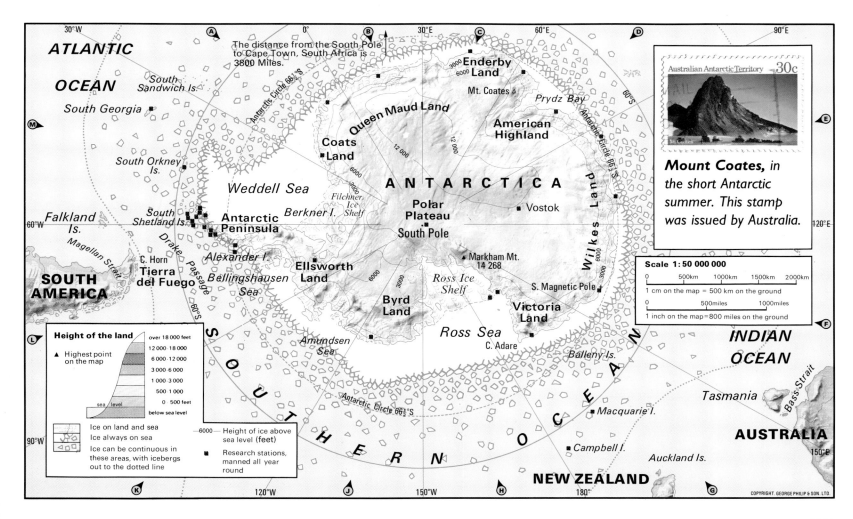

Mount Coates, in the short Antarctic summer. This stamp was issued by Australia.

Height of the land
over 18 000 feet
12 000-18 000
▲ Highest point on the map
6 000-12 000
3 000-6 000
1 000-3 000
500-1 000
0-500 feet
sea level
below sea level

Ice on land and sea
Ice always on sea
Ice can be continuous in these areas, with icebergs out to the dotted line

—6000— Height of ice above sea level (feet)
■ Research stations, manned all year round

Scale 1:50 000 000
0   500km   1000km   1500km   2000km
1 cm on the map = 500 km on the ground
0   500miles   1000miles
1 inch on the map = 800 miles on the ground

COPYRIGHT GEORGE PHILIP & SON LTD.

QUIZ QUESTIONS

A MYSTERY MESSAGE

Use the map of the countries of the world on pages 8–9 to decode this message. Each missing word is all or part of the name of a country. (For some answers, letters have to be taken out of or added to the name of the country.)

I was _ _ _ _ _ a _ _ (east of Austria), so I bought a large _ _ _ _ _ _ _ (east of Greece), some _ _ _ _ _ _ ns (east of Norway) and a bottle of _ _ _ _ ugal (west of Spain). Finally, I ate an _ _ _ land (west of Norway) -cream. I enjoyed my _ e _ _ i (east of Mauritania), but afterward I began to _ _ _ _ earia (south of Romania) and I got a bad S _ _ _ _ _ (south of France). A O _ _ _ (east of Saudi Arabia) told me: "Just eat Philip _ _ _ _ sapples (south of Taiwan) and _ _ gypt (east of Libya), cooked in a Ja _ _ _ _ (east of Korea). Tomorrow you can eat a Ghban _ _ _ (east of Ivory Coast) and some _ _ _ _ _ _ _ (east of Peru) nuts. It shouldn't _ _ _ _ _ a Rica (west of Panama) you too much." I said: "You must be _ _ _ _ agascar (east of Mozambique)! I think I've got _ _ _ _ _ ysr _ _ (north of Indonesia). I'll have _ _ / _ _ (west of Benin) to a doctor quickly, otherwise I'll soon be _ _ _ _ _ Sea (lake between Israel and Jordan)."

  Happily, the doctor _ _ bared (island country south of USA) me, so I am still M _ _ d _ _ _ s (islands west of Sri Lanka) today!

NAME THE COUNTRY

There is a long, thin country in almost every continent. Can you name the countries shown here – and name the continent in which they are found? (If you need help, look at pages 8–9 for a map of the countries of the world.)

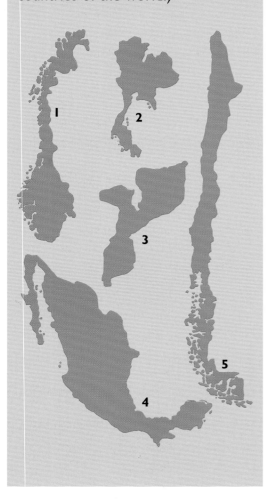

NAME THE ISLAND

The name of the continent where each island is found is marked on each outline. Do you know (a) the name of each island, and (b) to which country each island belongs (or are they island countries)?

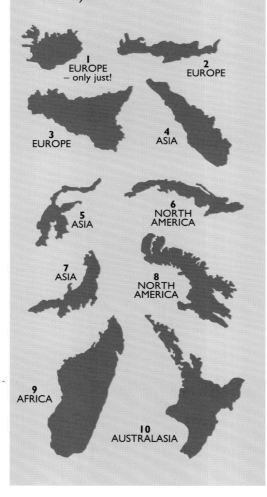

GREAT RIVERS OF EUROPE

Use pages 18–37 to discover which great river flows through or near each pair of cities.
1 Vienna (Austria) and Budapest (Hungary)
2 Rotterdam (Netherlands) and Bonn (Germany)
3 Avignon (France) and Lyons (France)
4 Worcester (England) and Gloucester (England)
5 Toledo (Spain) and Lisbon (Portugal)

PLACES IN ASIA

Move the letters to find:
Countries RAIN; CHAIN; MOAN; AWAIT N; PLANE
Capital cities ANIMAL; DIARY H; THE TANKS; A BULK; COOL MOB

FIND THE COLOR

Each answer is a color. Use the atlas index and the maps to help you.
Cover the right-hand column with a piece of paper and try to answer the
left-hand column only. Award yourself 2 points for each correct answer to
the left-hand column only, or 1 point if you used the clues in both columns.

1 A sea between Egypt and Saudi Arabia . . .

. . . and the river on the border of Oklahoma and Texas, USA.

2 **A big island east of Canada . . .**

. . . and a bay on the west side of Lake Michigan, USA.

3 The sea between Turkey and Ukraine . . .

. . . and a forest in Germany.

4 **The sea between Korea and China . . .**

. . . and a (stony) river in Wyoming, USA.

5 The sea on which Arkhangelsk lies, in Russia . . .

. . . and the river flowing north from Lake Victoria to Khartoum (Sudan).

6 **A town in southern France which is also a fruit . . .**

. . . and the river which makes the border between South Africa and Namibia.

7 The tributary of the River Nile that flows from Ethiopia to Khartoum (Sudan) . . .

. . . and a mountain ridge in eastern USA.

OCEANS AND SEAS

What ocean would you cross on an airplane journey . . .

What sea would you cross on an airplane journey . . .

1   From Australia to the USA?
2   From Brazil to South Africa?
3   From Canada to Russia?
4   From Madagascar to Indonesia?
5   From Mexico to Portugal?

6   From Saudi Arabia to Egypt?
7   From Korea to Japan
8   From Denmark to the UK?
9   From Vietnam to the Philippines?
10 From Cuba to Colombia?

THINGS TO DO

COLLECT STAMPS WITH A THEME
A stamp collection soon grows.
Try a thematic collection: choose
a theme (topic) and collect stamps
on that theme. For example, you
could collect:
Flags on stamps – such as the stamps
of Estonia and Latvia on page 37.
Map stamps – small islands often
issue map stamps to show everyone
where they are!
Traditional crafts on stamps.

COLLECT YOUR OWN COINS
Ask people who have been abroad
for any foreign coins they do not
want – you will have an instant
collection! If you cannot have the
coins to keep, you could make
pencil or crayon rubbings on
thin paper. The coin box on
page 16 is a good starting point for
making sense of the coins in your
collection: each coin has a date,
a value, a picture – and a country!

USA STATES QUIZ

All the answers can be found on
the maps on pages 62–3 and 66–9.
Do not include Alaska and Hawaii.

1   Which is the *biggest* state?
2   Which is the *smallest* state?
3   Which state reaches furthest *north*? (Careful!)
4   Which state reaches furthest *south*?
5   Which state reaches furthest *west*?
6   Which state reaches furthest *east*?
7   Which state is split into two by a lake?
8   Which state is split into two by an inlet of the sea?
9   Which two states are perfect rectangles in shape?
10 Which state is shaped like a saucepan?
11 In which state will you be if you visit Lake Huron?
12 In which state will you be if you visit Lake Ontario?
13 In which state will you be if you visit the Great Salt Lake?
14 In which state will you be if you visit the Mississippi delta?
15 Which state in *northern* USA is called South . . . . . ?
16 Which state in *southern* USA is called North . . . . . ?
17 There is only one place in the USA where four states meet: which states?
18 How many states have a border with Mexico?
19 How many states have a coastline on the Pacific?
20 How many states have a coastline on the Gulf of Mexico?

ANSWERS TO ALL QUIZ QUESTIONS ARE ON PAGE 96

INDEX

HOW TO USE THIS INDEX

The first number given after each name or topic is the page number; then a letter and another number tell you which square of the map you should look at.

For example, Abidjan is in square B2 on page 57. Find B at the top or the bottom of the map on page 57 and put a finger on it. Put another finger on the number 2 at the side of the map. Move your fingers in from the edge of the map and they will meet in square B2. Abidjan will now be easy to find. It is the capital city of the Ivory Coast, a country in West Africa.

If a name goes through more than one square, the square given in the index is the one in which the biggest part of the name falls.

Names like Gulf of Mexico and Cape Horn are in the Index as 'Mexico, Gulf of' and 'Horn, Cape'.

ANSWERS TO QUESTIONS

Page 6 "RSA" stands for Republic of South Africa.

Page 8 On this flag, the emblem of the United Nations is shown in white. This is the view of the world as it appears from above the North Pole. It is surrounded by olive branches of peace.

Page 18 This building is in Brussels, Belgium: it was the headquarters of the European Union. Many important decisions were made here.

Pages 18–19
SF = Finland (Suomi Finland); B = Belgium; L = Luxembourg; DK = Denmark; F = France; D = Germany (Deutschland in German); NL = Netherlands; I = Italy; E = Spain (España); S = Sweden; IRL = Ireland (Republic of Ireland); A = Austria; GB = Great Britain; P = Portugal; GR = Greece.

Page 22 The London landmarks featured on the stamp are (*from left to right*): Westminster Abbey; Nelson's Column (in Trafalgar Square); statue of Eros (in Piccadilly Circus); Telecom Tower; clock tower of the Houses of Parliament (containing the bell Big Ben); St Paul's Cathedral; Tower Bridge; White Tower of the Tower of London.

Page 24 Belgium has two official languages, Flemish and French. The coin on the right has the Flemish name for Belgium (*Belgie*); the coin on the left shows its French name (*Belgique*).

Page 24 The yellow objects are CLOGS. They are shoes made out of wood. A few Dutch people still wear clogs, but tourists also like to buy them.

Page 26 The photograph of the fruit stall shows: a watermelon, strawberries, blackberries, mangoes, pineapples, melons, cherries, avocados, tomatoes, apricots, peaches and nectarines.

Pages 38–39 The script reads *across* the two pages:
1 Australia; **2** Egypt;
3 Hong Kong; **4** United States;
5 Taiwan.

Page 39 The five countries which share the shoreline of the Caspian Sea are Russia, Kazakstan, Turkmenistan, Iran and Azerbaijan.

Page 40 The 15 "new" countries formed at the breakup of the USSR are (*from largest to smallest*): Russia, Kazakstan, Ukraine, Turkmenistan, Uzbekistan, Belarus, Kyrgyzstan, Tajikistan, Azerbaijan, Georgia, Lithuania, Latvia, Estonia, Moldova and Armenia.

Page 41 Moskva (= Moscow) to Vladivostok.

Page 44 Clockwise (*from the top right-hand corner*), the picture shows: samosas, ground coriander, coriander leaves, cumin, pakoras, rice, poppadums, red chilli powder next to yellow turmeric powder, green okra (also called "ladies fingers"), garlic and bay leaves.

Page 65 Australia, of course!

Page 68 The north shores of Lakes Superior, Huron, Erie and Ontario are in Canada, and the south shores are in the USA. Lake Michigan is entirely in the USA.

Page 69 El Salvador only has a coastline on the Pacific Ocean. Belize only has a coastline on the Caribbean Sea. (Honduras has a tiny coastline on the Pacific – look closely at the map!) One island has two countries on it: Haiti and Dominican Republic.

Page 73 Seattle to Miami is 3384 miles; New Orleans to Chicago is 925 miles.

Page 76 The Spanish words mean:
Amarillo = Yellow;
Colorado = Colored;
El Paso = The pass;
Los Angeles = The angels;
San José = St Joseph;
San Francisco = St Francis.

Page 81 The islands of Guadeloupe and Martinique are both part of France. Curaçao is owned by the Netherlands; Turks Is, Caicos I. and Grand Cayman are owned by the UK. Some of the Virgin Islands belong to the UK, and some belong to the USA.

ANSWERS TO QUIZ QUESTIONS (on pages 90–91)

NAME THE COUNTRY
1 Norway (Europe)
2 Thailand (Asia)
3 Mozambique (Africa)
4 Mexico (Central America)
5 Chile (South America)

NAME THE ISLAND
(Note: Name of country in brackets after name of island)
1 Iceland (Iceland)
2 Crete (Greece)
3 Sicily (Italy)
4 Sumatra (Indonesia)
5 Sulawesi (Indonesia)
6 Cuba (Cuba)
7 Honshu (Japan)
8 Baffin Island (Canada)
9 Madagascar (Madagascar)
10 North Island (New Zealand)

A MYSTERY MESSAGE
I was *hungry*, so I bought a large *turkey*, some *swedes* and a bottle of *port*. Finally, I ate an *ice*-cream. I enjoyed my meal, but afterward I began to *bulge* and I got a bad *pain*. A man told me: "Just eat *pineapples* and *egg* cooked in a *pan*. Tomorrow you can eat a *banana* and some *Brazil* nuts. It shouldn't *cost* you too much". I said: "You must be *mad*! I think I've got *malaria*. I'll have *to go* to a doctor quickly, otherwise I'll soon be *dead*".

Happily, the doctor *cured* me, so I am still *alive* today!

GREAT RIVERS OF EUROPE
1 Danube; **2** Rhine;
3 Rhône; **4** Severn;
5 Tagus.

PLACES IN ASIA
Countries
Iran; China; Oman; Taiwan; Nepal.
Capital cities
Manila; Riyadh; Tashkent; Kabul; Colombo.

COLOR QUIZ
1 Red (Red Sea/Red River)
2 Green (Greenland/Green Bay)
3 Black (Black Sea/Black Forest)
4 Yellow (Yellow Sea/ Yellowstone River)
5 White (White Sea/White Nile)
6 Orange (Orange/Orange River)
7 Blue (Blue Nile/Blue Ridge)

STATES OF THE USA
1 Texas
2 Rhode Island
3 Minnesota
4 Florida
5 Washington
6 Maine
7 Michigan
8 Maryland
9 Wyoming and Colorado
10 Oklahoma
11 Michigan
12 New York
13 Utah
14 Louisiana
15 South Dakota
16 North Carolina
17 Utah, Colorado, Arizona and New Mexico
18 Four (California, Arizona, New Mexico and Texas)
19 Three (Washington, Oregon and California)
20 Five (Texas, Louisiana, Mississippi, Alabama and Florida)

OCEANS AND SEAS
1 Pacific; **2** Atlantic;
3 Arctic; **4** Indian;
5 Atlantic; **6** Red Sea;
7 Sea of Japan; **8** North Sea;
9 South China Sea;
10 Caribbean Sea.

PICTURE ACKNOWLEDGEMENTS

Sue Atkinson 66 bottom center; **BBC Natural History Unit** /Keith Scholey 58 bottom left; **Colorsport** 22 center right, /Bryan Yablonsky 72 top; **Finnish Tourist Board** 20 bottom center; **Robert Harding Picture Library** 11 left, 11 right, 14, 20 top, 22 center left, 28 center right, 30 center right, 30 bottom, 41 middle center, 43 left, 44 top, 46 top, 48 center left, 49 top left, 64 center left, 64 center right, 70 top, 70 bottom left, 70 bottom right, 79, 80 top, 80 bottom left, 81 left, 82, 86 top, 24 center bottom, 34 bottom left, 36 center right, 48 top right, 66 top left, 22 top, /David Beatty 40 bottom left, /Nigel Blythe 50 center,

/P. Bordes 56 top, /C. Bowman 32 center, 78 top, /Rob Cousins 26 right, 46 bottom right, /Nigel Francis 26 center left, 74 bottom, /Simon Harris 77 top, /Kim Hart 19 left, /Gavin Hellier 77 bottom, /Dave Jacobs 75 bottom, /F. Jackson 12 top, /Carol Jopp 15 right, /Thomas Laird 45 bottom, /Louise Murray 25, /Roy Rainford 23, 33, 74 top, /Geoff Renner 55, 87 top, 89, /Christopher Rennie 84 bottom right, /Michael Short 34 top right, /Adina Tovy 49 top right, /J. H. C. Wilson 45 top, /Nick Wood 66 bottom left, /Adam Woolfitt 19 center; **James Hughes** 22 bottom right; **Hulton Deutsch Collection** 54 bottom left; **Hutchison**

Library 24 center, 40 center bottom, 68, /Sarah Errington 58 top, 85, /Bernard Gerard 20 bottom right, /Tony Souter 30 center left; **Image Bank** 24 top, /Walter Bibikow 22 bottom left, /Gallant 42 top, /L. D. Gordon 87 bottom, /Bullaty Lomeo 36 top right, /Michael Melford 32 top, /Kaz Mori 75 top, /Jeffrey M. Spielman 8, /Harald Sund 40 top right, /Hans Wolf 28 top, 28 bottom left; **Nina Jenkins** 54 center, 56 center right; **Japan National Tourist Organization** 50 top left; **Steve Nevill** 76 bottom; **Panos Pictures** /Gary John Norman 57 left; **Planet Earth Pictures** 60 top, /G. Cafiero 43 right, /John Eastcott 76 center, 6, 88 below, /John Lythgoe 54 bottom right, 78 center right, /John Waters/Bernadette Spiegel 39

top; **Reed International Books Ltd** /James Johnson 26 bottom, /Graham Kirk 78 bottom left, /NASA 4, /Paul Williams 46 bottom center; **Russia & Republics Photolibrary** /Mark Wadlow 40 bottom right, 41 top; **South American Pictures** /Tony Morrison 83; **Still Pictures** /B. & C. Alexander 88 top, /Chris Caldicott 53, 54 top, /Mark Edwards 56 bottom left, 84 bottom left, /Michel Gunther 58 bottom center, /John Maier 10 top, 61, /Roland Seitre 62; **Tony Stone Images** 28 bottom center, 50 top right, 66 bottom right, /Doug Armand 67 top, /John Beatty 86 bottom, /Stephen Beer 60 bottom left, /Richard Bradbury 69, /Suzanne & Nick Geary 64 center, 76 top, /Walter Geierserger 29, /George Grigoriou 34

bottom right, 35 top, /Gavin Hellier 36 bottom left, /Simeone Huber 19 right, /Dave Jacobs 72 bottom, /H. Richard Johnston 71, /Hideo Kunhara 64 top, /Alain le Garsmeur 48 center, 60 bottom right, /John Noble 84 bottom center, /Nicholas Parfitt 59, /Greg Pease 74 center, /Pete Seaward 30 top, /Ed Simpson 84 top, /Zygmunt Nowak Solins 37 center top, /Nabeel Turner 42 bottom right, 50 bottom, /Art Wolfe 63, /Trevor Wood 44 left; **Judy Todd** 38 top right; **David & Jill Wright** 10 bottom, 15 left, 16, 18, 20 bottom left, 21, 24 bottom right, 26 top left, 26 top right, 37 bottom right, 42 bottom left, 44 center, 46 bottom right, 52 bottom, 57 right, 58 bottom right, 60 bottom center, 67 bottom, 81 right.

  **AFGHANISTAN**

 ALBANIA

 ALGERIA

 ANDORRA

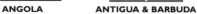 **ANGOLA**

 ANTIGUA & BARBUDA

 ARGENTINA

 **BARBADOS**

 BELARUS

 **BELGIUM**

 **BELIZE**

 **BENIN**

  BHUTAN

  BOLIVIA

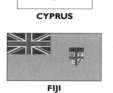 **BURUNDI**

 CAMBODIA

 CAMEROON

 CANADA

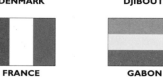 **CAPE VERDE**

 **CENTRAL AFRICAN REP.**

 **CHAD**

 CUBA

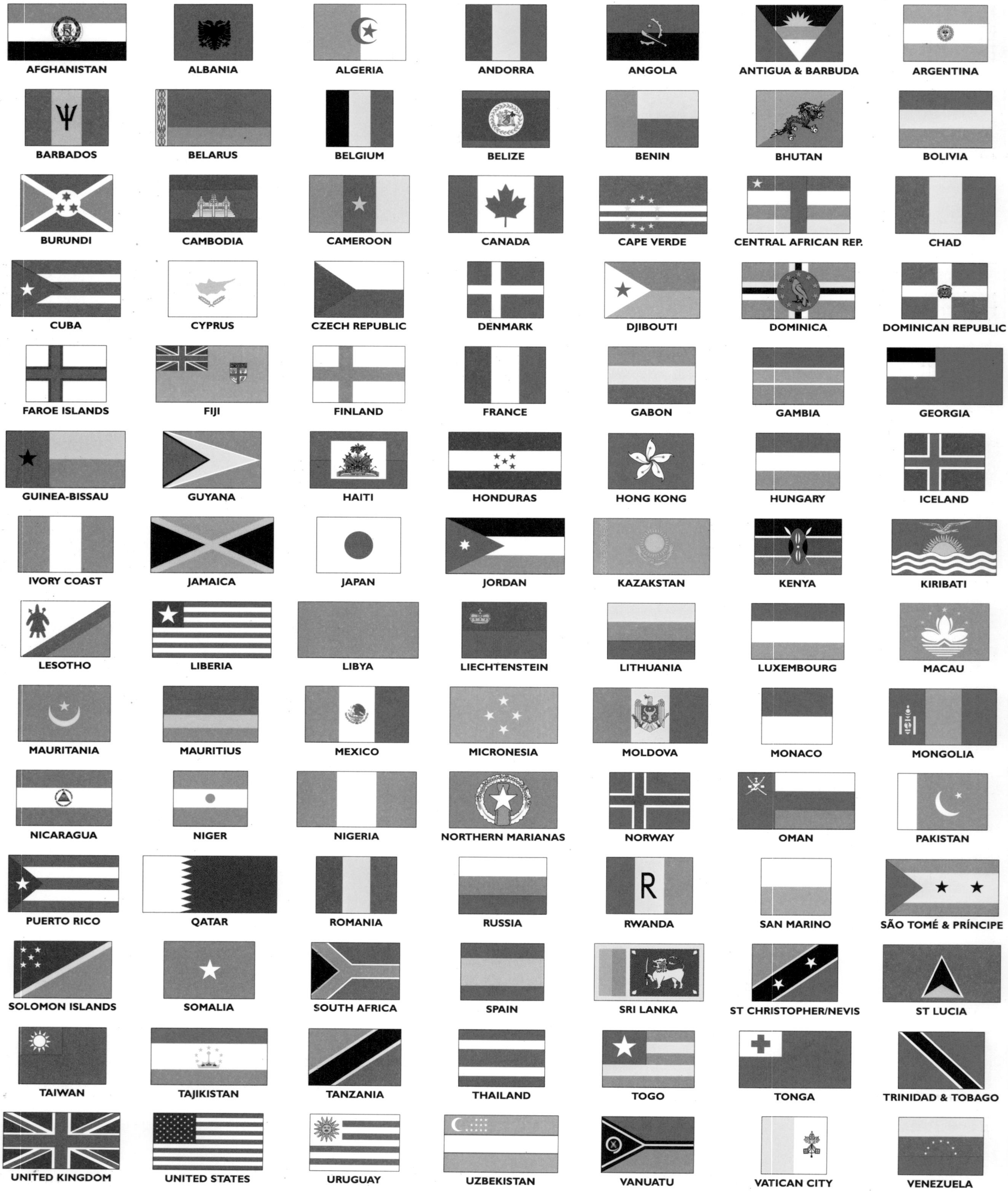

CYPRUS

 CZECH REPUBLIC

 **DENMARK**

 DJIBOUTI

 **DOMINICA**

 DOMINICAN REPUBLIC

FAROE ISLANDS

 **FIJI**

FINLAND

 **FRANCE**

 **GABON**

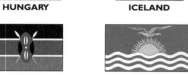 **GAMBIA**

GEORGIA

 **GUINEA-BISSAU**

GUYANA

 HAITI

 HONDURAS

 **HONG KONG**

 **HUNGARY**

ICELAND

IVORY COAST

JAMAICA

JAPAN

 **JORDAN**

 **KAZAKSTAN**

 **KENYA**

 **KIRIBATI**

 LESOTHO

 LIBERIA

 **LIBYA**

 LIECHTENSTEIN

 LITHUANIA

 **LUXEMBOURG**

MACAU

 MAURITANIA

 MAURITIUS

 MEXICO

 MICRONESIA

 MOLDOVA

 **MONACO**

 **MONGOLIA**

NICARAGUA

 NIGER

 **NIGERIA**

 **NORTHERN MARIANAS**

 **NORWAY**

 **OMAN**

 **PAKISTAN**

 **PUERTO RICO**

 **QATAR**

ROMANIA

 RUSSIA

RWANDA

 **SAN MARINO**

 **SÃO TOMÉ & PRÍNCIPE**

SOLOMON ISLANDS

SOMALIA

SOUTH AFRICA

SPAIN

 **SRI LANKA**

 ST CHRISTOPHER/NEVIS

 ST LUCIA

 **TAIWAN**

TAJIKISTAN

TANZANIA

THAILAND

TOGO

 TONGA

TRINIDAD & TOBAGO

UNITED KINGDOM

UNITED STATES

URUGUAY

 UZBEKISTAN

VANUATU

VATICAN CITY

VENEZUELA

GREAT
HISTORIC
PLACES OF
AMERICA

For Becky and Daniel

*The study at Monticello (**previous page**) seems to await Jefferson's return and the dome of the house he designed (**above**) shines brightly in the spring sun.*

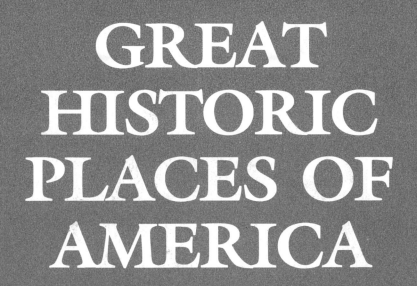

GREAT
HISTORIC
PLACES OF
AMERICA

David M. Brownstone
and
Irene M. Franck

AIRE DISTRICT
GALLERY BOOKS
An Imprint of W.H. Smith Publishers Inc.
112 Madison Avenue
New York City 10016

Contents

Design by Robert L. Pigeon, Combined Books
26 Summit Grove Ave., #207, Bryn Mawr, PA 19010

Produced by Wieser & Wieser, Inc., 118 East 25th St.,
New York, NY 10010

Published by W.H. Smith, Publishers, 112 Madison Ave.,
New York, NY 10016

Soldiers reenact the Battle of Yorktown in the October mist.

Philadelphia's Independence Hall (above) is reflected in a puddle on the cobblestones. Nearby, a child explores the crack in the Liberty Bell (right). At the Old North Bridge (overleaf), in Concord, the fight for the American republic began.

Preface

HERE ARE THE GREAT old American and Canadian historic places, presented in all their color and beauty. Here also are our very brief histories of the places we have chosen for this book, for while a picture really may be worth a thousand words, a few accompanying words are quite necessary, too.

Our aim throughout has been to create a work that provides the spirit, the "feel" of each historic place, and while doing so pleases both the eye and the mind. The success of the work is properly measured by the extent to which this has been accomplished.

Our thanks go to Olga and George Wieser, who in this book are our publishing partners, and without whom the work could not have been done. Our thanks also go to Domenico Firmani, who as photo researcher located and provided many of the illustrations for this work, all with apparent ease and aplomb; to our typists, Shirley Fenn and Mary Racette, for their excellent work; to the staff of the Chappaqua Library for their unfailing help; and to the many other people across the continent—in both Canada and the United States—who have been so very helpful throughout this project. We cannot possibly name them all, but the organizations they represent are listed in the photo credits at the end of the book. And finally our thanks go to Robert Pigeon, whose superb work in designing this book both speaks for itself and deserves our explicit recognition.

DAVID M. BROWNSTONE
IRENE M. FRANCK
Chappaqua, New York

NEW ENGLAND

Plymouth Rock

THE PILGRIMS came here, carrying with them the idea of democracy that is the essence of the American dream. It was not that the Pilgrims were the first Europeans to come to North America—or even to New England, for that matter. Nor did they land first at that particular place; indeed, they first went ashore at Provincetown, on Cape Cod, and then went on to Plymouth Harbor. But here, at Plymouth Rock, they stayed and planted the dissenters' view of real equality that was the heart and soul of the New England experience and then of the new American nation.

On August 15, 1620 (by the present calendar), the *Mayflower* and the *Speedwell* set out from Southampton for America. They were small ships; the larger *Mayflower* was about 90 feet long, with a beam of about 26 feet. The *Speedwell* soon developed leaks; after putting in at Dartmouth and then at Plymouth, England, it was abandoned. Some of the colonists then decided not to continue; those going on boarded the *Mayflower* and set sail for North America on September 16, 1620. Aboard were 101 colonists, and a crew of 20-30 seamen, captained by Christopher Jones.

After a long, difficult North Atlantic crossing, the *Mayflower* reached the tip of Cape Cod, at the harbor of what is now Provincetown, on November 21. A month later, after reconnoitering Massachusetts Bay for a permanent colony site, an exploring party settled upon Plymouth Harbor. Five days later, on December 26, the *Mayflower* came to Plymouth Harbor. There were still 101 colonists, but one was a baby born during the voyage to America, one colonist having died en route. The *Mayflower* sailed home to England without any passengers on April 15, 1621.

On the **Mayflower II (opposite)**, *passengers relive the crossing voyage of the first Pilgrims* **(opposite inset)** *to the New World. Plymouth Rock itself* **(below)** *is inscribed with the date of the Pilgrims' arrival. Today the Rock is covered by a protective canopy* **(above)**.

What is so notable about these Puritan immigrants from England is that they came to America seeking freedom, ready to live by their beliefs, and created a kind of faith in freedom that proved extraordinarily durable. That faith was embodied in the Mayflower Compact, signed by all of the able-bodied male immigrants at Provincetown, which provided for political equality among the male colonists. A sadly deficient document, by modern standards, leaving out half of humanity; yet still a foundation stone for the larger democracy that came later.

The idea of political equality, as ideas so often do, has proven even more durable than Plymouth Rock itself. It has split over the years, and been somewhat diminished by souvenir hunters, so it looks rather small inside the imposing columned enclosure in which it sits, at the foot of Coles Hill, overlooking Plymouth Harbor. A replica ship, the *Mayflower II,* is nearby, as is the Plimoth Plantation, a re-creation of some of the life of the time. Historians differ as to whether this was really the exact place at which the Pilgrims landed in Plymouth Harbor. It does not matter; the idea of freedom they carried did land hereabouts, and stayed to take root in American soil.

People at the modern Plimoth Plantation recreate Pilgrim daily life, occupying the same tiny houses, growing their own food **(above)**, making and repairing their own household items **(below)**, preserving food for safekeeping through the long winter **(opposite top)**, and reliving the first Thanksgiving feasts **(opposite bottom)**.

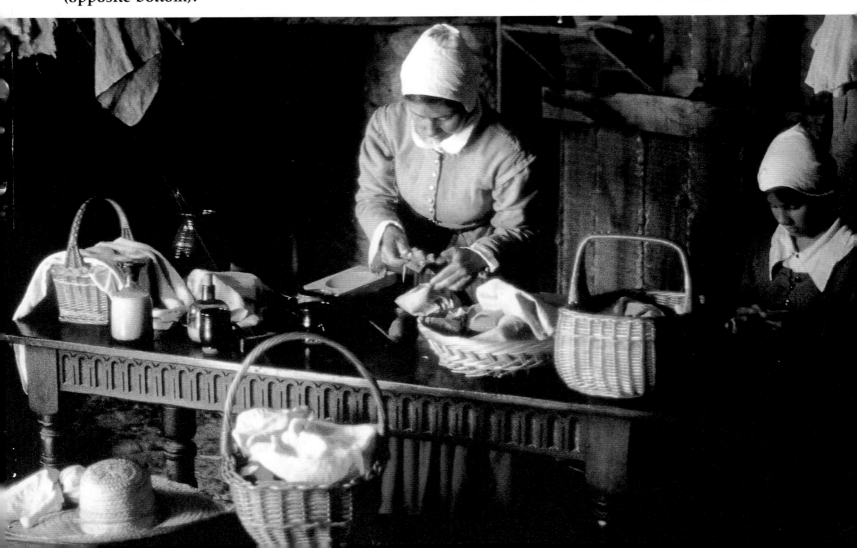

Lexington and Concord

By the rude bridge that arched the flood,
Their flag to April's breeze unfurled,
Here once the embattled farmers stood,
And fired the shot heard round the world.

from Concord Hymn
by Ralph Waldo Emerson

THE AMERICAN REVOLUTION started here, in two sharp skirmishes, and a long, running fight. One skirmish was at Lexington's Village Green and the other at Concord's Old North Bridge. The running fight started just outside Concord and went on all the way back to Boston; when it was over, the die was cast. The revolution had begun.

On the night of April 18, 1775, seven hundred British troops, commanded by Lt. Col. Francis Smith, set out along the sixteen-mile road to Concord, where they hoped to find and destroy large stores of munitions cached there by the local American Minutemen and militia units. They had hoped to do so secretly, but Paul Revere, William Dawes, Dr. Samuel Prescott, and other couriers roused the countryside before them. By the time the British reached Lexington, at daybreak, there was a small detachment of Minutemen on the Village Green, about seventy men in all. The British advance guard commander, Major John Pitcairn, ordered them to lay down their arms and disperse; their own commander, John Parker, ordered the Minutemen to hold their fire and retreat. After someone—from which side is not clear—fired a shot, the Redcoats fired into the ranks of the Minutemen, killing eight and wounding ten.

Daniel Chester French's Minuteman statue (above), on the bank of the Concord River, honors those early Americans who fought the British on that "rude bridge" (opposite), the Old North Bridge in Concord.

14

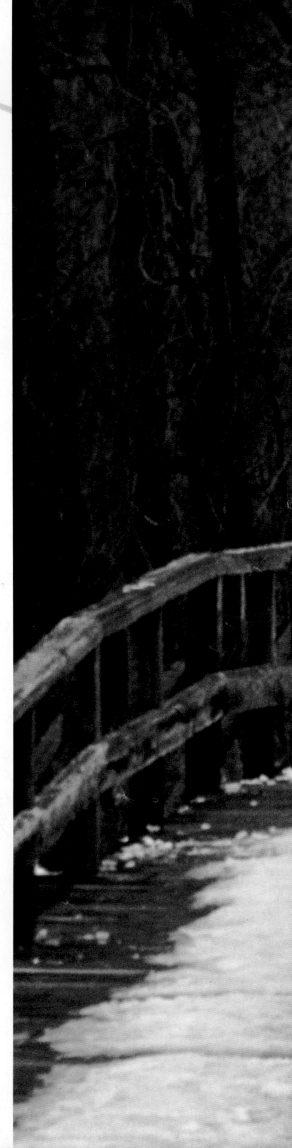

The British then moved on to Concord, where they discovered and destroyed very small quantities of munitions. But now the countryside was aroused; at the Old North Bridge in Concord, three companies of British soldiers skirmished with some 400 American militiamen, with both sides suffering a few dead. This was the first organized battle of the Revolution.

About noon, the British began to retrace their route toward Boston on what was later dubbed Battle Road. They soon began to encounter heavy fire from American militia hidden on both sides of the road, and suffered particularly heavy casualties because they continued to march forward on the road, without deploying for battle. By the time they reached Lexington, their column was under such heavy attack that it could have been destroyed; but here they met 1,000 more British troops, equipped with cannon, sent by General Thomas Gage out of Boston to relieve them. Ultimately, the combined British forces managed to fight their way back to Boston, through twice their number of American militia, and with many more dead and wounded than the Americans.

Today, much of the site of the Lexington and Concord battles is occupied by Minuteman National Historic Park, which includes both the Old North Bridge in Concord and Battle Road through to Lexington. On the western bank of the Concord River stands Daniel Chester French's Minuteman statue.

As the Concord River's spring waters flood the flats near Battle Road (below), *New Englanders* (above) *reenact the events of April 1775. At Minuteman National Historic Park, the Minuteman statue* (opposite) *is framed by early spring flowers.*

Boston: The Cradle of Liberty

THE FIRE OF REVOLUTION burned hottest in Boston. The main events that led to the American Revolution occurred here; and the Revolution itself began just outside Boston, in Lexington and Concord.

By 1768, Boston had clearly become the single most important source of resistance to British North American colonial policies. That year, matters worsened dramatically. In the spring, Britain's Board of Custom Commissioners, sitting in Boston, joined Governor Francis Bernard of Massachusetts in requesting that British troops be sent to Boston to enforce the hated Townshend Acts, which levied heavy import taxes on the Colonies. One regiment was sent. In June, after the Commissioners fled for safety to a British ship in Boston Harbor, two more regiments were sent, and by the spring of 1769 there were four British regiments occupying Boston. Two were withdrawn that year, but two remained. On March 5, 1770, in what became known as the Boston Massacre, a mob at the Customs House was fired upon, and five Bostonians were killed, including Black freedman Crispus Attucks.

Throughout those years preceding the Revolution, feelings in Boston ran high. At meeting after meeting in Faneuil Hall, itself often called the "Cradle of Liberty," Samuel Adams, John Hancock, James Otis, and a dozen other leaders attacked the British. From 1768 on, the crowds at Faneuil Hall were often too large, and meetings were often then shifted to the larger old South Meeting Hall. It was at Faneuil Hall, in 1772, that the first

From Boston's Copps Hill Cemetery (above), *with graves dating back to the 1660s, the British pointed their cannon toward Charlestown and Bunker Hill. Not far away, a statue* (opposite) *commemorates Paul Revere's famous ride; the Old North Church stands in the background.*

Committee of Correspondence was created, foreshadowing the body of committees that would, in only a few years, grow into the Continental Congress.

In 1773, the British government passed the Tea Act, which gave the East India Company a near-monopoly of the American trade. In angry Boston, this became an opportunity; the Sons of Liberty, Paul Revere among them, dumped English tea into Boston Harbor on December 6, 1773, at the Boston Tea Party. The British responded with more troops, and with a series of punitive acts in April, 1774. Among other things, they closed the port of Boston until the dumped tea had been paid for.

The response of the Colonies took the American-British dispute into a new stage. The First Continental Congress met in Philadelphia on September 5, 1774, adopted a Declaration of Rights, and declared common cause. Committees of Safety formed, ten colonies developed provincial congresses, militia began to gather, and munitions were gathered and stored throughout the Colonies.

The war that came was widely expected. It began on the night of April 19, 1775, with Paul Revere's arranged signal from Old North Church, that the British were moving on Lexington and Concord, in search of munitions. "One if by land, and two, if by sea" was the pre-arranged code; and the two lanterns in the belfry of Old North Church—indicating that the British would cross the Charles River by boat—signaled the beginning of the American Revolution outside the city at Lexington and Concord.

Boston itself saw the first substantial battle of the Revolution. By June 1776, the American militia had surrounded Boston, some 16,000 strong, and were putting maximum pressure on the British troops occupying the city. To that end, the Americans moved a substantial force out of Cambridge with orders to fortify Bunker Hill, across the Charles River from Boston.

In Boston harbor lies "Old Ironsides," the **U.S.S. Constitution (opposite)** *first launched in 1797. It was from the Old North Church* **(above)** *that Paul Revere received the signal that sent him on his ride. Revere's house* **(right),** *still stands, the only 17th-century building remaining in the heart of Boston.*

They fortified Breed's Hill instead, and that is where the British attacked them, in the early afternoon of June 17, moving 2,200 men and cannon up against the approximately 1,000 Americans defending the hill. After repelling two frontal attacks by the British infantry and inflicting heavy losses, the Americans began to run out of powder. The third frontal assault succeeded, and the British took the hill. For the British, it was a costly victory; they had over 200 dead and over 800 wounded, while the Americans had less than half that number dead and only a third as many wounded. For the Americans, the seeming defeat was actually a great victory, for here elements of what was to become the Continental Army had fully met the British army in battle and inflicted heavy losses.

Today, many of Boston's historic places are part of the Boston National Historical Park. In old Boston, there are still Faneuil Hall, Old South Meeting House, Boston Common and its adjoining Boston Massacre site, Old North Church, the Central Burying Ground, Old Granary Burying Ground, Old State House, the Paul Revere House, and a dozen other sites of great historic interest. Across the Charles River are the Bunker Hill Monument and the *U.S.S. Constitution*.

Numerous monuments, such as this one (below) on Dorchester Heights, mark the Freedom Trail, a walking tour in Boston National Historic Park.

From the Bunker Hill Monument **(above)** in Charlestown, visitors have a view of the battle sites of old Boston. The Sons of Liberty often met at the Old South Meeting House **(below)** to plan actions such as the Boston Tea Party.

Because so many large revolutionary meetings were held here, Faneuil Hall **(above)** is sometimes called the "Cradle of Liberty." In the Old State House **(below)**, John Hancock was inaugurated as Massachusetts' first governor in 1789.

Salem

FROM SALEM, NEW ENGLAND sailors made their mark upon the whole world. In its time, Salem was one of the greatest of New England's port cities, and one of the world's most important seaports. From the early 1600s right on through the American Revolution and into the mid-19th century, Salem's seafarers fished the Atlantic, sought whales in all the world's oceans, and traded on behalf of Salem's merchants around Cape Horn to China and in seaports the world over. The Salem Maritime Historic Site commemorates Salem's sailors and merchants, whose work was so vital for the development of England's American colonies and then for the new American nation.

During the period of trade restrictions that preceded the American Revolution, Salem's port, like most other American ports of the day, virtually came to a stop. During the Revolution, Salem's sailors responded; from 1776 on, scores of privateers operated out of Salem, harrying English merchant ships and engaging English warships throughout the North Atlantic. After the Revolution, Salem resumed its role as a major port, until its sailors went back to war against the English during the War of 1812.

The National Historic Site is an area of nearly nine acres, bordering Salem Harbor, and including the old Custom House and the restored Derby Wharf, which extends almost 2,000 feet into the harbor.

The old Custom House **(above)** is preserved as part of the nine acres of waterfront buildings **(opposite)** belonging to the Salem Maritime National Historic Site. In a restored office, an old warehouse scale **(below)** and other gear are reminders of Salem's days as a great international port.

Newport

TODAY, NEWPORT is far more widely remembered for its development as a playground for the rich before World War I than for its much longer history as one of New England's earliest and most prosperous seaports. Yet it flourished as a seaport for almost two and a half centuries before the Vanderbilts, Firestones, Belmonts, Goelets, and Havemeyers arrived. At Newport is Touro Synagogue, founded in 1763, the oldest synagogue in the United States. Also in Newport is the Redwood Library, built in 1748, the oldest continuously used library building in the country. Many other structures in Newport's national historic district have been preserved, some of them excellent examples of 18th-century Georgian architecture in the Colonies. Newport was even, for a time during the Civil War, the temporary home of the United States Naval Academy.

After the Civil War, wealthy summer residents began to build massive summer "cottages" at Newport, with some truly enormous mansions being built from the 1880s until the outbreak of World War I. The society that developed continued until the impact of the Great Depression ended all that, at least for that time and in that place. Many of the mansions remain, some occupied, some given over to institutional uses, and some open to public view. They include, among others, Richard Morris Hunt's Marble House, built for William K. Vanderbilt; Hunt's The Breakers, built for Cornelius Vanderbilt; Hunt's Belcourt Castle, built for Oliver H. P. Belmont; his Ochre Court, built for Ogden Goelet; and Horace Trumbauer's The Elms, built for Edward J. Berwind.

The Touro Synagogue **(above)**, built in 1763, is a remnant from the early days of Newport's history. Newport is also famous for the many mansions built in the late 19th century, including William K. Vanderbilt's Marble House **(below)** and Cornelius Vanderbilt's magnificent summer home, The Breakers **(opposite)**. Modern redcoats reenact the Battle of Saratoga **(overleaf)**.

THE MID-ATLANTIC

The Gateway: New York

Not like the brazen giant of Greek fame,
    With conquering limbs astride from land to land;
    Here at our sea-washed, sunset gates shall stand
A mighty woman with a torch, whose flame
Is the imprisoned lightning, and her name
    Mother of Exiles. From her beacon-hand
    Glows world-wide welcome; her mild eyes command
The air-bridged harbor that twin cities frame.
"Keep, ancient lands, your storied pomp!" cries she
    With silent lips. "Give me your tired, your poor,
Your huddled masses yearning to breathe free,
    The wretched refuse of your teeming shore.
Send these, the homeless, tempest-tost, to me,
    I lift my lamp beside the golden door!"

The New Colossus
by Emma Lazarus

FOR ALL THE WORLD'S PEOPLE, this Mother of Exiles, this statue called Liberty, is the single most powerful symbol of the best that America has to offer. That was so for the tens of millions who crowded past it on their way to Ellis Island in the great years of American immigration; it is still so today.

For a century, the Statue of Liberty, originally called "Liberty Enlightening the World," has greeted all those entering New York harbor, itself the main gateway to the United States. The torch she carries in her right hand is the torch of freedom; its light is a beacon illuminating the path out of the darkness of the Old World and into the New. The broken chains at her feet are the chains of

For over a century the Statue of Liberty (opposite) has stood on Bedloe's or Liberty Island (above) in New York harbor, greeting arrivals at that great gateway to America.

The sun glints on the buildings of lower Manhattan (above), viewed from out in the harbor—so near and yet so far for early immigrants waiting to enter the land of their dreams.

slavery. The book in her left hand carries the date July 4, 1776, Independence Day. Emma Lazarus' poem, *The New Colossus,* was engraved into her base in 1903, seventeen years after her dedication by President Grover Cleveland in 1886.

Liberty was designed by Frederic Auguste Bartholdi, who began to develop the work in 1874, as a gift from the French to the American peoples in commemoration of their Revolutionary War alliance and of the first centennial of the American nation, in 1876. It was built in Paris, shipped to New York in sections, and there reassembled and placed on a prepared pedestal on Bedloe's Island, now Liberty Island. It stands 305 feet above the level of the harbor, with a base 69 feet high, a pedestal 89 feet high atop that, and the statue itself a little over 151 feet high. It was completely rebuilt in the mid-1980s and rededicated as the centerpiece of an enormous national celebration of its first centennial, on July 4, 1986, and as part of the joint Statue of Liberty-Ellis Island restoration project.

It is entirely appropriate that the Statue of Liberty and Ellis Island be rebuilt together. If Liberty was the beacon lighting the gateway, then Ellis Island was the Golden Door. During the early years of this century, Ellis Island, then known the world over as the Island of Tears, was the last hurdle, the great portal through which flowed all the peoples of the Old World, and especially the peoples of southern and eastern Europe—Italians, Jews, Poles, Ukrainians, Russians, Greeks, Armenians, Serbs, Bohemians, and a score more ethnic groups. At the same time, the older immigration continued: Irish, British, German, and Scandinavian immigrants, among others, continued to flow across the Atlantic in great numbers early in the century.

In the process, Ellis Island became a major set of structures, and by far the largest immigration station in North America. At the start, it was little more than an unwanted three-acre sandbar out in the harbor, which had been successively a place of execution, a fort, and an ammunition dump

Ellis Island is a great monument to America's immigrants. Before restoration, all the buildings on 27-acre Ellis Island (above inset) *had been allowed to fall into grave disrepair, including the main building* (above) *with its Great Hall.*

during the 18th and 19th centuries. By the 1920s, it was a 27-acre set of structures built mainly on landfill, with a large immigration intake building—the Great Hall, with its high arched windows—and many auxiliary structures, including two substantial hospitals, dormitories, a bathhouse, a power plant, offices, and storage facilities. It is the Great Hall and a few related structures that are being rebuilt as a national shrine to the millions who came to America in those years and stayed to grow with the country.

The Ellis Island immigration station was opened on January 1, 1892. The first immigrant to pass through was Annie Moore, from County Cork, Ireland. It was officially completed on June 13, 1897, and burned to the ground the next day. It was then completely rebuilt, reopening in December, 1900. From then until 1914, and then again from 1919-1924, it handled as many as 10,000 immigrants a day, and in all, well over ten million immigrants. It was used as a detention center during the Red Scare just

The ferry (above) *that brought immigrants to Ellis Island for processing had foundered in its slip.*

after World War I and again as an internment center during World War II. It was—almost unbelievably—abandoned to the elements in 1954, only to be officially declared in 1965 the national monument it always had been. It was reopened for limited visiting in 1976, and is now being lovingly and rightly restored at enormous cost.

33

At The Battery in lower Manhattan stands the old fort of Castle Clinton **(above)** *with its small museum* **(below)**. *Gone now are any traces of the famous Castle Garden that once stood there, first a popular theater, then a 19th-century immigration station before Ellis Island took over.*

But New York was the main gateway to America long before the Statue of Liberty and the Ellis Island immigration station were built. From 1855 to 1890, an estimated seven to eight million immigrants came through the place now called Castle Clinton National Monument, on the section of the New York City shore known as The Battery.

Originally it had been a small island just off shore, called the West Battery. The federal government built a circular fort on the island in 1811, naming it after Dewitt Clinton, then governor of New York. In 1824, the fort was joined to the mainland by landfill, turned into a theater and amusement complex, and renamed Castle Garden; Jenny Lind, among many others, sang there. And it was as Castle Garden that the site became the earliest part of the immigrant gateway that was New York harbor. Castle Clinton National Monument on the mainland at the Battery is today a smallish, rather unimposing structure and museum. But in the 19th century, Castle Garden was

known to all the people of the Old World as the gateway to America. They called it Castle Garden, The Castlegarden, Kesselgarden, Kasselgarda, and a dozen other names in its time; indeed, many immigrants going through Ellis Island even in the 20th century thought it to be Castle Garden, and continued to think so all their lives.

The oldest surviving building in Manhattan, Fraunces Tavern dates from 1719. It was here that George Washington bade farewell to his officers in 1789. After a restoration early in the century, many of the rooms, including the Long Room (above) *and the Clinton Dining Room* (below), *have been kept as they were in that era.*

Federal Hall (above), with George Washington's statue before it, was built in 1842. Before that, this was the site of the young United States' first capitol building, where Washington was inaugurated and the first Congress met in 1789.

New York was also a major historic place for the new American nation. Not far from the Battery, on Wall Street, is the Federal Hall National Memorial, built on the site of New York City's 18th-century City Hall, which became the first capitol of the new United States under the Articles of Confederation. Then, enlarged and renamed Federal Hall, it became the first capitol of the United States under the Constitution. The first presidential inauguration of George Washington was held at Federal Hall, on April 30, 1789. The present building on the site is the old United States Custom House, completed in 1842. Fraunces Tavern, on Pearl Street a short distance away from Federal Hall, is the site of Washington's farewell address to the officers of the Continental Army, on December 4, 1783. It is the oldest surviving building in Manhattan, dating from 1719.

Saratoga

THE BATTLE FOUGHT at Saratoga decided the fate of the new American nation. Had the British won, they would have succeeded in splitting the country in two, and could then have turned at their leisure to destroy the remaining revolutionary forces. But the Americans won decisively, and their victory brought both new hope and a vital alliance with France, without which the war could probably not have been won.

Late in 1777, the British army moved to cut New England off from the country. Two main forces, one coming from Canada south along Lake Champlain under General John (Gentleman Johnny) Burgoyne and the other north from New York under General William Howe, were to meet at Albany, while a third, smaller force under Lt. Col. Barry St. Leger would come from the west through the Mohawk River valley.

But the plan failed, for Howe's forces moved only as far north as Bear Mountain, below West Point on the Hudson River. St. Leger's British and Iroquois troops were stopped by Nicholas Herkimer's frontiersmen at Oriskany, near Rome, New York.

Burgoyne's army came south along Lake Champlain in the spring. It consisted of approximately 9,400 men, including British regulars, Loyalists who had fled north to Canada at the start of the Revolution, German troops, and Native Americans. Starting south from St. Johns (now St. Jean), Canada, Burgoyne's army took Fort Ticonderoga, defeated the American rearguard at Hubbardton, Vermont, on July 7, and then slowly proceeded overland toward Albany, expecting to be joined there by Howe and St. Leger.

On September 13, Burgoyne began crossing the Hudson at Saratoga. By now, he was short of supplies. His attempt to scour

A modern redcoat is reflected in a brightly polished buckle (above).

the countryside for supplies and horses had been stopped by a defeat at Bennington, Vermont. Worst of all, he found the road to Albany blocked by 9,000 American troops under General Horatio Gates, strongly dug in and armed with cannon.

On September 19, the British and Americans fought an indecisive engagement at Freeman's Farm. Burgoyne then decided to dig in and await reinforcements. But reinforcements did not come; nor did supplies.

On October 7, desperate and running out of supplies, Burgoyne's army attacked. By now, though, they were fighting a much larger American army, well-provisioned and growing stronger every day. The attack failed. On October 8, the British began to retreat, moving back to Saratoga, to previously fortified positions. There the British were encircled by 20,000 American troops and surrendered on October 17, 1777.

Saratoga happened fairly early in the Revolutionary War; had the British won that battle, there might be no United States today.

The working center of a flintlock musket (above).

Saratoga National Historical Park occupies almost four square miles of land on the Hudson River, 28 miles north of Albany, between Stillwater and Schuylerville.

The British soldiers' basic weapon in the Revolutionary War was the "brown Bess," a flintlock musket (below) with a brown walnut stock and a long, smoothbore barrel, also of brown oxidized metal. Flint was struck against steel to produce the spark that ignited the gunpowder.

Facing the smartly uniformed British soldiers in this reenactment are the more modestly dressed farmers and frontiersmen who won the crucial victory at Saratoga. Near the battlefield, the home **(below)** of General Philip Schuyler, an American hero of that engagement, is preserved as a museum **(inset).**

West Point

DURING THE REVOLUTIONARY WAR, Washington ordered the fortification of West Point, after stationing a garrison at this key Hudson River crossing in January 1778. Polish engineer Thaddeus Kosciuszko began those fortifications in March 1778. They were strengthened all during the war, although the British never directly attacked West Point. Benedict Arnold was commander of the West Point post when his defection to the British cause was discovered.

The main significance of West Point lies in the location of United States Military Academy there, from its opening on July 4, 1802, until today. West Point has been the training ground of almost two centuries of American army officers, including Grant, Sherman, Sheridan, Eisenhower, Lee, and a host of others. Its key early commander was Major Sylvanus Thayer, who took command in 1817, after graduating from West Point in 1808. Robert E. Lee was its commander for three years, from 1852-1855.

Today, West Point is a massive set of military installations, most of them devoted to Military Academy functions, but including a substantial war museum and many memorials.

On the west bank of the Hudson River, West Point (above) rises above the trees, its foundations (opposite) giving an impression of solidity. On special occasions the cadets of West Point (below) put on a smart show for their superiors and for the academy's many visitors.

Hyde Park

The only thing we have to fear is fear itself.

Franklin Delano Roosevelt,
First Inaugural Address

THE LIFELONG HOME OF Franklin Delano Roosevelt is a place of extraordinary peace and beauty. Hyde Park is situated on a high ridge overlooking the Hudson River, the great valley that is the gateway to mid-America. It is, as presidential homes go, rather unusual, for it was his childhood home, his headquarters during much of his pre-presidential career, and his summer White House during his thirteen presidential years. It was therefore uniquely part of Roosevelt's life, work, and the history of his time. Here he worked on all the main matters and with all the key people of his age; here he delivered some of his fireside talks; here Roosevelt and Churchill launched the research program that led to the atomic bomb; here he delivered the last speech of the 1944 presidential campaign. And here, too, Eleanor Roosevelt worked on the great humanitarian projects that were to distinguish her as an extraordinary individual and the leading woman of her time.

James Roosevelt, Franklin's father, acquired this 116-acre estate a little north of Poughkeepsie in 1867, naming it Springwood. Franklin was born there in 1882. During his lifetime, James added to the house again and again. After his death, in 1900, Franklin and his mother, Sara Delano Roosevelt, continued the work of expansion, and by 1916 had created the fifty-room, three-story, H-shaped house that is on the site today.

Franklin Roosevelt gave his estate to the nation in 1939, and it became a National Historic Site in 1944. Eleanor Roosevelt and

The living room (left) at Hyde Park looks so much as it did that Franklin and Eleanor could walk in, perhaps for FDR to deliver one of his famous fireside chats.

During the long hot summers while Roosevelt was President, a room like this one (right) at Hyde Park served as the equivalent of the Oval Office of the White House.

Born here and buried here, Franklin Roosevelt considered Springwood (opposite), at Hyde Park, his permanent home.

their children gave over their lifetime interests in the estate in 1945, after his death, and the house and grounds were opened to the public as a national shrine in 1946. The Franklin D. Roosevelt Library, first of the federally administered presidential libraries, was built on the grounds in 1939-1940, and the President used an office in it during the last several years of his life.

In the rose garden, a little way from the house, are the simple white marble headstones marking the graves of Franklin Delano Roosevelt, 1882-1945, and Anna Eleanor Roosevelt, 1884-1962.

Independence Hall: Philadelphia

When in the course of human events, it becomes necessary for one people to dissolve the political bonds which have connected them with another . . .

We hold these truths to be self-evident, that all men are created equal, that they are endowed by their Creator with certain inalienable Rights, that among these are Life, Liberty, and the pursuit of Happiness.—That to secure these rights, Governments are instituted among Men, deriving their just powers from the consent of the governed.— That when any Form of Government becomes destructive of these ends, it is the Right of the People to alter or to abolish it, and to institute new Government, laying its foundation on such principles and organizing its powers in such form, as to them shall seem most likely to effect their Safety and Happiness . . .

We, THEREFORE, the Representatives of the UNITED STATES OF AMERICA, in General Congress, Assembled, appealing to the Supreme Judge of the world for the rectitude of our intentions, do, in the Name, and by Authority of the good People of these Colonies, solemnly publish and declare, That these United Colonies are, and of Right ought to be FREE AND INDEPENDENT STATES; that they are Absolved from all Allegiance to the British Crown, and that all political connection between them and the State of Great Britain, is and ought to be totally dissolved; and that as Free and Independent States, they have full power to levy War, conclude Peace, contract Alliances, establish Commerce, and to do all other Acts and Things which Independent States may of right do.—and for the support of this Declaration, with a firm reliance on the protection of divine Providence, we mutually pledge to each other our Lives, our Fortunes, and our sacred Honor.

from the Declaration of Independence

Independence Hall (opposite), where the Declaration of Independence was first proclaimed in 1776, today houses a museum with objects (above) recalling its historic past. Nearby stands the Liberty Bell (below), with its inscription: "Proclaim Liberty throughout the land unto all the inhabitants thereof."

IT HAPPENED HERE. The Declaration of Independence. The Constitution. The Liberty Bell. Here is where Jefferson, Franklin, Hancock, John and Samuel Adams, and the rest of the Founding Fathers signed the Declaration, on July 4, 1776. Here is

When the nation's capital was moved from New York to Philadelphia in 1790, Congress met at Congress Hall (above), while the Supreme Court met at Court Hall (opposite top). For less formal meetings, early legislators often gathered at the Assembly Room (opposite below), preserved in Independence Hall.

where the Continental Congress appointed George Washington Commander-in-Chief, where the Constitutional Convention met to frame the Constitution in 1787, where the Liberty Bell cracked while tolling the death of Chief Justice John Marshall in 1835. Boston is properly seen as the cradle of liberty; this place—Independence Hall in old Philadelphia—is where the nation itself was born.

The building that became Independence Hall was started in the 1730s, and completed in the 1750s as the State House of the Province of Pennsylvania. The Liberty Bell, engraved "Proclaim Liberty," from William Penn's Charter of Privileges of 1701, arrived in 1752. The First Continental Congress had met at Carpenters Hall, near Independence Square. The Second Continental Congress met at the State House and there adopted the Declaration of

Independence. In 1781, the Continental Congress adopted the Articles of Confederation at Independence Hall and then worked on the Constitution there in 1787. In 1790, the national capital was moved from New York to Philadelphia; there Congress met and nearby, at the new County Court House (now Congress Hall), George Washington was inaugurated for his second term and John Adams for his single term as president.

The Independence National Historic Park today includes Independence Hall, the Liberty Bell Pavilion, Independence Square, Congress Hall, Carpenters Hall, the Old City Hall, which was the first United States Supreme Court building, the First and Second Banks of the United States, the Deschler-Morris House, which was Washington's summer home in 1793 and 1794, and much more.

In 1774 the First Continental Congress met at Carpenters' Hall (above) to "consult upon the present unhappy State of the Colonies."

The flag that made her famous decorates the Philadelphia home (above) *of Betsy Ross, although it is far from certain that she actually made the first American flag.*

Valley Forge

A T VALLEY FORGE, a different kind of Revolutionary War battle was fought. For now it had become a long, hard war, testing the will of the Continental Army to survive—and testing its faith in its leader, George Washington, as well.

There had been a great victory at Saratoga, in the fall of 1777, and Burgoyne's whole army had surrendered. But further south, in the main arena of the war, the British had taken Philadelphia, as well as New York, and now occupied both major cities. Washington's army had been defeated at Brandywine, and his attack on the British at Germantown had failed. It was a defeated, half-starved, demoralized Continental Army that went to ground at Valley Forge on December 19, 1977.

As winter deepened, the army's situation worsened. Even at the beginning of the winter, there had been much exhaustion and illness, and far too little food and clothing. In the bone-chilling northern winter, sheltered only by the nine hundred rude huts they had thrown together on arrival, the men of the army found it extraordinarily difficult to even survive, much less to hold onto their resolve to stay on and fight. Many died; many deserted. Of the 11,000 men who entered the Valley Forge encampment, 6,000 were left in the spring.

Yet those 6,000 men were an army. What George Washington and his drillmaster, Friedrich von Steuben, created in the seemingly endless weeks and months of drilling and survival at Valley Forge was the core of the Continental Army that went on to defeat the British North American armies in the years that followed. The Valley Forge encampment is now the 2,800-acre Valley Forge National Historical Park and contains a memorial arch, reconstructions of the encampment, and Washington's headquarters.

The experience of the Continental Army during the winter of 1777–1778 at Valley Forge is commemorated with replicas of soldiers' and officers' log huts (**above and opposite**) and people wearing uniforms and using artillery from the time (**below**). It was here, with Washington's patient leadership and Baron von Steuben's careful drilling, that the American troops first truly became an army.

Washington's own headquarters have been preserved (above and below) *for today's visitors to Valley Forge. The Artillery Park* (opposite) *lies in the wide fields of the valley, named after a colonial iron-works nearby.*

Near the confluence of the Shenandoah and Potomac rivers lies Harpers Ferry, where some think the Civil War really began.

Harpers Ferry

John Brown's body lies a mould'ring in the grave,
John Brown's body lies a mould'ring in the grave,
John Brown's body lies a mould'ring in the grave,
But his soul goes marching on.

Glory, glory, Hallelujah!
Glory, glory, Hallelujah!
Glory, glory, Hallelujah!
His soul goes marching on.

HARPERS FERRY IS A SMALL PLACE in the hill country of West Virginia, where the Shenandoah and Potomac rivers join, about 55 miles northwest of Washington, D.C. Before 1859, it was chiefly notable for its federal armory and arsenal, sited there by George Washington in 1796. After October 1859, it was the place where John Brown had taken up arms against slavery and died for it. After John Brown's Raid on the Harpers Ferry arsenal, he was a martyr and a rallying cry for the anti-slavery forces of the North, and a foretaste of the death and destruction to come for the South. After John Brown, war was very much in the air; in a certain sense, the shots fired at Harpers Ferry can also be seen as the first shots of the Civil War.

Long an anti-slavery leader, John Brown and his sons turned to open warfare during the Kansas-Missouri guerrilla wars of the late 1850s. By October 1859, he had decided to try to develop a large-scale slave revolt in northwestern Virginia and then move south with a growing army of revolting slaves. On October 16, he and a small group of followers seized the federal arsenal at Harpers Ferry (then part of Virginia) and called for a slave revolt. But

The cemetery (above) recalls the old song about John Brown's body.

no revolt occurred. Instead, his small force was trapped in the armory by local militia units and then assaulted by the militia and a small federal force led by Colonel (later General) Robert E. Lee and Lieutenant (later General) J. E. B. Stuart. Two of John Brown's sons were killed in the battle, and he was soon hanged for treason in nearby Charles Town, West Virginia (then Virginia).

In military terms, John Brown's Raid was more skirmish than battle: ten killed on the federal side; seven killed and John Brown later executed on the raiders' side. In wider terms, however, it was one of the key events leading up to the outbreak of the Civil War, and John Brown's soul did go marching on, through four long years of carnage.

Harpers Ferry National Historical Park commemorates John Brown's Raid. Some of the structures of that time have been restored, including the building in which he and his followers made their last fight.

Today, many of the old buildings of Harpers Ferry (below) have been restored, some with exquisite detail, as this beautiful lamp (above). But the St. John's Episcopal Church (opposite), once a guard house and hospital, lies in ruins.

Antietam

S HARPSBURG IS A TOWN in western Maryland, seventeen miles north of Harpers Ferry and about fifty-five miles northwest of Washington, D.C. Nearby runs Antietam Creek. Here, on September 17, 1862, was fought the single bloodiest day of the Civil War, with over 22,000 casualties, including almost 5,000 dead. The Confederacy called the battle Sharpsburg; the Union called it Antietam.

After the Confederate victory at the second battle of Bull Run (Manassas), Robert E. Lee's Army of Northern Virginia moved north, crossing the Potomac into western Maryland. En route, he split his forces into four columns, sending three columns under Stonewall Jackson to take Harpers Ferry and its 11,000-man garrison. Those columns succeeded, but a copy of Lee' Special Orders 191, dividing his forces and detailing his plans, fell into Union hands, giving the 90,000-strong Union army under General George McClellan a major opportunity to move against the 19,000 men Lee had at South Mountain and then Antietam. McClellan delayed, Jackson partially rejoined Lee in time for the battle, and what might have been a major Union victory turned into an extremely long day, in which a much inferior, well-commanded Confederate force fought a much larger Union force to a standstill. There were 4,000 casualties at Bloody Lane alone.

It was in net effect a major Union victory, though. The next day, having suffered very heavy losses and still confronted with much larger Union forces, Lee pulled his army back across the Potomac. He was not to come north again in force until Gettysburg, then for only a short while. After Antietam, the war was to be fought almost entirely on Confederate soil, ultimately resulting in a scorched land and a broken people.

Today, the battle is commemorated by Antietam National Battlefield Site; a Union cemetery is nearby.

The cemetery **(above)** *gives melancholy testimony to the terrible losses at Antietam, known in the South as Sharpsburg. Rough-built field fences* **(opposite)** *line a lane that winds through the old battle site.*

Gettysburg

Four score and seven years ago our fathers brought forth on this continent, a new nation, conceived in Liberty, and dedicated to the proposition that all men are created equal.

Now we are engaged in a great civil war, testing whether that nation, or any nation so conceived and so dedicated, can long endure. We are met on a great battlefield of that war. We have come to dedicate a portion of that field, as a final resting place for those who here gave their lives that that nation might live. It is altogether fitting and proper that we should do this.

But, in a larger sense, we can not dedicate—we can not consecrate—we can not hallow—this ground. The brave men, living and dead, who struggled here, have consecrated it, far above our poor power to add or detract. The world will little note, nor long remember what we say here, but it can never forget what they did here. It is for us the living, rather, to be dedicated here to the unfinished work which they who fought here have thus far so nobly advanced. It is rather for us to be dedicated to the great task remaining before us—that from these honored dead we take increased devotion to that cause for which they gave their full measure of devotion—that we here highly resolve that those dead shall not have died in vain—that this nation, under God, shall have a new birth of freedom—and that government of the people, by the people, for the people, shall not perish from the earth.

Abraham Lincoln's Gettysburg Address
*November 19, 1863, dedicating
Gettysburg National Cemetery*

THIS WAS BY FAR LINCOLN'S GREATEST SPEECH; for these words he and his America are best remembered. And it is appropriate that he said these words at Gettysburg, for there, in the greatest battle of the Civil War, during the first three days of July 1863, the war turned. Gettysburg has most often been described as the "high water mark of the Confederacy." In fact, it

These are but two of the more than 1200 monuments honoring those who fought and died on the field at Gettysburg.

In the agony of battle, these soldiers, who might have been from either North or South, press forward.

was a last, ultimately failed attempt to take the war to the North, to relieve Union pressure in the West, to stir failing European support. After Gettysburg, the end was in sight, although the war would go on for two more long, bloody years. After Gettysburg, on July 4, 1863, Robert E. Lee began the long retreat south that would end at Appomattox Courthouse. The same day, the great fortress of Vicksburg, on the Mississippi, finally fell to Ulysses S. Grant's Union army.

In June 1863, Lee's Army of Northern Virginia, 70,000-75,000 strong, moved north across the Potomac, through western Maryland and into central Pennsylvania. The Union Army of the Potomac, under General Joseph Hooker, numbering about 85,000 men, moved with them, anticipating the engagement that would inevitably come. On June 28, Lincoln replaced Hooker with General George Meade. On July 1, the battle was joined at Gettysburg,

first by a single division of Confederate infantry against two brigades of Union cavalry, and then by large forces, as elements of both armies came up.

The battle raged for three days, with both sides taking enormous casualties, over 43,000 dead, wounded, or missing in all. Finally, on the afternoon of July 3, Lee ordered a frontal assault by 15,000 marching infantry from General George Pickett's division against the center of the Union line, defended by cannon and well-entrenched infantry. This was the bloody action called Pickett's Charge. The ill-advised attack failed; foot soldiers obeyed their orders, charged, and were slaughtered. The next day, Lee's army began its long retreat.

Today Gettysburg National Military Park occupies the site of this, one of the most pivotal engagements in the history of North America. The park includes Gettysburg National Cemetery, site of Lincoln's Gettysburg Address.

Visitors to the Gettysburg cyclorama (above) can feel the sweep of the battlefield. Off to the side of the main field of battle stands Leister House (below), headquarters of Union General Meade.

Annapolis

Annapolis was an old Colonial town long before it became the home of the United States Naval Academy. The area was first settled in 1649 by Puritan families from Virginia and by 1694 had become the capital of the Maryland colony. After the Revolution, it was for a short time in 1783 and 1784 the American national capital. It has long held a substantial number of early buildings; Colonial Annapolis Historic District, incorporating much of the old town and harbor district, is a national landmark.

Since 1845, Annapolis has been the home of the United States Naval Academy, training ground of the American naval and marine officers' corps. Not uninterruptedly, though. During the Civil War, the Naval Academy moved to Newport, Rhode Island, and the Annapolis buildings became a hospital.

Naval cadets on parade (opposite) *always present a stirring sight. On the campus of the Naval Academy at Annapolis, a monument* (above) *honors dead midshipmen. Another is a replica of a figurehead* (inset above) *from the* U.S.S. Tecumseh, *once called the* U.S.S. Delaware.

Fort McHenry

O say can you see by the dawn's early light
What so proudly we hail'd at the twilight's last gleaming . . .

from The Star-Spangled Banner
by Francis Scott Key

LATE IN THE WAR OF 1812, on September 13, 1814, British ships began what would become a 25-hour bombardment of Fort McHenry, in Baltimore Harbor. The British had earlier captured Washington, D.C., and were now moving to assault Baltimore by land and sea.

Francis Scott Key, detained by the British aboard an American truce ship in the harbor, watched the entire bombardment. During the day, as the bombardment continued and the flag continued to fly over the fort, he was reassured. Shortly after midnight the bombardment stopped, and he could no longer see the flag; he thought the fort had been taken. But the ships had stopped firing only because a strong landing party was attempting to take the fort. The assault failed. The landing party was repulsed, the British troops were withdrawn to their transports, and the Battle of Baltimore was concluded. Many of these same British troops were to participate in the costly assault on New Orleans in February of the next year, after the war had actually ended.

In the morning, Key saw the flag again, still flying over Fort McHenry. That day, he wrote the first version of the poem that was to become the American national anthem. Today Fort McHenry has been restored as a national shrine.

And the star-spangled banner in triumph shall wave
O'er the land of the free and the home of the brave.

Spectacular fireworks (opposite) at Fort McHenry simulate the night gunfire that lit Francis Scott Key's original "star-spangled banner." The classic five-point fort itself is seen in an aerial view (above).

THE CAPITAL DISTRICT

Washington, D.C.

I have a dream...
Martin Luther King, Jr.

HERE ARE ABRAHAM LINCOLN, George Washington, Thomas Jefferson, Frederick Douglass, John Kennedy, and Martin Luther King, Jr. Here are the Declaration of Independence, the Constitution, and the Bill of Rights. Here are the White House, the Capitol, and the Supreme Court. Here are the Library of Congress, the Smithsonian, the National Gallery, the Mall, and Pennsylvania Avenue. Here, then, are many of the great buildings, memorials, documents, artifacts, and main working institutions that are at the heart of the American nation. This is Washington, the capital city set in its own District of Columbia.

It was meant to be that way; the city was from the first designed as a national capital. After the Revolution, the new States of the Union could not really agree as to a proper site for the new nation's capital, moving it several times in the first decade of independence. Ultimately, they agreed to set up a new capital altogether; to that end, George Washington picked a site for the new city in 1791 and commissioned French engineer Charles L'Enfant to plan a city. L'Enfant did, and although he left the project in 1792, it was his basic design for Washington, carried through by Andrew Ellicott and Benjamin Banneker, that is to-day's massive national capital.

The city's first building was the White House, started in 1792 and finished in 1799. The Capitol was started in 1793 and finished in 1827. When the federal government moved the national capital to Washington in 1800, the White House and one wing of the Capitol had been completed; little else was there. The Capitol was

The heart of Washington is the Mall, with the Washington Monument (opposite) at one end and the Capitol (above) at the other. Southwest of the Mall, on the edge of the Tidal Basin, the sun sets behind the Jefferson Memorial (previous page).

surrounded by marshland, and the members of Congress had to live in Georgetown, leading many of them to call repeatedly for relocation of the national capital. Fourteen years later, during the War of 1812, the British took Washington, burning the Capitol, the White House, other public buildings, and the Navy Yard. All was rebuilt, and the city grew with the nation, coming fully into its own as the working headquarters for Lincoln and for the Union army during the Civil War.

For Americans, Washington is full of symbols and memories, places and people.

... RON F SMITH · MARION B WEARING · ...G McDONNELL · HENRY L OLSON · DEAN J CRAIG · JOHN W...
KENNETH R JACONETTI · ...G WILKINSON · ... JAMES M THOMAS...
JAMES H BUSH Jr · PATRICK C CASSIDY · EDWARD J CLEMMON · BARRY L RUNYON · RICHARD A...
MICHAEL P RUANE · ERNEST MAY · JOSEPH MORGAN Jr · MARSHALL L RITZ · ROBERT J GRANDE · JAMES D...
JOHN D BARNETT Jr · DENNIS L SENZ · LARRY D TRAASETH · BENNIE ALSTON · GEORGE X ROCHA ·
EDGAR A CAMPBELL · RALPH D BOBIAN · JAMES L BROWN · WALTER O BROWN Jr · DAVE E ASHFORD ·
WILLIAM R FURLONG Jr · CHARLES CARPENTER · GEORGE P COLANGELO · ANTHONY V C...
PATRICK L HENSHAW · CALVIN A GREENE · THOMAS E GRINER · ROGER D EVANS · LEROY E...
ROBERT D KLINE · THOMAS S HENSHAW · CHARLES R HOLLAND · DONALD P HAMILTON · LARRY A...
ANTHONY R MANTOUVALES · JAMES M KLOPMEYER · RAY TAYLOR · JEROME F LEVASSEUR Jr · JOHN F HOLZ · RODNEY L H...
ERRY LEE NATIONS · RICHARD E MEHL · EUGENE MILEY · JUNIOR E LOTT ·
LESTER L RIDINGS · GARY L NORMAN · LOUIE PETE PINA · RANDALL B PURDY · GREGORY McCRAY · WILLIE C M...
WINSTON A TAGGART · JOHN F RIEGEL · JUNIOR L SCHRINER · WINFIELD A SPOEHR Jr · STEVEN N RADU...
RAYMOND L ZIMMERMAN · EDDIE L LANCASTER · MURRAY D VIDLER · THOMAS M WEBSTER · BRUCE W St LOUIS...
DANNY JAY FISHER · DAVID ANTOL · TERRENCE D BECK · GLEN D BELNAP · JIMMY LEE...
WILLIAM C JANES · CARL E MURRAY · GREGORY GORE · JOHN H HOLMES · CHARLES L HOUSLEY · WILLIAM A CART...
FRANK G MICHULKA · LEROY JEFFERSON · HORATIO L JONES · WILLIAM C JONES · BERNARD P MEINEN...
GARY M RIST · RICHARD F GITTINGER · JEREMIAH D McGARRY · MORRIS G McPHAIL · RICH...
RONALD S ALLEN III · HERBERT ROBERTS Jr · TERRY ROBERTS · BARRY A THOMPSON · RAFAEL A VALPAIS-MO...
JAMES L BURNS · RUDOLPH J BILLIOT · JAMES H BROWN · FRANK H BUCK · DANIEL S BUKALA ·
OSE ANTONIO TINAJERO · ARTHUR P COPELAND · MITCHELL J DUNCAN · MICHAEL J FEAGAN · LARRY E GON...
THOMAS R KISNER · RICHARD J JANSKI · RICHARD A KASKE · CARROL G KEEHNER · WILLIAM...
OSE MEDEL MENDOZA · FRED D LAMBERT · EUGENE MANIGO · ROBERT D MASON · THOMAS R MATTY...
JAMES M McLEAN · DAVID W MILDE · WILLIAM C MOORE Jr · DAVID R MYERS · RICHARD H M...
GLENN H SIMMONS · GLENN L McMASTER · LES H PASCHALL · DONNIE D PRESLEY · LEE D SCURLOCK...
ANE A TILSON · LARRY E SMEDLEY · DONALD L SMITH · MURRAY L SMITH · CHARLES F SORRO...
EDWARD L POLSON · MICHAEL T HOKE · DANIEL A VERDUGO · ROBERT L WALLS · FREDERIC P WEBB ·
PHILLIP G CANTRELL · WILLIAM H BORCHART · WILLIAM E BRIDGES Jr · TED W BURROUGHS Jr · PETER...
GARY H FORS · WILMER P COOK · ROBERT W COOPER · MARIAN J DOMINIAK Jr · STANLEY W J...
HARRY W HORTON Jr · JOHN F FULLER · ROBERT A HANSELMAN · RODGER D HASTE · MERLIN C HOLLENBA...
CLARENCE W OBIE III · STANLEY R HUTCHISON · ROBERT L LONG · STEVEN W MUELLER · PETER E NA...
EARL E TYREE · CHARLES C PETERSON · LARRY P BLACK · TIMOTHY H RINEHART · THOMAS D...
LEWIS W SIGEL · MARTIN P SCHWARTZ · JOSEPH L SEEKFORD · MICHAEL M SENGER · GEORGE C SIGAL...
GARY LEE WEAVER · GARY S STICKEL · MICHAEL E SUNIGA · EDWARD RODRIGUEZ · ANGEL VEGA ·
OE EDDIE CARTER · KENYON G WELLMAN · DENNIS R WOOD · FRANK G ANTONE · GOOD...
HOUSTON GRANT Jr · JAMES N CLEMONS · MICHAEL J... · LEE B...
THOMAS E LAYNE Jr · EUGENE H HARRIMAN · DUDL... · R PH...
KENNETH E THRESHER · PAUL R MADDOX · THOMAS L N... · JOHN L...
BOBBY JOE LAWRENCE · NICHOLAS G WALZ · RAYMO... · OLEKA...
JOHN M NEALON · WALERIJA CHULCHATSCHINO... · LARRY W P... · ...TTON...
GRADY M JORDAN · RONALD A PARSONS · LARRY W P... · LICKI...
ANDREW M HUDAK · MICHAEL B SWEENEY · MATTHEW...
THOMAS A GRUD · DANNY W JETER · BERNARD D...
KENNETH F OLENZUK · DELBERT O LEWIS · JOHN D MOR...
PHILLIP E NEFF · HUGHIE OXENDINE · DONAL...
RAYMOND S ADAMS · JERRY A SELLERS · JOE T SHUMPERT · R...
...H CAMPBELL III · LANCE B BARTON · MICHAEL E... · ...Y K...
...JOSEPH T CLARK · TOMMY... · DAVID...
...GAMBLE · DARRELL D GEHRKE · DONALD F...
...THEW P MALCZYNSKI · JAMES L RUSS Jr · KENNY D SCHOE...
...MATTHEW P MALCZYNSKI · ...RT E WOODS · CARL E...

North of Washington's Reflecting Pool, near the Lincoln Memorial, lies the Vietnam Veterans Memorial (below), designed by then-student Maya Lin after a nationwide contest. The long, low-lying, V-shaped memorial, opened in 1982, lists the names (opposite) of over 58,000 people lost in the war, in the general chronological order of their deaths. A great book aids visitors, some of who leave tributes (opposite inset), in finding specific names on the memorial. In 1984, "Three Servicemen" (right), sculpted by Frederick Hart, was added to the memorial.

Ghosts of slavery and the Civil War still hover over Washington. The home **(below)** of Frederick Douglass, a former slave who became Minister to Haiti and a great Black leader, is preserved as a museum; its contents include several busts of Douglass himself **(right).** On April 14, 1865, only five days after the end of the Civil War, Abraham Lincoln was killed at Ford's Theatre **(opposite)** by a bullet from John Wilkes Booth's single-shot derringer **(opposite inset.)**

Lincoln Memorial

With malice toward none, with charity for all; with firmness in the right, as God gives us to see the right, let us strive on to finish the work we are in; to bind up the nation's wounds; to care for him who shall have borne the battle, and for his widow, and his orphan—to do all which may achieve and cherish a just, and a lasting peace, among ourselves, and with all nations.

from Lincoln's Second Inaugural
Address, *March 4, 1865*

DANIEL CHESTER FRENCH's magnificent statue of Abraham Lincoln sits here at the Lincoln Memorial, as it has since 1922, looking out over the Mall toward the Washington Monument and the Capitol dome beyond. In chambers to either side of the statue are inscribed Lincoln's Gettysburg Address and his Second Inaugural Address. All are set in a Parthenon-like memorial structure, with a long, wide flight of steps leading down to ground level. It is at this memorial and on those steps that some of the most memorable events of this century have happened, the most notable of them being the huge, Mall-filling meeting at which Martin Luther King, Jr., delivered his "I have a dream . . ." speech to 250,000 Americans on August 28, 1963.

The compelling statue of Abraham Lincoln (above left and opposite right), in its Greek-style setting (above right), has long symbolized justice and equality for Americans. So it is that demonstrators often gather here, marching down the Mall past the Washington Monument to the Reflecting Pool (right) and then on to the steps of the Lincoln Memorial in the distance. Since this photograph was taken, the Vietnam Veterans Memorial has been built to the right of the Reflecting Pool.

The White House

THE WHITE HOUSE has been the residence of all the American presidents since John Adams. George Washington approved the site and James Hoban's plans for the building, but never lived in this, the President's House, as it was officially called for many years after completion. Popularly, it has from the beginning been known as the White House, since its grey sandstone walls were painted white during the years of construction.

Only once for several years, from 1814 to 1817, did American presidents live elsewhere. After the British burned the White House in 1814, James and Dolley Madison lived in a private residence for the balance of his term in office, as did James Monroe for most of his first three years in office. Theodore Roosevelt, Calvin Coolidge, and Harry Truman moved out for short periods during some of the many major renovations and expansions of the building that have occurred in almost two centuries. But since 1800 the White House has uninterruptedly been the symbol of the American Presidency, the main base of operations for every president, and a magnet for visitors from all over the world.

For Americans, and for people the world over, the White House (opposite) *is a symbol of America's promise and power. Many a dignitary has been greeted in the gardens of the White House; this garden* (above) *is the traditional province of the First Lady.*

The Capitol

THE CAPITOL is the great workplace of American democracy, the center upon which all the multifold pressures generated by a huge, diverse American nation converge. For all of its well-advertised weaknesses, and however much it can be improved, to watch the American Congress at its labors is to see that American democracy does indeed continue to work.

The Capitol is a huge, ornate, Romanesque dome flanked by two large columned wings, the wings being occupied by the House of Representatives and the Senate. The whole structure dominates the Washington skyline. It was positioned at the hub of Washington's street system by Charles L'Enfant, who designed the city; the Capitol itself was designed by Dr. William Thornton. George Washington laid the cornerstone in September 1793, and Congress moved into its north wing, the only portion then completed, in 1800, when the federal government moved from Philadelphia to Washington. Much of it was burned by the British in 1814, and Congress met elsewhere until 1819. The building was developed and greatly expanded in the period before the Civil War, being substantially completed in its modern form during that war. Until 1935, when the present Supreme Court building was completed, the Court also met in the Capitol.

From the west facade of the Capitol, the main view is across the Mall to the Washington Monument and the Lincoln Memorial beyond. The east facade faces the Supreme Court building and the Library of Congress; these are the steps on which the American presidents are inaugurated, symbolizing the joinder between the three equal institutions at the top of American democracy—the Congress, the Presidency, and the Supreme Court.

The sight of the Capitol building (opposite) *in the spring, rising above Washington's many flowering trees, draws visitors from all over the world. The interior of the building has its own attractions, such as the beautiful architectural details of the Rotunda* (opposite left inset), *and paintings and statues commemorating great people and events* (above and opposite right inset).

The Supreme Court

FOR LAWYERS, the Supreme Court is a hallowed place; for all Americans, it is a decisive place. This is the court of Chief Justice John Marshall, who made the Supreme Court the final interpreter of the Constitution, and of all who came after him, once that great principle had been established; of Holmes, Cardozo, Brandeis, Black, and Douglas, and of such greatly different modern Chief Justices as Warren and Burger.

The present home of the Court is a three-story classical marble building facing the east facade of the Capitol, which was designed by Cass Gilbert, completed in 1935, and occupied in 1936.

The classical Greek style of the Supreme Court building (above) is a reminder that democracy is an old, deeply rooted idea. In front are two statues by James Earle Fraser, a female, "Contemplation of Justice," and a male (above inset), "Guardian of Law."

Washington Monument

The Washington Monument (above right) is one of the capital's most striking and best-known landmarks. Seen from the Lincoln Memorial (above left), the obelisk is mirrored in the Reflecting Pool.

IN THE CITY he started, which bears his name, it is right that the tallest memorial structure be Washington's. The Washington Monument is a 555-foot-high obelisk, standing on the Mall, with the Capitol to the east and the Lincoln Memorial to the west; with them, it is one of the American nation's greatest memorials and symbols, in the United States and throughout the world.

The Washington Monument was started in 1848 and progressed very slowly in the years before the Civil War; when work stopped because of that war, it stood only 176 feet high. After the war, work was not started again until 1880, but then progressed far more rapidly; the Monument was capped on December 6, 1884, and dedicated by President Chester Arthur on February 21, 1885.

Since 1888, the monument has been open to the public. Today the top can be reached either by elevator or by climbing 898 steps; however ascended, the view from the top is magnificent.

WE HOLD THESE TRUTHS TO BE SELF-EVIDENT: THAT ALL MEN ARE CREATED EQUAL, THAT THEY ARE ENDOWED BY THEIR CREATOR WITH CERTAIN INALIENABLE RIGHTS, AMONG THESE ARE LIFE, LIBERTY AND THE PURSUIT OF HAPPINESS, THAT TO SECURE THESE RIGHTS GOVERNMENTS ARE INSTITUTED AMONG MEN. WE··· SOLEMNLY PUBLISH AND DECLARE, THAT THESE COLONIES ARE AND OF RIGHT OUGHT TO BE FREE AND INDEPENDENT STATES···AND FOR THE SUPPORT OF THIS DECLARATION, WITH A FIRM RELIANCE ON THE PROTECTION OF DIVINE PROVIDENCE, WE MUTUALLY PLEDGE OUR LIVES, OUR FORTUNES AND OUR SACRED HONOUR.

Jefferson Memorial

Thomas Jefferson wrote the Declaration of Independence when he was 33 years old. Fifteen years later, he became the third President of the United States. He was a diplomat, sometime dissenter, philosopher, farmer, architect, classicist, linguist, patron of the arts and sciences, and more. His books formed much of the nucleus of the Library of Congress. Jefferson was truly one of the greatest of America's children and founding fathers. This round classical structure in which his image sits was dedicated on April 13, 1943, the 200th anniversary of his birth. It is his physical memorial. But his truest memorial is the idea of freedom that is at the heart of the American dream.

On the edge of Washington's Tidal Basin, the Jefferson Memorial (above) honors the author of the Declaration of Independence, parts of which are carved in the wall (inset above).

Arlington

ACROSS THE POTOMAC RIVER from Washington, D.C., at Arlington National Cemetery, is a different kind of memorial. Here are the Tomb of the Unknown Soldier and the graves of tens of thousands of others, most of them war dead, others veterans, and their family members. President John F. Kennedy, and his brother, Senator Robert F. Kennedy, are buried here, as are President William Howard Taft and many other political and military leaders. The 420-acre cemetery, opened in 1864, was earlier part of the Robert E. Lee estate in Arlington, Virginia, which was seized by the federal government during the Civil War. The nearby Custis-Lee mansion has been restored and is a national memorial.

Thousands of war veterans and other honored Americans are buried at Arlington National Cemetery **(above)**; *President John F. Kennedy's gravesite there is marked by a perpetual flame* **(inset above).**

THE SOUTH

Jamestown

A T JAMESTOWN, on May 13, 1607, began the long, slow unfolding of English settlement and power in North America. Here, to Jamestown Island, (then a peninsula), came three ships of the Virginia Company of London, the *Susan Constant,* the *Goodspeed,* and the *Discovery,* to establish what became the first successful English settlement in America.

The first three years were extraordinarily difficult, with survival at stake every step of the way, in spite of the efforts of Captain John Smith, an early leader of the colony. About to give up, the colony was saved in June 1610 by the arrival of Lord Delaware with supplies from England. Economic survival was assured in 1612 when colonist John Rolfe developed tobacco as a valuable export crop. The colony's physical survival was in those years largely dependent upon the good will of its Native American neighbors; John Rolfe's marriage to Pocahontas, daughter of chief Powhatan, made survival possible for a decade more. Later relations worsened and the Native Americans made a successful attack on the colony in 1622, but the colony still survived and continued to grow. In 1624, the Virginia Company was dissolved by the crown, and Jamestown became a royal colony.

Jamestown can properly claim two other "firsts" in North America, both occurring in 1619. In that year began the Virginia House of Burgesses, the first representative body in North America; the *Mayflower* was not to land at Provincetown and Plymouth until a year later. And Jamestown can claim a far more dubious distinction, as well; in that same year, 1619, the first African slaves were brought to the North American shore to Jamestown.

Jamestown was until 1699 capital of the Virginia colony, later succeeded by Williamsburg. It was never a commercial center, and

Statues honor important figures in Jamestown's history, including early leader John Smith (opposite) and Native American princess Pocahantas (below). Artists have recreated the look of a typical house (above) in the fledgling settlement. The massive walls of the Castillo de San Marcos (previous page), standing in St. Augustine, Florida, testify to the early Spanish presence in the South.

with the removal of the seat of government went into rapid decline. During the Revolutionary War, the Jamestown peninsula was the scene of some of the fighting that led to the British surrender at Yorktown. But by the end of the 18th century, it was little more than a group of structures on a fast-eroding peninsula, which by the middle of the 19th century became the island it is today.

Today Jamestown is part of colonial National Historical Park, which includes Williamsburg and Yorktown. At Jamestown, itself, the outlines of the old town have been excavated; at adjacent Jamestown Festival Park, replicas of the *Susan Constant, Goodspeed,* and *Discovery* are on view, as well as reconstructions of the settlers' original James Fort and several other early buildings.

*The rough shelters **(above)** typical of the settlement's early days are recreated in modern Jamestown, and crafts like glassmaking **(below)** live again there. Excavations have uncovered old foundations **(opposite inset)**, while elsewhere ivy-covered walls **(opposite)** speak of the age of the surviving Old Church Tower.*

Castillo de San Marcos

ST. AUGUSTINE, FLORIDA, site of this massive old Spanish fort called Castillo de San Marcos, is the oldest city in the United States. Both fort and city date all the way back to 1565, though many earlier wooden forts preceded the building of this masonry fort, which was started in 1672 and completed almost 25 years later.

St. Augustine was founded by a Spanish expedition commanded by Pedro Menendez de Avilés, who sighted land here on St. Augustine's Day, August 28, 1565. Its early history reflects the century and a half of British-Spanish conflict in the Caribbean, a conflict that continued in Florida between the new American nation and Spain until full control of the area passed to the United States in the early 1820s. From St. Augustine, Spanish fleets controlled the whole north Florida coast and raided north into the Carolinas; they attacked Port Royal, North Carolina, in 1681. Against St. Augustine came fleet after fleet, out of the Caribbean and from the English colonies to the north. Francis Drake captured the fort and burned the city in 1586; John Davis took it in 1665; raiders from the Carolinas burned the city in 1702; and expeditions against the city from the Carolinas continued through the mid-1700s.

The present fort is the oldest masonry fort in the United States. It is made of coquina, a local stone composed of small seashells, with mortar made of shell lime, and has walls thirty feet high and up to twelve feet thick. Built by Spanish engineers employing Spanish artisans, the main work on the fort was for 25 years supplied by the forced labor of local Native Americans. Later, during the 19th century, by then part of the United States

On the shores of Matanzas Bay rise the walls of the Castillo de San Marcos **(opposite)**, *begun in 1672 after earlier wooden forts were burned in British raids. Often used as a military prison, the fort* **(above and below)** *was used to house "rebels" during the Revolutionary War and American deserters during the Spanish-American War.*

and renamed Fort Marion, the fort was used as a prison for Native Americans. These were at first local Seminoles, but later included people transported from the Southwest, mostly Kiowas, Comanches, Southern Cheyennes, and Apaches, many of whom died because of the conditions of their captivity.

In addition to Castillo de San Marcos, St. Augustine today contains a notable body of preserved and restored structures, many dating back to Colonial times, including the oldest house in the United States and a group of restored buildings collectively called the Restored Village.

The oldest house surviving in the United States is this one (below) in St. Augustine, Florida, which dates back to the early 1700s. George Street (opposite), in the restored historic district of the city, gave its name to the George Street Players (above), shown celebrating the city's 415th anniversary in 1980.

Charleston

HERE THE CIVIL WAR BEGAN.
South Carolina had seceded from the Union on December 20, 1860. The federal garrison at Fort Sumter, in Charleston harbor, had refused to surrender the fort, while the small garrison at Fort Moultrie, also in the harbor, had evacuated and gone to Sumter. Long negotiations failed; South Carolina, set on seceding and maintaining slavery, was determined to take Fort Sumter. On April 12, 1861, Confederate artillery began a massive bombardment of the fort. The federal garrison held out for three days, but then surrendered on April 14. On April 15, President Abraham Lincoln called for 75,000 volunteers to save the Union, and so took the first steps on the long, bloody road that led to Appomattox.

During the Civil War that followed, Charleston continued to be held by the Confederacy, and even through the long Union blockade of 1863-1865 was a port through which some supplies flowed to the Confederate army. In February 1865, as Union troops led by General William Tecumseh Sherman neared, marching from Atlanta to the sea, Charleston was evacuated, and then occupied by the Union forces.

Charleston had figured in another American war, as well. Early in the Revolution, a British squadron had failed to take Fort Moultrie and sailed away. Four years later, a 45-day British siege of the city was successful, and 5,000 American troops led by General Benjamin Lincoln surrendered.

Today, Charleston focuses far more on its Colonial and post-Revolutionary heritage than on its Civil War history. The Charleston historic district contains over a thousand 18th- and 19th-century historic places and structures, many of them restored and some of them excellent examples of the architecture of

Fort Moultrie **(above)**, *originally a sand-and-log structure, has guarded Charleston from an island in the harbor since Revolutionary days. The larger Fort Sumter* **(below)**, *on the mainland, refused to surrender to Union forces, sparking the Civil War in 1861. Charleston's famed Magnolia Gardens* **(opposite)**, *covering some 55 acres, date back to the 1670s.*

the time. The gardens of Middleton Place, home of Henry Middleton, President of the Continental Congress, are the oldest landscaped gardens in the United States and a national historic landmark, as are several buildings in the area. There is also a substantial reconstruction of Old Charles Towne, at the site of the original Charleston settlement in 1670, the first by Europeans in South Carolina.

The Joseph Manigault house (above), built in 1803 in the Adam style, is one of the many fine historic houses open to Charleston's visitors.

Cabbage Row (below), once a Black tenement section, was the inspiration for Catfish Row in Du Bose Heyward's novel Porgy and George Gershwin's resulting musical Porgy and Bess.

Henry Middleton, president of the Continental Congress, built Middleton Place (above) and its famous landscaped gardens near Charleston in the mid-18th century. The Dock Street Theatre (below), later made part of the Planters Hotel, began serving as the first full-time theatre in the country in 1735.

Williamsburg

WILLIAMSBURG WAS THE CAPITAL of Colonial Virginia from 1699 to 1780, as well as a major cultural center of the time. Here sat Virginia's House of Burgesses, with such representatives as George Washington, Thomas Jefferson, and Patrick Henry, who here delivered his stirring "Give me liberty, or give me death!" speech.

For that part of its history alone, Williamsburg would be a major historic place. But in our time, it is notable for something more, as well. Since 1926, the most substantial of all the American restoration projects has been developed here, funded primarily by John D. Rockefeller, Jr., and his and his Colonial Williamsburg corporation. During the past sixty years, hundreds of structures, gardens, monuments, and streets have been moved, restored, reconstructed, and furnished, all to the end of reconstituting that portion of 18th-century Williamsburg known as the Middle Plantation. And with conspicuous success: The Williamsburg restoration is one of the most visited and most satisfying of all the American restoration projects and has served as a model for much of what has followed, as towns and cities all over the country have sought to capture and preserve their past.

Today Colonial Williamsburg is part of the Colonial National Historical Park, which includes nearby Yorktown Battlefield and historic Jamestown; all are linked by the Colonial Parkway.

When Virginia was still a colony, the Governor's Palace (**opposite**) *at Williamsburg was the residence of the Royal Governor. The Capitol* (**above**), *where Patrick Henry made his famous speech, was the meeting place of the House of Burgesses.*

In Colonial Williamsburg, where cars are banned during the day, visitors can take carriage rides **(opposite)** through the historic district. Among the many attractions of this popular and successful restoration are gardens **(above)** and homes showing rooms like this kitchen **(below)** as they were in Colonial days.

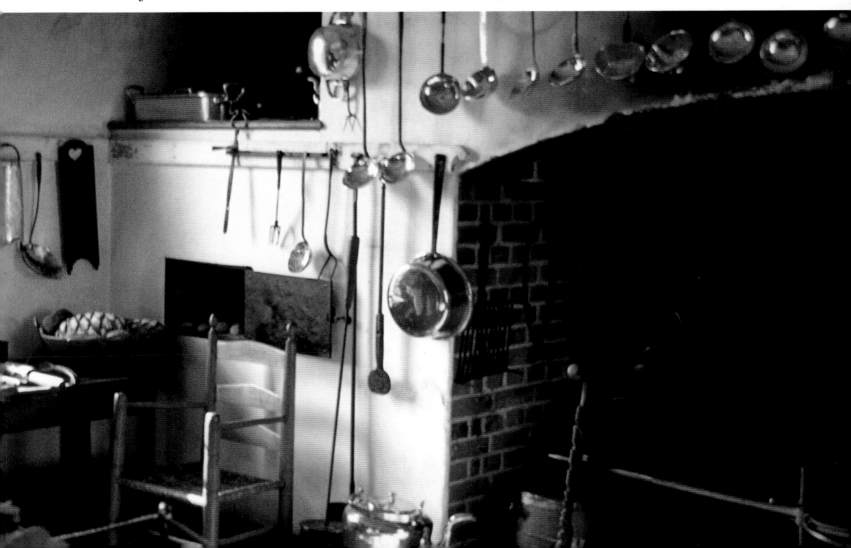

In Williamsburg's cemeteries, old headstones and grave markers (right and below) give some semblance of immortality to people long gone. The restored area even includes an old windmill (opposite).

Mount Vernon

THE GEORGIAN MANSION that was the plantation home of George and Martha Washington stands on a hill looking east over the Potomac River, about fifteen miles south of the city that carries his name. Nearby on the grounds are their plain brick tombs, marking his death in 1799 and hers in 1802.

The 2,400-acre estate had been in the family for eighty years when George Washington took possession of it in 1754, first by lease and later by inheritance. During his 45 years of ownership, he enlarged the four-room wooden building on the site into the present mansion, built many of the outbuildings still on the property, and developed the estate into what was at its height an 8,000-acre working plantation, originally in tobacco and later mainly in wheat and other grains. Washington occupied Mount Vernon mainly between his return from the French and Indian War in 1758 and his reluctant assumption of the commander-in-chief's role in 1776, a period of sixteen years. After that, he returned to his plantation only infrequently for the next two decades, going home finally in 1797.

Mount Vernon was the family home of the man who has come to be known as the father of his country; it was also to a large extent a house built on the fruits of slavery. Most of those who worked on and in both house and plantation were slaves, even though Washington declared himself to be against slavery, telling Jefferson (himself a slaveholder) that it was "among his first wishes to see some plan adopted by which slavery in his country might be abolished by law." In his will, Washington directed that at his death his slaves be freed.

Today Mount Vernon is a magnet for visitors from all over the world and is administered by a private trust.

*The Washington family home at Mount Vernon is furnished with numerous artifacts (**right and below**) from George and Martha's day.*

*The image of Mount Vernon (**opposite**), the mansion on the crest of the hill, is sharp in the minds of everyone interested in Washington and his role in the making of the American republic. Today many visitors are also attracted by Mount Vernon's beautiful gardens (**below**).*

Monticello

Here was buried Thomas Jefferson, Author of the Declaration of American Independence, of the Statute of Virginia for religious freedom, & Father of the University of Virginia.
Inscription on the tomb of Thomas Jefferson at Monticello

HAD HE BEEN A VAIN MAN, Thomas Jefferson might have said much more. He had also been third President of the United States, Secretary of State, Ambassador to France, member of the Virginia House of Burgesses and of the Continental Congress, Governor of Virginia, author, President of the American Philosophical Society, classicist, linguist, bibliophile, and intimate of many of the other great people of his time. Beyond that, he was the innovative architect of the building called Monticello (Italian for "Little Mountain").

Jefferson's site was on a hilltop two miles east of Charlottesville, Virginia, looking east over a twenty-mile-wide plain to the Blue Ridge Mountains. He had begun to level the site in 1768 when he was 25 years old; two years later he moved into Monticello's small southern pavilion, after a fire had destroyed his nearby home and birthplace at Shadwell. Jefferson lived alone there until his marriage to Martha Skelton in 1772; Monticello was their home from then on. The few rooms they lived in during their early years together are still called the "Honeymoon Cottage."

Jefferson built, expanded, and rebuilt Monticello for the next forty years, the present structure being fully completed only in 1809 and then continued to occupy it until his death at 83 in 1826. In those years, he created and maintained one of the most innovative buildings of his time, which included what was then the major innovation of placing the service structures of his plantation underneath the terraces of the main house, rather than in a series of small outbuildings. He also installed such ingenious devices as a seven-day calendar clock, dumbwaiters, and weathervanes readable from inside the house.

The mansion at Monticello (opposite) is a tribute to its creator, Thomas Jefferson, both in its architecture and in the many innovations he introduced, some of which are still displayed in public rooms (above) of the home.

Yorktown

THE AMERICAN-FRENCH VICTORY at Yorktown was the last major battle of the Revolutionary War. Here, on October 19, 1781, while British army bands played "The World Turned Upside Down," General Charles Cornwallis's southern army of over 7,000 men surrendered to the joint American-French forces that had besieged them by land and sea.

In a sense, Yorktown was Saratoga all over again, with strong British forces in New York failing to relieve a trapped British army under attack by superior forces. At Saratoga, in 1777, the British army in New York had failed to move up the Hudson River valley to join General John Burgoyne, which would have allowed them to split the new American nation and probably win the war. At Yorktown, four years later, Cornwallis dug in on a strong position by the sea, after having been assured by General Henry Clinton, in New York, that a strong British fleet carrying large reinforcements would come to relieve him.

That fleet never came. The Americans and French came instead. In May, a French fleet arrived at Newport, Rhode Island, carrying 4,800 troops who moved to join Washington's army in the Hudson Valley. In mid-August, the French informed Washington that a French fleet under Admiral the Comte de Grasse was sailing out of the West Indies for Virginia, carrying over 3,000 more French troops. By then, Cornwallis had settled into Yorktown and was building fortifications.

Washington and his French allies decided to attempt to trap the British at Yorktown. He moved south with his combined American-French forces toward the southern Jersey shore, there to meet de Grasse's ships and go by sea to Yorktown. Meanwhile, the French fleet had met and defeated a British fleet in Chesapeake Bay, sealing the fate of Cornwallis, who could not then be either resupplied or relieved.

On the field of Yorktown today, visitors can see cannon from the Revolutionary War (below) and sometimes reenactments (opposite) of the battle that ended the war. Nearby, at Moore House, they can visit the Surrender Room (above) where the Articles of Capitulation were drafted.

The rest was easy. Between September 18 and October 15, the combined American-French army of over 15,000 men besieged and entrapped a British force half its size, while the French fleet stopped access from the sea. By October 17, it was over, with the formal surrender occurring on October 19.

The peace treaty establishing the new nation was not signed until two years later, in 1783, but Yorktown was in fact the decisive and concluding battle of the American Revolution.

Today Yorktown Battlefield is part of Colonial National Historical Park, which also includes Jamestown Island. It is thirteen miles east of Williamsburg, with its major Colonial restoration.

Bull Run-Manassas

THE BULL RUN is a minor stream winding through the Virginia countryside about thirty miles west of Washington, D.C. Near that stream, with the village of Manassas close by, two early, massive Civil War battles were fought, both of them won by the Confederate army. The battles were both called Bull Run by the Union, and Manassas by the Confederacy.

The first Bull Run fight was the earliest major battle of the war, occurring on July 21, 1861. After a series of moves and counter-moves on both sides, it brought an unseasoned force of a little under 30,000 Union soldiers against an equally unseasoned, but slightly larger Confederate force. Early in the battle, General Irvin McDowell's Union forces turned the Confederate left flank, but were held by General Thomas Jackson's brigade, earning Jackson his nickname, "Stonewall." Later General P. G. T. Beauregard's Confederate forces turned McDowell's right flank, forcing retreat. That retreat soon turned into a rout, as the green Union troops began to panic and run, side by side with the carriages and horses of all the notables who had come out from Washington to see what they thought would be an easy Northern victory. The Union rout was so complete that the Confederates might very well have taken Washington had they realized how decisive their victory had been.

The second Bull Run battle occurred over a year later, on August 29-30, 1862, and on much the same ground as the first battle. It ended with a decisive victory for General Robert E. Lee and the withdrawal of the Union army from northern Virginia. This opened the way for Lee's first invasion of the north, into nearby Maryland.

A century and more after the battles, the 3000 acres of fields **(above and below)** at Bull Run-Manassas *show little sign of the battles and their more than 24,000 casualties, but an abandoned caisson* **(opposite)** *hints at the site's bloody past.*

Shiloh

AT SHILOH CHURCH, near Pittsburgh Landing in western Tennessee, the second great battle of the Civil War was fought. Here, on April 6 and 7, 1862, a Confederate army of about 40,000 men, led by General Albert Sydney Johnston, met an army of similar size commanded by General Ulysses S. Grant. Grant's army was moving south along the Tennessee River after a decisive early victory at Forts Henry and Donelson, in which over 11,000 Confederate soldiers were captured.

On April 6, Johnston attacked Grant's army, taking it by surprise. On that day, although General Johnston died on the battlefield, the Confederates prevailed, driving the Union forces back toward the Tennessee River, with very large casualties on both sides. But on the second day of the battle, Grant's remaining forces were joined by much of another Union army, led by General Don Carlos Buell. The combined Union forces counterattacked, driving the Confederate army from the field; by the time that battle had ended, Shiloh had seen almost 24,000 casualties. The way was now clear for further Union advances. Ultimately, Grant was to take Vicksburg, thereby splitting the Confederacy, and opening the South to such devastating attacks as Sherman's later march through Georgia.

Today, Shiloh National Military Park occupies the battlefield site, commemorating the long and bloody battle that was Shiloh.

Union forces camped and fought near the original of this modern Shiloh Church **(above)**. In a position fronting a sunken road **(below)**, some were surrounded and forced to surrender by Confederate troops in an area called the Hornet's Nest, today marked by Potter's Stump **(opposite)**.

Appomattox

HERE IS WHERE LEE SURRENDERED to Grant, on April 9, 1865. Here is where the long, bloody Civil War that had begun at Harpers Ferry and Fort Sumter effectively ended, with the nearly 27,000 soldiers left in General Robert E. Lee's Army of Northern Virginia disbanding and going home. There were still some Confederate units in existence, and a few small armed engagements, but after Lee's surrender the war was really over.

The journey to Appomattox Courthouse had commenced almost a year earlier, when General Ulysses S. Grant took the Army of the Potomac through northern Virginia and into the battle of The Wilderness, on May 5 and 6, 1864. Grant's army took very heavy losses—over 17,000 dead, wounded, or missing—in The Wilderness, but was by this time so much stronger than the Confederate army that it was able to continue south toward Richmond even after the battle.

The battle of The Wilderness was fought about fifty miles southwest of Washington, D.C. Only four days later and ten miles further on, Grant and Lee fought another major battle, this one at Spotsylvania. In a very heavy three-day battle, peaking on May 12 at the "Bloody Angle," the Union forces again suffered heavy losses—11,000 to Lee's 6,000— but again moved south, with Lee's army retreating before it.

One month later, the Union and Confederate armies, again further south, settled in for what became the climactic series of battles of the war, at the siege of Petersburg. For over nine months, from June 14, 1864, to April 2, 1865, the Union army confronted the Confederate army, cutting off its sources of supply, whittling it down engagement by engagement. Ultimately, on April 2, after a total of over 70,000 casualties on both sides,

Near the Appomattox Court House (**above and opposite**) *Lee surrendered to Grant and Confederate soldiers laid down their arms, piling them in the open area thereafter called Surrender Triangle.*

Lee broke off, evacuated Petersburg, and moved west, hoping to reach General Johnston's forces in North Carolina. But blocked by General Sheridan's cavalry, and suffering heavy losses from repeated engagements with the Union army on his heels, Lee's army lasted only one more week. The Union army surrounded Lee's remaining forces at Appomattox Station on April 8. After a brief engagement on the morning of April 9, Lee surrendered his command—still almost 29,000 strong. The Army of Northern Virginia was no more; the war was over.

Today the site of Lee's surrender is Appomattox National Historic Park, which includes a restoration of some of the village as it was in 1865, and includes McLean House, where Lee's surrender to Grant took place.

Cumberland Gap

This was the way west, for Daniel Boone and a million who came after him. Here, in this wild and beautiful Appalachian country, is Cumberland Gap, the only good path through the mountains between Georgia and the Mohawk River valley in New York.

The Native Americans of the southern Appalachians had long used this path; Cumberland Gap is part of the great old Warriors Trail, used for hundred of years by Cherokees, Shawnees, and many other peoples on both sides of the mountains.

In the middle of the 18th century, as the people of the American colonies began to chafe under restrictive British colonial policies, they began to look west, beyond the mountains that for a century and a half had held them on the Atlantic plain,—even while French and Spanish explorers and settlers had moved out into the continent, north from Mexico and New Orleans, and south from the Great Lakes and out along the Mississippi. By 1750, Dr. Thomas Walker had discovered Cave Gap, which he later called Cumberland Gap. By the early 1770s, Daniel Boone and other frontiersmen were moving through Cumberland Gap and into the vast and rich continent beyond.

In the spring of 1775, after land speculator Thomas Henderson "bought" twenty million acres of Kentucky from the Cherokees, who probably did not have it to sell, he sent Boone and thirty axemen to clear a path through the Cumberland Gap to Kentucky. They did so rather easily, between March 10 and March 20, 1775, moving on the Warriors Path out into Kentucky, surviving Shawnee attack on the other side of the Gap, and moving on to found Boonesborough on the Kentucky River. The road they cleared was later called the Wilderness Road; by 1792, 70,000

Americans poured westward on Daniel Boone's Wilderness Road, through the famous Cumberland Gap (above).

settlers had poured west through Cumberland Gap, and Kentucky was a state in the Union. Hundreds of thousands more came in the decades that followed, until even easier paths became available south of the mountains and north through Pennsylvania and New York's Mohawk Valley.

Today Cumberland Gap National Historical Park commemorates Daniel Boone and the surge of the people of the new United States westward after the Revolution.

New Orleans

NEW ORLEANS IS ONE of the world's great port cities. It has for all of its history been the gateway to the Mississippi River, and therefore also to the heartland of North America.

Of the Europeans, the French came here first—and from the north—when Robert Cavalier, Sieur de La Salle, reached the mouth of the Mississippi in 1692; he was completing the long journey from the North Atlantic that had started 130 years earlier, when Jacques Cartier entered the St. Lawrence. In 1700 Pierre le Moyne, Sieur d'Iberville, coming in from the Gulf of Mexico, founded a colony near the mouth of the Mississippi, and colonization of the lower Mississippi basin began. Eighteen years later his brother, Jean Baptiste le Moyne, Sieur de Bienville, founded New Orleans farther upriver. Soon there were plantations along the river, and substantial numbers of French settlers, along with many Native American and Black slaves. By the end of the century, the river was bringing to New Orleans cotton, furs, sugar cane, rum, and molasses. Meanwhile, in 1763, New Orleans passed from France to Spain, and then back to France in 1800. By then, New Orleans was an extraordinarily cosmopolitan city, reflecting its French, Spanish, Black, and Native American heritage. Many of the French were Acadians, expelled by the British from French Acadia, then renamed Nova Scotia.

In a very real sense, all this was prologue for New Orleans, for after the American Revolution the people of the new nation came west in droves over and around the Appalachians, their sheer numbers soon overwhelming the earlier populations. In 1803, Thomas Jefferson's government acquired the Louisiana Territory, including the whole lower Mississippi Valley and New Orleans with it. By 1812, the cotton gin and the steamboat had been

Tradition has it that freebooter Jean Lafitte and future president Andrew Jackson met at Old Absinthe House (above), on Bourbon Street, to prepare for the British attack on New Orleans in 1815. Many buildings (below) nearby look much as they did then. Outside the city proper are remains of a different lifestyle, as at Greenwood Plantation (opposite).

invented, and New Orleans was well on its way to becoming one of the world's wealthiest ports, tapping the wealth of some of the richest farmlands on Earth.

By that time the Americans and the British were at war. At Chalmette, six miles from the center of the old city, on January 8, 1815, an American army led by Andrew Jackson repelled a large-scale British attack on the city. This was the Battle of New Orleans, which occurred after the war was over and wasted a great many lives on both sides—especially on the British side, for they sent troops marching in close order against an American line defended by good riflemen supported with cannon.

Much of old New Orleans remains, even today reflecting the diverse ethnic and cultural heritage of the city, especially at Mardi Gras time. The Vieux Carré, or French Quarter, consists of the eighty blocks in which the city was originally laid out by French military engineers. Most of the buildings in the Quarter date from after the disastrous fire of 1794, but a few landmark earlier buildings still remain, including the Ursuline Convent and St. Louis Cathedral. Jackson Square, at the heart of the Quarter, also remains. The old Spanish administrative center, The Cabildo, dates from after the fire, having been built in 1795.

Visitors to modern New Orleans can sample life in a typical southern mansion, such as Longue Vue House (right) with its fine formal gardens, and can tour Chalmette (above), site of the Battle of New Orleans.

The most famous part of New Orleans is probably the Vieux Carré ("Old Square"), better known as the French Quarter, where street musicians (opposite top) and sidewalk vendors (opposite below), among others, give the area a special life, night and day.

THE SOUTHWEST

Pueblo Country

LONG BEFORE THE EUROPEANS CAME, several great Native American cultures flourished in the Southwest. These were peaceful farming peoples—mainly Hohokam, Mogollon, and Anasazi—many of them from or strongly influenced by the agricultural peoples to their south, in what would become Mexico. Later nomadic tribes came from the northern plains, notably the Navajos and Apaches, related by language and in that era by their predatory habits. By the time the Navajo and Apache came, the Anasazi were the dominant people in the region; "Anasazi" is a Navajo word meaning "The Old Ones." Conversely, "Apache" is a Zuni word meaning "enemy."

To the Spanish invaders, all the Native American farming peoples, regardless of their cultural origins, were collectively known as the Pueblo Indians, because *pueblo* was the local word for the striking towns they inhabited. And it is as the Pueblos that they and their descendants are popularly known today.

There are Hohokam and Mogollon ruins in the Southwest; some of them, like the Hohokam village at Casa Grande National Monument in southern Arizona, and the Mogollan village at Gila Cliffs National Monument in New Mexico, are part of the National Park System. However, the main body of the spectacular Pueblo sites of the Southwest are those of the Anasazi, who from about 700 A.D. through about 1300 A.D. developed their villages into the truly extraordinary cliff, cave, canyon, and mesa-top town-dwellings of the Southwest. After 1300, a process of withdrawal began for reasons not yet clear. Some large Anasazi villages were populated into the 1500s, but most were abandoned before the Spanish came. What remains are the large abandoned

Over a thousand years ago the Anasazi built the extraordinary dwellings of Canyon de Chelly (below). Some of the most strikingly beautiful of these are found in the canyon's Mummy Cave (opposite) and at Moca (above). At Pecos (**previous page**), not far from Santa Fe, ruins of Spanish missions stand near more recent adobe pueblos.

Anasazi towns at such places as Chaco Canyon, Mesa Verde, Canyon de Chelly, and Wupatki.

Today's Pueblo people are the direct descendants of the Anasazi; their pueblos are some of the oldest towns in the United States. One of them, Acoma Pueblo, is generally recognized as the oldest continuously inhabited settlement in the United States, having been founded in approximately 1200 A.D., some 300 years before the Europeans came.

The Anasazi towns and villages at Chaco Canyon, in New Mexico, are especially complete. Here, especially after 1000 A.D., a whole culture developed, with many towns and villages, road networks, and irrigation projects. In a sixteen-square-mile area, well over four hundred sites have been excavated, including several of the large apartment blocks that were the main feature of the Pueblo towns. Some of these have hundreds of rooms and are capable of housing well over a thousand people. The one at Pueblo Bonito, for example, is five stories high and has over eight hundred rooms. Many Great Kivas are found here, as well; these are underground religious sites, some of them fifty to seventy feet in diameter, developed from the earlier Anasazi underground pit houses.

Similarly, Mesa Verde National Park, in southwestern Arizona, contains hundreds of Anasazi pueblos, many of them built of stone and several stories high, out on the mesa tops, and others built into more easily defensible cave mouths at the heads of canyons.

At Canyon de Chelly, in Arizona, there are the remains of hundreds of pueblos; at Wupatki, also in Arizona, over eight hundred ruins have been excavated; at Aztec Ruins, in New Mexico, there is a restored Great Kiva. Throughout the Southwest, at scores of sites, archaeologists are working to uncover and better understand the remains of these great Native American cultures.

Among the red sandstone cliffs of Canyon de Chelly (right) *are literally hundreds of buildings, sometimes built in naturally sheltered spots, as in the famous Mummy Cave* (above and opposite right). *At Casa Grande, the remains of a four-story adobe building* (opposite left) *are protected from the elements by a modern shelter.*

At Wupatki (left), only ruins remain from a three-story building that once held over 100 rooms. Native Americans lived at Pecos (above), near Santa Fe, for over 500 years, until the early 19th century.

The Great Kiva at Pueblo Bonito in Chaco Canyon was a traditional underground chamber for ceremonial use. Like other kivas, it was probably covered with a wooden roof and entered—generally by men only—by means of a ladder.

The ruins at Mesa Verde **(above)** give some sense of how the multi-storied dwellings of the Pueblos once looked. Lying close to Santa Fe, in a modern mecca for artists and tourists, the Taos Pueblos **(below)** are among the best known of the surviving Native American habitations.

Santa Fe

I N THE HEART OF SANTA FE, at a specific place, three cultures and two great old American trails meet. That place is The Plaza, with its Palace of the Governors occupying the north side of the old square. Here met the Native American, Spanish, and Anglo-American cultures; here are the ends of both the Santa Fe and Chihuahua Trails.

The Palace of the Governors in Santa Fe's Plaza is the oldest continuously occupied government building in the United States. It—and the city—were founded in 1610, by Pedro de Peralta, then governor of Spanish New Mexico, as The Royal City of the Holy Faith of St. Francis of Assisi (La Villa Real de la Santa Fe de San Francisco de Asis). The site was then an old Native American village; for the next 376 years, and until today, the city has been the capital of the region, under a succession of Spanish, Mexican, and United States governors.

This is the great crossroads city of the Southwest. From the east, starting in 1821, came the Santa Fe Trail, opened up by William Becknell as a direct result of Mexico's independence from Spain. For over 200 years under Spain, the people of the region had been forced to trade south exclusively, on the old Chihuahua Trail through Mexico City to Spain. Only after independence could the new Mexican government turn toward the far shorter trading routes to the Mississippi. The Santa Fe Trail ran west from the Mississippi, near Independence, Missouri, through Council Grove and then west across the plains through Pawnee and Comanche country all the way to Santa Fe; in American folklore, it is quite properly synonymous with Kit Carson, wagon trains of prairie schooners, and the opening of the old Southwest. At Santa Fe, Americans met traders who had come north through central

Santa Fe's San Miguel Mission (below), dating from the early 1600s, is the oldest church still in use in the United States, and the San Francisco de Asis Mission Church at Ranchos de Taos (opposite), north of Santa Fe, is one of the most beautiful. The strong Spanish and Mexican influence in the area is shown in these folk dances (above) at nearby Ranchos de la Golandrinas.

Mexico by way of Durango, Santa Barbara, Chihuahua, El Paso, and Albuquerque, hugging the Rio Grande—to the Mexicans, the Rio Bravo—for water much of the way through the desert country.

Today much of old Spanish and Mexican Santa Fe remains in and around The Plaza and throughout the city. Much of the older Native American culture is also to be found, as at nearby and still occupied Taos Pueblo and throughout the Southwest.

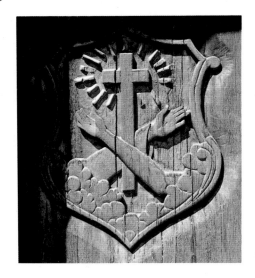

Santa Fe is the center of a whole historic region, with Spanish influence strong throughout. At Laguna **(above left)** *the handcarved door* **(above right)** *testifies to the church's Christian mission. Near Gran Quivira, at Salinas, ruins of pueblos and Spanish missions* **(below)** *lie side by side.*

Throughout the year Santa Fe is home to many fiestas and festivals, some commemorating historic dates, others celebrating seasonal events with Native American dances **(below)** *and the occasional burning of ceremonial effigies* **(above).**

The Alamo

SAM HOUSTON WAS AN ASTUTE LEADER of his people. Early in the Texas War of Independence, he learned that a Mexican army of several thousand men, with artillery, commanded by General Antonio Lopez de Santa Anna, was marching north to reclaim Texas for Mexico. Houston ordered Colonel William B. Travis, commander of The Alamo, to abandon and burn the fortress with his garrison of a little over 150 men and retreat to join the main Texas force. Houston's small army numbered, in all, less than a thousand men; even the tiny force in The Alamo was significant to such an army.

Travis did no such thing. Instead, with the agreement of Colonel Jim Bowie and frontiersman Davy Crockett, he sent out a call for more men to augment his small band of volunteers. Thirty-two men responded, leaving his force at still under 200 men. Travis and the others then set about defending The Alamo—by agreement among themselves, to the last man.

The place in which they decided to die had started its own life as the first Franciscan mission in San Antonio, Mission San Antonio de Valero, built in 1718. It was fortified and became a military post near the turn of the 18th century, acting as a Mexican military headquarters during the Mexican revolution against Spain. When revolution broke out in Texas, in 1835, Texans seized and garrisoned The Alamo.

Travis, Bowie, Crockett, and the other Texans did die there at The Alamo, to the last man. After a siege lasting thirteen days, with substantial casualties on both sides, The Alamo fell, its defenders fighting until the end. No quarter was asked; no quarter was given. And so The Alamo and its defenders passed into Texas history.

Once a church, now a shrine, The Alamo (above and opposite)—named after the native cottonwood, or álamo, trees—draws visitors from all over the United States. The former convent is now the Long Barrack Museum (below), preserved in the heart of San Antonio. Split Rock (overleaf) marked the Oregon Trail for many travelers on the way west.

Sam Houston, then very astutely using "Remember the Alamo!" as a rallying cry, proceeded to build his very small force, while retreating before Santa Anna's larger army. Six weeks later, on the Rio San Jacinto, near what would later be Houston, his force of 800 men surprised the Mexican army, attacking and killing 800 men and capturing 200 more, while themselves losing only 6 dead and 30 wounded. Within a day, they had captured Santa Anna and 700 more Mexican soldiers. It was an utterly decisive victory, and essentially won the Texas Revolution.

Today, The Alamo and San Jacinto Battlefield are both National Historic Landmarks, while The Alamo is by far the best-known historic site in Texas.

SPLIT ROCK

A famous natural landmark used by Indians, trappers, and emigrants on the Oregon trail.

Site of Split Rock pony express 1860-1861, stage, and telegraph station is on the south side of the Sweetwater.

Split Rock can be seen as a cleft in the top of the Rattlesnake Range.

Erected by the Historical Landmark Commission of Wyoming 1956

MOUNTAIN AND PLAIN

Springfield

When lilacs last in the dooryard bloom'd,
And the great star early droop'd in the western sky in the night,
I mourn'd, and yet shall mourn with ever-returning spring.

Ever-returning spring, trinity sure to me you bring,
Lilac blooming perennial and drooping star in the west,
And thought of him I love.

O powerful western fallen star!
O shades of night—O moody, tearful night!
O great star disappear'd—O the black murk that hides the star!
O cruel hands that hold me powerless—O helpless soul of me!
O harsh surrounding cloud that will not free my soul.

from When Lilacs Last in the
Dooryard Bloom'd,
by Walt Whitman

AFTER HIS ASSASSINATION AT FORD'S THEATRE, Abraham Lincoln's body was returned here, to his home in Springfield. He, his wife, and three of their four sons are buried here at Lincoln's Tomb, in Oak Ridge Cemetery, which was completed in 1874.

His home, the only home Lincoln ever owned, is also here, and has been preserved as a national historic site, along with the four surrounding blocks. It was purchased in 1844, from Reverend Charles Dresser, who had married Abraham and Mary Todd Lincoln. Their four sons were born here. The Lincolns lived in this house between 1844 and 1861, with a year away during his term in Congress, in 1847 and 1848. In this house, he received word of his presidential nomination in 1860; from this house, he conducted his presidential campaign. He left Springfield to assume the Presidency on February 11, 1861; only his body came home again.

Lincoln's Springfield house (opposite) was a far cry from the log cabin that was his birthplace. The sitting room (above) was furnished and decorated in a manner befitting a rising politician, though the kitchen (left), with its spare furniture and central stove for cooking and heating, still retained some of the essential simplicity always associated with Lincoln.

Mount Rushmore

FOUR HUGE SCULPTURES —the faces of Abraham Lincoln, George Washington, Thomas Jefferson, and Theodore Roosevelt—are carved into the smooth granite of 6,000-foot-high Mount Rushmore. This is the masterwork of sculptor Gutzon Borglum, whose other work includes the large head of Lincoln in the rotunda of the Capitol in Washington and the huge unfinished Confederate monument at Stone Mountain, Georgia.

The work was conceived by South Dakota historian Doane Robinson as a monument to Western heroes; Borglum's conception was that of a massive set of sculptures dedicated to the four presidents. The state and federal governments recognized the site as a national memorial and Borglum dedicated the site on October 1, 1925. He then turned to the task of fundraising, and actually started work two years later, in 1927. But there were money problems, and he stopped work within a few months; the work resumed only after a Congressional appropriation had been secured, in February 1929.

Washington's face was unveiled on July 4, 1930. Six years later, President Franklin D. Rossevelt traveled to Mount Rushmore to dedicate Jefferson's image. Lincoln was dedicated in September 1937; Theodore Roosevelt in July 1939. Borglum felt that the work was not yet finished, though, and continued to work at the site, aiming to carve a huge hall of records into the interior of the mountain, reached by an enormous flight of steps. He died in 1941, with that part of the work undone, but his masterwork remains.

These four sculpted faces **(above)**—*Washington, Jefferson, Teddy Roosevelt* **(opposite inset)**, *and Lincoln* **(opposite)**—*have made Mount Rushmore famous.*

Mackinac

THE STRAITS OF MACKINAC, joining the northern ends of Lakes Michigan and Huron, lie between Upper and Lower Michigan, south of Sault Ste. Marie. From the late 17th century until the end of the War of 1812, this was one of the most highly strategic and hotly contested areas in North America, first between the French and the British, and later between British Canada and the new American nation.

The French were the first Europeans to come in force, from the east along the Great Lakes and then south on the Mississippi River. French explorers and traders were in the American heartland of the continent almost a century before the British colonists, now become Americans, began to move west through the Appalachians into the Ohio River valley and then beyond to the Mississippi. By 1720, the French had completed Fort Michilimackinac, on the south shore of the straits, at the present site of Mackinaw City. The British took that fort during the French and Indian War, lost it in 1763 during Pontiac's War, and occupied it again in 1764. In 1781, fearing American attack, they moved their headquarters to the more easily defensible Mackinac Island. The island and its fort passed to the Americans after the Revolution, was taken back by the British during the War of 1812, and finally passed back to the United States in 1815.

From 1812-1830, during the great early years of the fur trade, John Jacob Astor's American Fur Company was head-quartered on Mackinac Island. Late in the 19th century, the island became a very popular summer resort, as it still is today.

Native Americans called Mackinac Island **(opposite)** the "great turtle" for its mound-like shape. Over four-fifths of the island is now a national park, and the Grand Hotel **(below)** and many well-kept Victorian homes **(above)** testify to its popularity as a resort.

South Pass

THE SOUTH PASS was the way west through the Rocky Mountains for hundreds of thousands of emigrants on the Oregon and California Trails. Through this great pass came Oregon and California settlers, goldseekers, Mormons, overland freighters, soldiers, preachers, gamblers, prostitutes, lawmen, outlaws, and all the others who settled the American West in the last half of the 19th century.

This is the Sweetwater River valley, a 20-mile-wide, 7,500-foot-high pass through the mountains, with a grade so gentle that many did not even know when they had reached the top of the pass—which is also the crest of the Continental Divide—and were beginning to descend on the other side. For wagons and walkers the South Pass is by far the best pass through the northern Rockies. Discovered by Jedediah Smith, it is also the main entry point into the old Oregon Territory; when travelers were through South Pass, they were up out of the Great Plains and into the West, about halfway between the Missouri and the Pacific, and well on their way to their final destinations. All of them went through the Pass; after that, some forked to Oregon, some to California, and some to the Mormon country of the Great Salt Lake. In later years, some went shorter distances, settling in the mountain country itself.

Today South Pass is a national historic landmark, though it is no longer an active link in the routes from Atlantic to Pacific. The transcontinental railroad took a different route in the late 19th century, as did the transcontinental highways of the 20th century. The old Oregon Trail, traversing a thousand miles of flat and rolling country from the Missouri River and along the Platte River to the Rockies is no more. The thousand miles beyond,

either through the Rockies and Cascades to Fort Vancouver and Oregon's Willamette valley, or across the Rockies, the desert, and the Sierras to Sacramento, is partly paralleled by modern highways, but is no longer a single main route. What remains, in South Pass and other such places on the Oregon Trail, is the memory of the way west, and the completion of the long journey from Jamestown and Plymouth Rock to the Pacific.

Passing through the Sweetwater Valley **(above)**, *the South Pass took the Oregon Trail—and thousands of westward travelers—easily through the Rocky Mountains. Along the way there grew up towns like South Pass City* **(opposite)** *and Atlantic City* **(below)**; *some later became ghost towns, like Miner's Delight* **(above inset).**

The Little Bighorn

ON JUNE 25, 1876, in Montana's Little Bighorn River valley, Lt. Col. George Armstrong Custer, leading about one-third of the Seventh Cavalry, made the literally fatal error of attacking a considerable portion of the Sioux and Cheyenne nations. The forces he attacked numbered in all somewhere between 4,000 and 5,000 of the finest light cavalry in the world, rested and ready to fight. His own force consisted of 220 exhausted troopers on equally exhausted mounts; as a direct result, he and his small force were annihilated.

Exactly how Custer's last fight ended is not clearly known, as none survived to tell that part of the story. How it started was with greed for gold.

In 1875, after a gold strike, the federal government had reneged on existing treaties and thrown the sacred Black Hills of the Sioux open to mining and prospecting, making armed clashes inevitable. Many Sioux then left their reservations, moving farther west to join those in the Powder River country. The government insisted that they return to their reservations; when they refused, the army moved against them. In the ensuing campaign, Custer's Seventh Cavalry was sent on ahead to the Little Bighorn valley, with instructions not to engage, but rather to wait for the slower-moving infantry, artillery, and additional cavalry to arrive. But on reaching the Little Bighorn valley, and being sighted by Sioux scouts, Custer decided to attack immediately. While six companies were sent in two different directions, Custer himself led the remaining five companies into a confrontation with thousands of enemy cavalry. They were attacked in a series of small company-sized actions, ultimately being dismounted and slaughtered to the last man on what is now known as Custer Hill. The remainder of

*The I company cemetery **(above)** lies between Calhoun Ridge and Custer Hill **(above inset)**, where Custer's final stand was made and many who died in the action are buried. For years Native Americans called those who preserved the site **(opposite)** "ghost herders."*

the Seventh Cavalry ultimately rejoined forces and held their ground until relieved the next day by the forces that Custer had chosen not to wait for. This was the battle that has since been glorified in song and story as Custer's Last Stand.

The Sioux and Cheyenne could not long stand against the American army. Within two years, most had surrendered, been killed, or fled north of the border to Canada. Today the site is the Custer Battlefield National Monument.

Wounded Knee

THE "BATTLE" OF WOUNDED KNEE was precisely what the Sioux, General Nelson Miles, and many others called it at the time—a massacre. On Wounded Knee Creek, at the Pine Ridge Sioux Reservation in South Dakota, on December 29, 1890, five hundred American cavalry, with cannon, annihilated a captive Sioux band under their dying chief, Big Foot. Afterward, the soldiers counted 153 Sioux dead and 44 wounded, but Sioux casualties were higher, the Sioux having removed many of their dead and wounded before the soldiers began their count. The army reported 29 dead and 44 wounded, making no estimate of how many of these casualties were caused by the army's firing into the camp while their own cavalry was attacking it.

What is clear is that the entire Seventh Cavalry, with an artillery detachment, commanded by Colonel James W. Forsyth, had turned the easy task of disarming an already-captive Sioux band, numbering 230 women and children and 120 men, into a massacre. During the disarming, a single shot was fired from a Sioux rifle, probably accidentally. The soldiers surrounding the camp then opened fire on the Sioux, as did the artillery on the hill overlooking the camp. As men, women, and children fled, they were pursued by the troopers, who killed them indiscriminately. At the end of the "battle," the soldiers buried the Sioux in a mass grave. Later General Miles, commander of the United States forces in the area—who was at that time involved in the series of engagements with the Sioux called the Ghost Dance wars—preferred charges against Colonel Forsyth, who was then exonerated by an army court of inquiry.

In a wider sense, this was the last battle of the last Indian war . . . or perhaps of the single long war that had started over 400 years earlier, at Roanoke Island and Jamestown. That war was at first between the Native Americans and the English and then between the Native Americans and the new Americans who invaded and ultimately colonized the entire area of what is now the mainland United States.

Today Wounded Knee is part of the Oglala Sioux Reservation. The Big Foot Massacre Memorial, erected by the Sioux in 1903, stands over the mass grave of those Native Americans who died at Wounded Knee.

A simple monument **(opposite),** *surrounded by an unassuming metal fence* **(above),** *marks the mass grave of many of the Native Americans who were killed at Wounded Knee.*

Deadwood

WITHIN A YEAR OF CUSTER'S DEFEAT at the Little Bighorn, and while the Sioux and Cheyenne were still fighting the United States army, tens of thousands of prospectors had poured into the Black Hills, seeking and finding gold. These were the sacred Black Hills of the Sioux—of Sitting Bull, Gall, and the great cavalry commander and war chief, Crazy Horse, but by the spring of 1876, Deadwood alone was a town of over 7,000 and one of the prototypical boom towns of the West. In and around Deadwood and Lead, only three miles away, were at least fifty working gold mines, including the Homestake mine, one of the richest strikes in history, and the greatest mine in the territory.

This was the Deadwood of Wild Bill Hickok, and of Calamity Jane, both of whom are buried in Deadwood's Mount Moriah cemetery. But it is more than that; Deadwood is typical of all the little mining boomtowns of the West, so many of them now ghost towns. Tombstone, Cripple Creek, Placerville, Nevada City, and scores of other towns sprang up overnight on news of a strike, had their brief heyday as the mines were worked and then played out, and then all but disappeared, a few to be revived mainly as tourist attractions. Among them, Deadwood is rare, for it has survived as a small, but working town, with some of its original buildings and its famous cemetery intact.

The bygone days of gold strikes and boom towns are celebrated in Deadwood with annual parades (above) and the Adams Memorial Museum (below). Many who did not survive those times, including Wild Bill Hickok, ended up in Deadwood's version of "Boot Hill," Mt. Moriah Cemetery (opposite).

THE PACIFIC

Point Loma

POINT LOMA, the long, high ridge of land jutting out into the Pacific Ocean at San Diego Bay, is one of the most beautiful places in the world. It is also the site of Cabrillo National Monument. Here, in September 1542, came the Portuguese navigator Juan Rodríguez Cabrillo, seeking the mythical island called California, earlier sought by Hernando Cortés. He sought also that elusive northern passage that was said to link the Atlantic and Pacific oceans, known to many generations of explorers as the Northwest Passage. What he discovered instead was the coast of California—known to the Spanish as Alta (Upper) California.

Cabrillo sailed north along the coast of Mexico out of Navidad, near modern Acapulco, in two small Spanish ships, the *San Salvador* and the *Victoria*, becoming the first European to enter San Diego Bay, which he called San Miguel Bay. With their ships anchored behind Point Loma, Cabrillo's landing parties explored the region around the present-day San Diego harbor, although they were attacked by local Native Americans. His ships then sailed north along the California coast, making landfall in many places, as far as what is now southern Oregon. Cabrillo himself died en route, at San Miguel Island, in 1543.

Cabrillo National Monument commemorates that earliest California coast landing; the national monument area also includes the San Diego Lighthouse, dating from 1855.

At Point Loma, the most southwesterly part of mainland United States, a monument **(above)** *honors its European discoverer Juan Rodriguez Cabrillo. Today visitors often congregate near Point Loma's 1855 lighthouse* **(opposite inset)** *or on the shore below it* **(opposite)** *to watch the whale migrations. Russians, too, settled on the Pacific shore, as at Fort Ross* **(previous pages).**

The California Missions

A COASTAL STRING OF twenty-one Franciscan (later Dominican) missions and a few small military garrisons allowed Spain to develop a fragile hold on early California, and gave the region some of its distinctive character and style. The role of the missions was twofold: to convert—and often enslave—the local Native American population, and to provide a series of lodgings, roughly one day's journey apart, for travelers and traders between Mexico and Alta (Upper) California. To those ends, Father Junipero Serra and Captain Gaspar de Portolá led an expedition out of Baja (Lower) California in the spring of 1769, blazing a fresh trail along the coast; others had tried before, by sea, but heavy coastal winds made the ocean route very difficult. When they reached San Diego (visited over two centuries earlier by Juan Cabrillo), de Portolá went on, north along the coast to Monterey, on the path that would later be the California Mission Trail, while Serra stayed behind to found the first of the missions, Mission San Diego de Alcala. His second was the mission located first at the Presidio in Monterey in 1770 and then relocated as the Mission San Carlos Borromeo del Rio Carmelo to its present site in Carmel in 1771; this was Father Serra's headquarters and, in 1784, his burial place. Others carried on the work of extending the chain of missions.

Spanish control was not to last long in California; it took 44 years to build the missions, from the founding of the first one at San Diego in 1769 to the completion of the last, at Sonoma, in 1823. Only 23 years later, the "Bear Flag Revolt" of the American settlers in northern California ushered in the period of United States control.

The stained glass window (above) *at the Mission Dolores Basilica in San Francisco honors Father Junipero Serra, who opened the California Mission Trail. Father Serra's home mission and burial place is the beautiful mission at Carmel* (opposite).

Today the missions serve to link California with its Spanish past. Many have been restored, such as the Mission San Luis Rey de Francia, in Oceanside. Eighteenth and largest of all California missions, it was known as the "King of Missions." Father Serra's Mission San Carlos Borromeo at Carmel has also been restored, as has the Santa Barbara Mission, destroyed by the massive earthquake in 1925. The La Purisma Concepcion Mission, near Lompoc, is one of the best restored of the missions.

The mission at Carmel (left) is the site of many festivities honoring the region's Spanish past.

The Mission San Carlos Borromeo del Rio Carmelo (below) at Carmel was founded by Father Junipero Serra in 1770 and served as headquarters for all the California missions.

The Mission San Miguel Arcangel **(above)**, *founded in 1797 as the 16th in California's mission chain, was noted for its healing mineral waters.*

The white-sided, red-roofed adobe construction of the Mission San Juan Bautista **(above, left and right)**, *with its graceful Spanish arches, was typical of the California mission style.*

The Mission San Diego de Alcala **(below)**, dating from 1769, was the first of the California missions founded by Father Junipero Serra himself, while the Mission San Buenaventura **(above)** was the ninth and last, founded in 1782.

Founded in 1776, the Mission San Francisco de Asis **(below)**, *now known as the Mission Dolores, is somewhat dwarfed by the towers of the modern Basilica, with its fine windows* **(above)**, *this one of St. Francis.*

Monterey

MONTEREY WAS THE CAPITAL of Spanish, later Mexican, Alta (Upper) California, from its founding in 1770 to its capture by Commodore John Sloat's American squadron in 1846.

Monterey Bay and its peninsula were sighted by Juan Cabrillo, sailing north on the California coast in 1546. He did not land there; the first to do so may have been Spanish Captain Sebastián Vizcaíno, who in 1602 quite erroneously described Monterey Bay as "all that can be desired as a harbor . . . surrounded by settlements of friendly Indians . . . with plenty of food and water."

It remained for Captial Gaspar de Portolá, breaking a new trail north 168 years later, to explore Monterey. In 1770, he and Father Junipero Serra founded the Presidio and a mission in Monterey. Father Serra moved the mission to its present location in Carmel the following year; the Presidio and its garrison remained in Monterey, which soon became the capital of Alta California.

Monterey today possesses a substantial set of historic sites. The Old Custom House, where Sloat raised the American flag, is the oldest public building in California. The restored Mission San Carlos Borromeo del Rio Carmelo nearby was Father Serra's headquarters and home mission. The Royal Presidio Chapel is the only surviving portion of the original Monterey Presidio.

When Monterey was the capital of California, whalers and traders were guided into the bay by Point Pinos lighthouse (opposite) and brought their trade goods to the Custom House (above), which dates from 1827. Today several of Monterey's historic homes are open to the public, this one (below) having been specially decorated for Christmas.

Fort Ross

O N THE NORTHERN CALIFORNIA COAST, a little way north of Russian River, stands a restoration of Fort Ross. This marks the southernmost penetration of the Russian Empire into North America.

For over three centuries, French, British, Canadian, and American explorers, trappers, and traders moved west in North America, following and progressively exhausting the supply of fur-bearing animals. During the same three centuries, Russian explorers, trappers, and traders moved east, across the whole face of Eurasia, following the fur trade to the Pacific. By 1639, they had reached the Pacific, and by the mid-1700s were voyaging to Alaska. By 1804, they had founded Sitka. Moving swiftly, and by now with the Russian-American Company in full control of exploration and settlement, they began to trap and trade south, following the sea otter supply they were so rapidly depleting in Alaska. The result was the founding of Fort Stawianski in 1812 and its completion in 1814. The Spanish called it *El Fuertos de los Russos,* which the English and Americans transmuted to its present name: Fort Ross.

Fort Ross was considerably more than a fur trading and some-time farming center. Like the Hudson's Bay Company forts in Canada, it was both a trading post and an outpost of empire. The Russian-American Company was chartered by the czar and included members of the czar's family and other high nobility in its directorate. Fort Ross was a very substantial post for its time and place, housing as many as four hundred Russians, Aleuts, and local Native Americans, and containing fifty cannon. The Spanish government viewed this Russian penetration into California with alarm, as did the British and American governments.

California shows Russian influence, a heritage celebrated in the reconstruction of Fort Ross's Russian Orthodox chapel **(above)** *and its seven-sided blockhouse* **(opposite).** *Some original artifacts, like this mill stone* **(below),** *also remain.*

Ultimately, the Russian trappers used up much of the local sea otter population, as they had in Alaska. Nor was the farming the Russians attempted productive; this section of the California coast is, for many reasons, rather inhospitable to agriculture. Most importantly, the Russian Empire decided to withdraw from the Americas, under heavy British and American pressure. In 1841, the Russians sold Fort Ross and other lands to John Augustus Sutter for $30,000 in cash and goods and left California. Sutter, in turn, mounted twelve of the Russian cannon from Fort Ross on the walls of his fort in Sacramento; they are there yet.

Sutter's Fort

SUTTER AND GOLD. The name of the man and the California Gold Rush are inextricably intertwined. Old Sutter's Fort, now in the heart of modern Sacramento, and built by John Augustus Sutter in 1839, was the main takeoff point for the tens of thousands of Forty-Niners who poured into California after gold was discovered at Sutter's Mill in Coloma, only eight miles away.

It was Sutter's need for lumber that triggered the gold strike. In January, 1848, at Sutter's new mill on the American River, mill-wright James Marshall picked up a gold nugget in the millrace. He reported the find to Sutter, and the two men decided to keep the strike a secret. Within a very short while, the find was a secret no more, and goldseekers began to pour into the area.

Sutter's Fort and old Sacramento signify much more than gold, for here also was the end of the California fork of the great Oregon-California Trail, which started almost two thousand miles away, on the Missouri River. The Oregon-California overland migration had started a few years before the Gold Rush; when the Gold Rush was over, the migrants kept on coming, in long wagon trains and by the hundreds of thousands, over the Great Plains, the Rockies, and the Sierras to California. This was the main way west, on the long road that, over two and a half centuries, led from Jamestown and Plymouth to the Pacific.

At Marshall Gold Discovery State Historic Park in Placerville, where James Marshall first discovered traces of gold, are a working replica of Sutter's Mill (bottom left), Marshall's cabin (bottom right), and a marker (left) commemorating the event. Soon after the gold strike, Forty-Niners were gathering at Sutter's Fort (opposite) in nearby Sacramento. Parts of old Sacramento (above) have been preserved or reconstructed to show how it was when the Gold Rush first made the city a boom town and capital of California.

Fort Vancouver

FORT VANCOUVER is properly seen as a shared Canadian-American historic place, for it is located today in the United States, but is mainly important in the history of the Canadian way west and the Canadian fur trade.

Fort Vancouver is in Vancouver, Washington, across the Columbia River from Portland, Oregon. Before the British-American Oregon Treaty of 1846, which fixed the border at its present position far to the north, this fort was the great western fur trading outpost of the Hudson's Bay Company, and a center of the political, economic, and cultural life of the Canadian Far West.

In the 1820s, 1830s and 1840s Hudson's Bay Company chief factor and fort commander John McLoughlin built Fort Vancouver into by far the largest fur trading post on the Pacific coast, in the face of major American competition. At the same time, he was extraordinarily hospitable to the American settlers who began moving into the Oregon country in the 1840s; indeed, his Hudson's Bay Company superior, George Simpson, accused McLoughlin of encouraging them and of being pro-American. But as American settlers moved into the territory in larger numbers, friction grew between British and Americans, and between Native Americans and the new American settlers. In time, the 1846 treaty resolved the situation; with it, Fort Vancouver was abandoned by the British, who moved their operations farther north. It later became a United States army installation and then the restored national historic site it is today.

At Fort Vancouver National Historic Site, many buildings have been reconstructed, including the bastion (left). The Ulysses S. Grant house (above), where the future Civil War general and United States president headquartered in the early 1850s, has been kept as a museum.

Sitka

Sitka's harbor (above), once thronged by trans-Pacific trading ships, is now home to many sightseeing and fishing boats. Totem poles (opposite) by local Tlingit artists are displayed in a woodland setting; in Sitka itself, a popular statue (below), "The Prospector," celebrates the pioneers who helped build Alaska.

FOR SIXTY-THREE YEARS SITKA —in those years named New Archangel—was the main center of Russian power in the New World. It was the base from which the Russian Empire ruled Alaska and the Aleutians, exploring and colonizing as far south as Fort Ross, on the California coast north of San Francisco. The city is in southeastern Alaska, on Baronof Island in the Alexander Archipelago, and enjoys both the warm Pacific Current and shelter from the mountains to the north.

In 1799, with the chartering of the Russian-American Company by the czar, further Russian expansion eastward from the earlier base on Kodiak Island began. That year, Alexander Baronof, the company's manager, founded Fort St. Michael, a few miles north of present Sitka; it was destroyed and its inhabitants massacred by the local Tlingit people in 1802. In 1804, Baronof came again, with a stronger force, defeated the Tlingits (the battle site is now Sitka National Monument), and re-established the colony as New Archangel, which two years later became capital of Russian America.

New Archangel became a substantial Russian town and a chief port of call for ships engaged in the China trade, for Alaskan sea otter skins and other furs fetched substantial prices in China, and the trade was therefore enormously profitable. In Sitka were the Governor's residence, occupied by Baronof until his retirement in 1818; St. Michael's Cathedral; and a substantial number of warehouses, foundries, and port facilities.

In 1867, New Archangel passed to the United States with all of Alaska, and from then until 1900, now called Sitka, it was the territorial capital.

Skagway

GOLD MADE SKAGWAY. This is the gateway to the Yukon and to the great Klondike gold strike of 1896-1898. Only the slightest of settlements before the Klondike strike, Skagway was by 1898 a lawless boomtown of 15,000-20,000 people, all in some way connected with Klondike gold.

Skagway is a port city at the northern end of the Lynn Canal, about 75 miles northwest of Juneau. It is a warm water port, and the natural means of entry into the Klondike region, over either the White or Chilkoot passes. The White Pass route was the one favored by the railroad; in 1900, the White Pass and Yukon Railway was completed and is still in use today. The town is in use, as well, as a shipping and supply center for miners and trappers.

It is also in use as a major living museum of North America's mining frontier. In Skagway are over one hundred structures built in gold rush days, including the still-used narrow gauge railway through the 45-mile-long White Pass, the railway depot, many commercial buildings, and the old Federal Court building, now a museum.

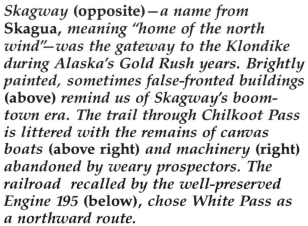

Skagway **(opposite)**—*a name from* **Skagua,** *meaning "home of the north wind"—was the gateway to the Klondike during Alaska's Gold Rush years. Brightly painted, sometimes false-fronted buildings* **(above)** *remind us of Skagway's boom-town era. The trail through Chilkoot Pass is littered with the remains of canvas boats* **(above right)** *and machinery* **(right)** *abandoned by weary prospectors. The railroad recalled by the well-preserved Engine 195* **(below)**, *chose White Pass as a northward route.*

Pearl Harbor

FOR AMERICANS, the war that was to end in Berlin and Tokyo began here, with the massive disaster that was the Japanese attack on Pearl Harbor, on December 7, 1941.

The disaster might have been much worse in net effect, had the aircraft carriers in the American fleet also been berthed at Pearl Harbor at the time of the attack. Had those few carriers and their airplanes been destroyed, the entire course of World War II and of world history might have been quite different.

It was bad enough. Of the eight battleships jammed together and wholly unable to maneuver in the crowded harbor, seven were sunk and one severely damaged, and ten other ships were sunk or destroyed. There were 2,400 American dead, 2,100 of them on the *Arizona*. Of the 394 aircraft on Oahu, 188 were destroyed and 159 more damaged. The Japanese navy lost 29 planes; at this very small cost, it had gained superiority in the whole Pacific basin, making the invasion of the Philippines, all of southeast Asia, and the Pacific islands possible. After Pearl Harbor, it was going to be a long, long war.

Today Pearl Harbor is a national historic landmark; the *Arizona* Monument stands as a memorial to the Americans who died there.

For Americans, Pearl Harbor **(below)** is forever associated with the Japanese attack of December 7, 1941. The more than two thousand sailors killed on the **Arizona** alone are honored in the Arizona Memorial **(opposite)**. A more peaceful and pleasant image of Hawaii is given by Oahu's famous Diamond Head **(above)**, near Waikiki Beach and Honolulu.

CANADA

L'Anse Aux Meadows

HERE, ON THE NORTHERN TIP OF NEWFOUNDLAND, facing the Strait of Belle Isle, at the entrance to the great waterway into the heart of North America, is the oldest European settlement so far discovered on the main body of the continent. It is the Norse settlement at L'Anse Aux Meadows, dating back to the 11th century A.D., almost 1,000 years ago—to the time of Eric the Red and of Leif, his son. It was Leif Ericson who, four centuries before Columbus, sailed from Greenland to the land he called Vinland, long supposed to be the mainland of North America.

We may never know precisely where Vinland was, but the L'Anse Aux Meadows site makes it clear that the Norse did indeed visit—and settle—on the mainland in those years. The L'Anse Aux Meadows National Historic Park is not only a great Canadian or even North American historic place, but also a world historic place as well; it was the first site to be placed on UNESCO's World Heritage List.

The L'Anse Aux Meadows settlement discovered by Helge Ingstad and George Decker in 1960 consists of eight buildings, similar to Norse buildings in Greenland and Iceland of the 11th century. Archaeologists have found a wide variety of Norse artifacts—knitting needles, spindle whorls, a bronze pin, stone oil lamp, rivets and wood debris from the Norse shipwrights' workshop, slag from their ironmaking furnaces (found in three of the eight buildings), and a great deal more. This was in all probability a ship repair and reprovisioning place, implying that Norse ships were in that period exploring much farther, south along the Newfoundland coast and perhaps through the Strait of Belle Isle into the Gulf of St. Lawrence and beyond, as Jacques Cartier was to do four centuries later, during the second European exploration of North America.

Based on the results of their "digs" nearby, archaeologists have reconstructed three Viking-style sod houses (above and previous pages) at L'Anse Aux Meadows, on the shores of northernmost Newfoundland.

Built of turf taken from the grassy plain around them, the sod roofs of the houses at L'Anse Aux Meadows sprout flowers in the springtime (above). Inside (below) they are furnished with replicas of articles that archaeologists actually found on the site.

Quebec

QUEBEC IS BY FAR the greatest of French Canada's historic places. New France was born here in 1608, when Samuel de Champlain established his trading post, a Habitation much like the one he and Sieur Pierre De Monts had founded at Port Royal three years earlier. New France died here 151 years later, on the Plains of Abraham.

Quebec has been aptly called the "Gibraltar of America;" its great rock dominates this place where the St. Lawrence River narrows sharply before broadening out again a little beyond. The name *Quebec* in fact means "narrowing of the river." Jacques Cartier passed here in 1535, landing near the Huron village of Stadacona. He named the rock, on which Quebec's Upper Town would later be built, Cape Diamond.

Champlain's Habitation was the beginning of Quebec's Lower Town, which has always been the center of the commercial life of the city. The Upper Town, on Cape Diamond, has been the military and administrative center. It was on Cape Diamond that Champlain built Fort St. Louis in 1620, near what is now Dufferin Terrace (to the French Canadians, *Terrasse Dufferin*). But in 1629, an English expedition besieged and took the city; this was only the first of the long series of military actions that were to reach a climax on the Plains of Abraham.

The first missionaries arrived in 1615; the first farmer-colonist, Louis Hébert, in 1619; the first school was opened by the Ursuline nuns in 1639. The first bishop, Francois-Xavier de Laval, came in 1859, and it was he who established the Quebec Seminary, in 1663. Quebec was still a very small place, but it was also by then the heart of New France—and a target for attack by British colonial rivals. In 1690, a New England fleet commanded

Fortifications and Quebec go hand in hand, as above at the Gate St.-Jean. At the Place Royale (opposite), in the Lower Town, many 18th and 19th-century buildings are being restored.

by Massachusetts governor Sir William Phipps attacked Quebec, but was repulsed by Governor Frontenac's forces. In 1711, a British fleet headed for Quebec was wrecked in heavy fog on the St. Lawrence River.

In 1759, during the worldwide Seven Years War—known to the British North American colonies as the French and Indian War—the final battle came. Having already taken the fort at Louisbourg, a British fleet, carrying an army under the command of General James Wolfe, was able to enter the St. Lawrence to attack Quebec. It arrived off Quebec City on June 25 and laid siege to the city. By July 12, British guns were firing on the city from the heights across the narrow river. During July, August, and early September, Wolfe found himself unable to cross the river, scale the cliffs on the other side, and engage the French, under the command of the Marquis de Montcalm. But on September 9 the British located the dry streambed called L'Anse au Foulon, ascending the cliffs on the French side of the river. On the night of September 12, an advance party took the French guards atop the cliffs, and then Wolfe's army moved up to the Plains of Abraham, where an astonished Montcalm found them the next morning.

The resulting battle took only a few minutes. The British regulars stood their ground under French fire. The French, mostly militiamen, advanced, took severe casualties from two British rifle volleys, and then were defeated when the British regulars charged. Wolfe died on the field of

battle; Montcalm died the next day, of battlefield wounds.

And so ended New France. The French army later regrouped, beat the British garrison at Sainte-Foy in the spring, and then themselves laid siege to the city. But it was too late. A British fleet raised the siege, and that summer a large British army took ill-defended Montreal without a fight. In North America, the war was over, and the British were—for sixteen short years, until the American Revolution—in control of all of Atlantic North American north of Florida.

New France was gone; French Canada remained, as it has ever since. Quebec City today is still the foremost center of French Canadian life and achievement and is easily recognized as a unique city in North America. The city has preserved its past; the whole old city is a historic place, with several major areas designated as such. At the Place Royale, site of Champlain's second Habitation, built in 1824, there is a major restoration of the 17th- and 18th-century structures. At Cartier-Brébeuf National Historical Park, there is a full size replica of one of Cartier's three ships, *La Grande Hermine*.

Up on the Plains of Abraham is the National Battlefields of Quebec National Historical Park, while atop the great rock of Cape Diamond is the Citadel, built by the British in the 1820s on the site of earlier French fortifications. Throughout the old city, in Upper Town and Lower Town alike, French Canada's past still lives.

At the Citadel on Cap Diamant, first fortified in 1693, visitors can still see the Changing of the Guard (opposite), *at least during the summer months. It was on these wide Plains of Abraham* (above) *that the French lost North America to the British. Small, very old churches abound in and around Quebec, such as this one* (left) *at La Vieille Eglise.*

Built on the site of a chapel dating back to 1658, the Basilica of Sainte-Anne-de-Beaupré **(opposite)**, *just outside Quebec, is regarded as the oldest place of pilgrimage in North America. The interior of the Basilica* **(above)** *has been given much rich and fine detail, such as the stained glass windows, painted statue* **(inset right)** *and the carved pews* **(inset left)**.

Annapolis Royal

PORT ROYAL, now Annapolis Royal, occupies a major place in the shared French and British heritage of the Canadian nation. Here in 1605 came Samuel de Champlain and Sieur Pierre de Monts, to establish Port Royal, one of the first successful European settlements in North America, and the first successful French settlement in Canada. The small fort they built then they called The Habitation; three years later, Champlain was to establish Quebec City with a similar Habitation.

The original Port Royal, built on the north side of Annapolis basin, lasted only until 1613, when it was destroyed by Captain Samuel Argall's Virginia expedition. In 1635, a new French fortress was built, this time on the south side of the Annapolis basin, the site of the present Annapolis Royal. For the next three-quarters of a century, it was one of the most hotly disputed places in North America, being taken and retaken by French and British forces again and again. From 1667 until the final capture by the British in 1710, it was the capital of French Acadia. From 1710 until 1749, it was the capital of British Nova Scotia.

In 1938-1939, the original Habitation at Port Royal was reconstructed, to Champlains' original plan, and is now Port Royal National Historic Park.

Across the basin, at Annapolis Royal, the fortress, renamed Fort Anne by the British, is Canada's oldest National Historic Park.

In the late 1930s, archaeologists reconstructed The Habitation at Port Royal **(above)** on the basis of surviving records and remains, recreating the simple, sparse lifestyle **(below)** of the time. Today guides in period dress **(opposite)** show visitors around this replica of the oldest successful French settlement in North America.

Grand Pré

*This is the forest primeval; but where are the hearts that beneath it
Leaped like the roe, when he hears in the woodland the voice of the
   huntsman?
Where is the thatch-roofed village, the home of Acadian farmers . . .
Waste are those pleasant farms, and the farmers forever departed!
Scattered like dust and leaves, when the mighty blasts of October
Seize them, and whirl them aloft, and sprinkle them far o'er the
   ocean.
Naught but tradition remains of the beautiful village of Grand-Pré.*
                    from Evangeline,
                    by Henry Wadsworth Longfellow

GRAND PRÉ was a garden reclaimed from the sea. Here, at the head of the Minas Basin, northwest of Halifax in present-day Nova Scotia, 17th-century Acadian farmers began the long task of reclaiming rich farmland from the waters of the basin. Their success in the next quarter-century made Grand Pré the largest community in Acadia.

But the long French-British war for North America did not leave Acadia unscathed. In 1704, troops from New England attacked and razed much of Grand Pré, destroying the dykes and flooding the land.

After the British took Acadia in 1713, the Acadians refused to take an oath of allegiance to Britain and continued to refuse, right through the 1740s and another British-French war. Ultimately, on July 28, 1755, a sad and bitter day in Canadian history, the British expelled most of the French-speaking population of Acadia—women, children, and men alike—forcing them at bayonet-point aboard ships bound for the British colonies to the south. Of about 10,000 Acadians, some 6,000 were deported, and

Symbol of her people's trials, a statue of the fictional Evangeline stands in modern Grand Pré, sculpted by Phillippe Hébert and his son, descendants of early Acadians. Elsewhere in the village stands an old-Acadian-style blacksmith's shop (opposite).

at least 2,000 more fled to the countryside, many to take up a very effective guerrilla war against the British in the province now renamed Nova Scotia. The deportees were scattered; many later settled in French-speaking Louisiana, while some thousands eventually found their way home to Acadia.

Today, at Grand Pré National Historical Park, there is a chapel where once the Church of St. Charles stood; it was in this church that the order expelling the Acadians was read.

Louisbourg

THIS IS THE GREAT FRENCH FORTRESS on the Atlantic, now massively restored as the Fortress of Louisbourg National Historic Park.

Here, at the eastern edge of Isle Royale, now Cape Breton Island, the French in 1719 set about building the enormous fort that was to guard the eastern approaches to French North America. Most of Acadia and all of Newfoundland had been lost to the British in 1713; Louisbourg to be was the new center of French power on the Atlantic and a safe harbor for a large fishing fleet, trans-Atlantic commerce, and French privateers.

Construction was nearly complete 26 years later, in 1745, when the 150-gun fortress was besieged for seven weeks and fell to a force of 4,000 New England militia joined by a British naval squadron. Louisbourg was returned to France by treaty in 1748 and continued to be the main French fortress on the Atlantic until 1758. In that year, it was attacked and captured by a large British army led by Major General Jeffrey Amherst.

The British held the fortress for two years and then systematically destroyed it, to prevent any further military use of the site. When they left, there was nothing more than a grassy knoll where the fortress of Louisbourg had been. Just over 200 years later, the Canadian government began the tremendous undertaking that was the restoration of about one-fifth of the original town and its fortifications, using in large part artifacts collected on the abandoned site itself, which had not been touched for two centuries. That restoration is Louisbourg today.

Once the largest French fort in North America, Louisbourg was leveled to the ground in 1760. Today one-fifth of the fort **(above)** has been rebuilt, complete with guards **(opposite)** and guides in period costume, and even restaurants **(below)** serving 18th-century fare.

Signal Hill

FIVE-HUNDRED-FOOT-HIGH SIGNAL HILL dominates the old port city of St. John's, Newfoundland. St. John's dates its origin back to John Cabot's landfall here in June 1497, only five years after Columbus reached the Americas and almost four decades before Jacques Cartier was to sail through the Strait of Belle Isle into the Gulf of St. Lawrence. It is the oldest and easternmost city in North America, dating back to the year after Cabot's discovery, when a small settlement was founded. European sailors knew this coast long before Cabot, though. Norse ships and settlers had been here as early as 500 years before, and Icelandic, Basque, British, and Portuguese sailors had fished the Grand Banks off Newfoundland for hundreds of years before St. John's was founded.

For centuries simply called The Lookout, Signal Hill was the place from which the town was alerted to approaching ships; from 1704, signaling was formally instituted, with flags hoisted on a yardarm to communicate with the town.

The British built Fort William in St. John's in the 1690s, during the long French and British contest over North America; and from then until the end of the Seven Years War in 1762, it passed back and forth between them several times. The French took Fort William in 1696, 1709, and 1762; the British took it back for the last time in September 1762, after seizing French guns on Signal Hill and using them against Fort William. That was the last battle between British and French forces in North America.

The present substantial fortifications on Signal Hill date from Napoleonic War times and were never used in battle. They are part of Signal Hill National Historic Site, as is Cabot Tower,

Only decades ago, the first wireless transmission was sent across the Atlantic from Marconi Tower on Signal Hill (opposite), at St. John's, Newfoundland. In a military tattoo (above), players in redcoats relive something of Signal Hill's earlier history during the French-British struggle for North America, which ended here in a final British victory.

which was built between 1898 and 1900 to celebrate Queen Victoria's Diamond Jubilee and the 400th anniversary of Cabot's landing.

Signal Hill was also the scene of a different sort of famous signal. Here, in 1901, Guglielmo Marconi received the first trans-Atlantic wireless transmission.

Province House

In the hearts and minds of the delegates who assembled in this room on September 1st 1864 was born the Dominion of Canada. Providence being their Guide, they builded better than they knew.
Plaque in Province House.

IN PROVINCE HOUSE the Canadian nation was born. Not in the heat of battle; rather as the culmination of a long, peaceful, yet intense struggle for independence.

Province House, at Charlottestown, on Prince Edward Island, was in September 1864 host to the first meetings of the Fathers of Confederation. Here, in the room later known and preserved as Confederation Chamber, delegates from all over the land—from what would in 1867 become the Dominion of Canada—met to discuss the confederation of all the British North American colonies into a single new nation. John A. MacDonald, George-Etienne Cartier, and the other delegates signed no delcarations at that set of meetings; all that was to come later, after much hard bargaining, at Quebec in October of that year, and at the London Conference, in 1867. Yet it was at Province House—also called Confederation House—that the idea of Canada was really born; this then is the birthplace of the nation.

Today the building has been restored to be much as it was in 1864 and is Province House National Historic Site. It continues to be the seat of the Prince Edward Island provincial legislature, as it has been since 1847.

*Built of local stone by Prince Edward Island artisans, Province House (**opposite**) was where the provincial delegates met to shape Canada's fate. The Fathers of Confederation gathered in Confederation Chamber (**above**); the island's provincial legislature used a separate assembly room (**below**).*

Ottawa

IN OTTAWA PAST AND PRESENT intertwine; the great working institutions of the Canadian nation are, by their nature, also great Canadian historic places. That is so for all historic capital cities, and nowhere more so than in Canada, whose massive Houses of Parliament, topped by the Peace Tower, are by far the best recognized symbol of Canada around the world.

Until the turn of the 19th century, this was wholly Native American land, forest and river. By then, furs had been traded east along the Ottawa River for two centuries. Samuel de Champlain stopped here in 1613, on his way west, but the first settler in the area was American Philemon Wright, who in 1800 began lumbering operations across the river in what is now Hull. Nicholas Sparks was a little later the first settler on the Ottawa side of the river.

Settlement of the area accelerated with construction of the Rideau Canal, built to provide an east-west passage safe from American interference should war come again between the two nations, as it had in 1812. The canal was built under the direction of Lt. Col. John By, and the resulting town was named Bytown. It became Ottawa in 1855, as national debate grew over where to locate the new capital.

That debate was resolved by Queen Victoria in 1857: She chose Ottawa. Construction of government buildings began there in 1857. When some buildings were completed, in 1865, government departments began to move in. But it was with the British North America Act and Confederation in 1867 that Ottawa became a fully working capital city.

Ottawa is both symbol and power. Most of all, it is Parliament Hill, with its three enormous Victorian Parliament buildings. In the Center Block, the House of Commons, the Senate, and the

Ottawa is the heart of the modern Canadian nation, especially the Parliament buildings (opposite) dominated by the Peace Tower (below) on Parliament Hill. The building of the Rideau Canal (left), after the 1812 battles with the Americans, led to the founding of the city; today the canal delights its modern residents.

Peace Tower; in the East Block, the offices of the prime ministers, the cabinet, and other notables; in the West Block, more offices and committee rooms. In the top floor of the Peace Tower is the carillon; below the carillon the Memorial Chamber, with its Books of Remembrance, commemorating the Canadian war dead. The Center Block also houses Confederation Hall. Just behind the Center Block is the Parliamentary Block, dating back to the completion of the original structure in 1876; the balance of the structures were built after the disastrous fire of 1916, which all but destroyed the earlier Parliament buildings. Ottawa is the home of many other major institutions as well—the Supreme Court, the Royal Canadian Mint, National Library, Public Archives, National Gallery, National Arts Centre, and Canadian War Museum, among others.

Ottawa is also many great houses, full of the history of the nation. It is 24 Sussex Drive, the residence of the Prime Minister; and Stornowaye, too, the residence of the leader of the Opposition. It is Earnscliffe, the home of John A. MacDonald, first Prime Minister after Confederation, now Government House; Laurier House, home of Wilfrid Laurier and Mackenzie King; and of Rideau Hall, the residence of the Governor-General.

Ottawa is also a very beautiful modern city, with the Rideau Canal coming right through the center of the city and now devoted to recreational pursuits. In winter, the Rideau Canal is a nearly five-mile-long ice-skating stream, and many skate to work in the city that is the center of the Canadian nation.

Montreal

MONTREAL IS CANADA'S LARGEST CITY, with over two million inhabitants; it is also the second-largest French-speaking city in the world, behind Paris. It is a place of huge underground shopping complexes, skyscrapers, Expo, massive international trade, and all the cultural events and creature comforts that go with being one of the world's great trading cities.

And that is what is has always been—a trading city *par excellence*. As a chief contributor to the growth of the Canadian nation, it is, in a sense, Canada's greatest economic historic place.

Situated at the confluence of the St. Lawrence and Ottawa rivers, Montreal is one of the great crossroads cities of North America. Until the 1820s, no ships of any substantial size could go beyond Montreal, because of the Lachine Rapids nearby. And not until the advent of the St. Lawrence Seaway in the mid-20th century could ocean-going ships pass into the heartland of North America. So it was that Montreal has always been one of Canada's greatest ports and was from the first the logical eastern terminus of the all-important fur trade. In the process, Montreal became the largest inland seaport in the world, although it lies one thousand miles from the sea.

Jacques Cartier came here in 1535, to the large Huron village called Hochelaga, on the slopes of the mountain he called Mont Réal (to the later British, Mount Royal). Samuel de Champlain came later, three years after the founding of Quebec, to build a fur trading post, seeking both the Northwest Passage and beaver. Two years later, Champlain went west for the first time, along the Ottawa River, taking the first long Canadian step away from the Atlantic and the St. Lawrence, on the route that would eventually

At the heart of Old Montreal lies the Place D'Armes (above), where the early French fought and won their first battle with the local Iroquois. The oldest church in the city is Notre-Dame-de-Bonsecours (below), built in its present form in 1772, but founded in 1657. One of the finest is the Notre Dame Church (opposite), with its strikingly beautiful interior detail (right inset).

take Alexander MacKenzie to the Pacific.

Champlain's trading post, which he called Place Royale, gave way to the settlement Paul de Chomedey, Sieur de Maisonneuve, founded on the site in 1642; this prospered and ultimately became the city of Montreal.

Montreal saw little of the wars that wracked Atlantic North America during the 17th and 18th centuries. It surrendered to the British in 1760, after the fall of Quebec, and was briefly occupied by American forces under Benedict Arnold in 1775, but continued to trade and grow all during the period.

In recent years, Montreal has been restoring some of its most important historic places. In Old Montreal, many of the buildings, squares, and streets in this earliest waterfront portion of the city have been rebuilt, and much more is in progress. Montreal continues to trade, to look forward; today, it also looks back, with appreciation of its historic past.

Citadel Hill

THE VIEW FROM CITADEL HILL, especially out over Halifax harbor to the sea, is one of the best known in Canada. The large star-shaped fort that is The Citadel dominates the city of Halifax, largest of the Maritimes cities, capital of Nova Scotia, and historic center of British, and then Canadian, power on the Atlantic.

The forts at Halifax—The Citadel, York Redoubt ten miles away, and several associated fortifications—have never been tested in battle. Had they been, the result might very well have been the same as at Louisbourg, for developments in military technology made such forts obsolete as early as the middle of the 18th century.

This fort, The Citadel, was the fourth fort to be built on the site. The first fort at Halifax was little more than a series of five stockades, built in 1847, when—after the first return of Louisbourg to the French—the British wanted a competing center of power. The second was a substantial star-shaped fort, built in 1761 on the direction of General Jeffrey Amherst after the destruction of Louisbourg. The third was built during the Napoleonic Wars. The fourth, and present, Citadel was completed in 1856, essentially as a possible defense against the growing power of the new American nation to the south, which had been at war with Great Britain earlier in the century and—it was feared—might attack Canada again.

Today, The Citadel, York Redoubt, the restored buildings of the Halifax waterfront, and the Prince of Wales Martello Tower are all major national historic places, and are together the most visited historic sites and parks in Canada.

Dominating the capital of Nova Scotia from its hilltop position, the Halifax Citadel (opposite) has never seen true battle. But throughout the year, the fort echoes with the sound of marching feet—those of students in period uniforms(below). The region's Scottish traditions show clearly in the dress of the young 78th Highlanders (above) and the ever-present bagpipe player (right).

Lower Fort Garry

LOWER FORT GARRY NATIONAL HISTORIC PARK, at Selkirk, north of Winnipeg in Manitoba, is the oldest surviving stone fur trade post. It is a substantial historical restoration, evoking the history of the fur trade and the role it played in the making of the Canadian nation.

It was to a large extent fur that took Canadian explorers from the Atlantic to the Pacific. When Jacques Cartier entered Chaleur Bay, on the coast of New Brunswick, he was met by "a large number of Indians, who set up a great clamour and made frequent signs to us to come on shore, holding up to us some furs on sticks. . . " When Samuel de Champlain first went west along the Ottawa River, he was following the fur trade routes of the Ottawa people, and going to meet the Hurons, in search of new supplies of the rapidly disappearing beaver. When the British established posts on Hudson's Bay, and from there went on to explore and colonize all of western Canada, it was fur that was the main goal. Indeed, Alexander MacKenzie himself was a Northwest Company fur trader at the time of his great western explorations.

The restoration at Lower Fort Garry faithfully reproduces this Hudson's Bay Company post and fort. It preserves thirteen structures, including the Big House, at one time the home of George Simpson, Governor of the Hudson's Bay Company.

People in period costume attempt to recreate the life of Lower Fort Garry, during its 150 years of active service. One young man (opposite) acts as clerk in the office of the fur loft, while two young women (above) walk outside the Big House, once home of the Hudson's Bay Company governor.

Bella Coola

Alex MacKenzie
from Canada
by land
22 d July 1793

GEORGE VANCOUVER, exploring up the Pacific coast a few days later, saw this inscription, written "in large characters" of vermilion and grease by Alexander MacKenzie, on a rock in Dean Channel, north of what is now Vancouver Island.

The inscription might have read:

Alexander MacKenzie, Leif Ericson, Jacques Cartier, John Cabot, Henry Hudson, Samuel de Champlain, Robert La Salle, Jean Nicolet, Jacques Marquette, Pierre Radisson, Anthony Henday, Simon Fraser, David Thompson, and others, by land and waterway across Canada from sea to sea.

Bella Coola is the far end of the Canadian way west, of the long journey that had started when Jacques Cartier's little ship passed though the Strait of Belle Isle into the Gulf of St. Lawrence 259 years before.

For Alexander MacKenzie, too, it was the end of a long, long journey of exploration and discovery. Scottish-born MacKenzie was the greatest of all the explorers of the western North America, being both the first to reach the Arctic Ocean overland in western Canada, and the first to reach the Pacific overland north of Mexico. MacKenzie eventually retired to Scotland, but his rock is still there, at Bella Coola, with his words embedded in red cement; it is the centerpiece of British Columbia's Sir Alexander MacKenzie Provincial Park.

Lying on Dean Channel near the west coast of North America is the town of Bella Coola (above), where Alexander MacKenzie marked (opposite) his completion of the European overland journey to the Pacific. Today the town's modest wharf (below) symbolizes the joining here of the land and water routes from the Atlantic to the Pacific.